# ENTERPRISES

## THAT

# CHANGE LIVES

Edgar Parnell

i

ISBN: 978-1720898436

English (United Kingdom) version

First published in 2018 by Edgar Parnell
Witney, Oxfordshire, United Kingdom

Available from Amazon.com and other booksellers

# ENTERPRISES THAT CHANGE LIVES

## CONTENTS

*Continued...*

## Dedication

This book is dedicated to all the people that I have worked with in self-help enterprises, they have contributed to my experience and understanding of this transformative form of enterprise. I pay tribute to those leaders with the vision to identify the root causes of the challenges facing their communities, and who found both the courage and determination to lead the mutual action necessary to bring about positive change to their members' lives.

## Acknowledgements

I acknowledge the help of all those that have contributed to the development of this book, especially those whom I have worked with in various kinds of self-help enterprises in diverse parts of the world. Two influential mentors have provided me with their wise guidance over the course of many years. Explicitly, Prof Ian MacPherson (1939 – 2013) who led the process and authored the Cooperative Identity Statement adopted by the International Co-operative Alliance (ICA) in 1995, and Trevor Bottomley (1921 – 2017) who I first met in 1966 when he was the Registrar of Cooperatives in Botswana. I also thank Kate Targett, a Fellow of the Plunkett Foundation, and my eldest daughter, Susan. Both have contributed their expertise towards making my book more readable than it would have been without their help. However, as its author, I accept sole responsibility for the book's content.

*To Myra Parnell for everything.*

# INTRODUCTION

The term 'the market' is used throughout this book to describe the mechanisms that allow buyers and sellers to exchange anything of tradeable value. All of us are all both buyers and sellers of goods and services in a wide variety of markets, the leading causes of people living miserable lives arise due to their unequal power in the markets they rely upon for their well-being.

The market regularly works against the mass of ordinary people. Whenever people can't access the goods or the services, they need on terms that are both fair and reasonable, they are inevitably exploited by those holding power in the market. When the market doesn't work as it should, because it's not free, fair and open; or, where those using the market have no choice but to take the 'deal' that's on offer. In these circumstances, those dominating the market reap excessive profits at the expense of all others using the market. Likewise, when people can't get a fair price for their labour, knowledge, and skills, or for the things they produce, grow or supply, they suffer in any market that doesn't work correctly.

Faced with adverse market conditions, individuals can sometimes secure the improvements they want through their own efforts alone, but when powerful forces are ranged against them within a market, they need to work with others similarly disadvantaged in the same market. Ordinarily, the most effective response is to join an existing self-help enterprise or, where there are none, set up a new one.

Self-help enterprises include, for example, cooperatives, credit unions, mutual insurers, building societies, friendly societies, and community enterprises. These are all organizations with the function of intervening in the market in the best interest of their members. Groups of people work together with the aim of improving their position within a market; this may be in their capacity as consumers, producers, workers or as a community. The primary objective of their joint intervention is to secure a 'better deal' for their members. The alternative to mutual action is to remain at the mercy of those who dominate or manipulate the market.

Throughout history, people have developed ways of working together to achieve their common objectives. Successful self-help enterprises, of diverse types, began to emerge during the Industrial Revolution. Initially, these were mostly in Europe but soon spread rapidly throughout the world. During the 18th century, following much trial and error, various methods were developed for running specific types of this form of enterprise. Over the next two centuries, they became involved in a wide range of markets, most notably food retailing and wholesaling, agriculture, housing, financial services, and insurance.

Today, around the world many enterprises are working toward improving the lives of their members. In recent times the world has fundamentally changed, especially in the markets for most goods, services and labour. These changes have often occurred because of the globalisation of markets, fuelled by developments in transport and communications, and more recently by the application of digital technologies. Simultaneously, socio-economic events have affected most countries, bringing about shifts in what people spend their money on, and how and where they spend it. The ways that both work and production are organized are radically changing, creating new threats, opportunities and challenges for both existing and emerging self-help enterprises.

It's easy enough to see the need to take mutual action to improve peoples' lives but setting-up and running the kind of organization necessary to achieve the outcomes that members want is by no means easy. Where the 'self-help mindset' takes root and when authentic leaders emerge, then such enterprises flourish. Despite the huge potential for mutual action to improve peoples' lives it needs to be acknowledged that many such enterprises are not as effective as they ought to be, and where this happens millions of individuals, their communities and their national economies, all suffer due to the absence of effective market interventions on behalf of ordinary people.

One of the most significant factors impeding the accelerated development of this form of enterprise has been the failure to adopt an easy-to-understand 'self-help enterprise model'. A model that can make self-help enterprises much more effective, dynamic and resilient. My book explains this enterprise model and its practical application. The model takes full account of centuries of international know-how and includes the 'foundation practices' that sustain this form of enterprise. The model is designed to ensure self-help enterprises always focus on achieving their real purpose and work in the best interest of their members.

The book is arranged in two parts; the first outlines the essential concepts that leaders need to fully comprehend if they are to fulfil their responsibilities, while the second details the practices required to construct the systems crucial to running successful self-help enterprises.

Edgar Parnell
November 2018

*Enterprises that change lives*

---

# PART ONE:

## SELF-HELP ENTERPRISES

## - THE ESSENTIALS

---

# 1. WHAT THIS BOOK IS ABOUT

**What's in this book?**

This book explains how a family of enterprises, collectively referred to as 'self-help enterprises', work in support of people wishing to improve their lives. It describes the characteristics of these enterprises, how to run them so that they achieve their objectives and deliver the results that members want. It also sets out why individuals, communities and nations need self-help enterprises if they are to prosper, and what policy-makers can do to help grow and sustain them.

**Self-help enterprises**

Self-help enterprises are set-up (and run) by people seeking to get a better life by harnessing the power of mutual action. The term 'self-help enterprises' embraces all of the many types of this form of enterprise, which, for example, includes: cooperatives, credit unions, mutual insurers, building societies, friendly societies, community enterprises, as well as many others. The acronym 'SHEs' is used throughout the book to refer to all the diverse types of this form of enterprise. The activities of such enterprises can encompass any category of goods or services where a market exists; see *Annex I - Types and activities of self-help enterprises.*

Each type of self-help enterprise follows typically a set of practices grounded in their own unique history, which have become the main characteristics of each specific type. The people involved with SHEs usually refer to them by the name of each type, for example – 'credit unions', 'cooperatives', etc. However, it's not always realised that all these diverse types of SHEs are driven by the same motivator, and all belong to the same 'family' of enterprises. The fact is, they all rely on people taking mutual action for their shared benefit and conduct their enterprises to help-themselves by joining with others to take mutual action. This requires that they 'co-operate' and hold any assets needed using a system of 'mutual ownership'.

## Understanding SHEs

The starting point for understanding the self-help form of enterprise is to identify what it is members want from their enterprises; this may be summed up as:

- A **better deal** - not solely measured in monetary terms;
- A **better organization** - one that can always be relied upon to act in the best interest of members;
- A **better future**.

Together, the above three objectives provide the basis for a holistic purpose for self-help enterprises; see *Chapter 6*, which further explains this concept.

The kind of organization necessary to deliver these three 'betters' is one that is:

- Purpose-driven
- Function-focused
- Organized to deliver its purpose
- Operating a sustainable market-intervention strategy
- Deploying dynamic and complete systems
- Undertakes a continuous process of organizational renewal.

The self-help enterprise model, detailed in *Chapter 9*, is designed to achieve the outcomes listed above

## Who is it for?

The main aim of the book is to help leaders of SHEs gain a deeper understanding of their enterprises. Starting with a straightforward explanation of what SHEs are, how they differ from any other form of enterprise and the way this impacts how SHEs need to be run in today's world. It should help all those wishing to create and develop SHEs and assist current leaders in making them more effective.

The book is written by a practitioner and is primarily aimed at those with leadership roles in SHEs. However, it's also intended to help all those involved with SHEs, especially those who seek to gain a greater insight into how such enterprises are best organized, run and developed. This includes grassroots members, employees and anyone else trying to increase their understanding of self-help enterprises, including - community-developers, policy-makers, professionals supplying services to SHEs, educators and researchers.

## Not an easy task

Setting-up and running SHEs is no easy task; it requires hard work, persistence and a commitment to learning how the enterprise needs to work if it is to do whatever it is that their members want to achieve. At the same time, making sure that their enterprise remains under member-control; and, responds positively and swiftly in an ever-changing world.

The book doesn't offer a new doctrine or a complete package of answers to the multitude of issues facing SHEs as they develop and grow. Instead, it provides some essential concepts and tools that can transform how such enterprises are organized and managed. The intention is to help leaders think-through the issues involved so that they can make better decisions, which are decisions that only leaders have the power to take.

## Changing lives

The extent of the impact that SHEs have on the lives of their members depends upon both the nature of the problems facing them and on the current quality of their lives. At the top-end of the scale of impact are those SHEs formed to counter gross injustice within a market, in these circumstances, their intervention can result in transforming member's lives. For example, where:

- Farmers and fishermen aren't getting anything like a fair price for their produce.
- Unhealthy foodstuffs, at unaffordable prices, are the only goods available to consumers.
- There is no access to health care or other essential services.
- Unscrupulous traders, moneylenders or property owners, are exploiting vulnerable people.

At the other end of the scale, measured by the degree of impact upon members' lives, some SHEs provide members with modest but crucial differences in their lifestyle, for example, by running social clubs, public-houses (pubs), cultural activities, sports facilities, or supporter-led sports clubs.

Midway between such interventions is those where SHEs deliver considerable improvements to the lives of millions of people worldwide. Examples include those providing:

- Community services in places where commercial businesses find it unprofitable to operate
- Insurance services that people can trust to cover the significant risks that arise in their everyday lives

- Facilities for savings and credit at rates that are honest and fair.
- Services that meet the health and care needs of people at various stages in their lives
- Healthy food at reasonable prices
- Livelihoods for people in workplaces that they control.
- Joint-marketing and other services in support of small and medium-scale enterprises (SMEs).
- Affordable homes that meet peoples' actual needs.

When SHEs are run correctly, they enhance the quality of life for their members and give them more control over their lives.

**Achieving their potential**

Throughout the world, there are countless examples of highly successful SHEs of all types, - long may these prosper. Conversely, are other enterprises needing to make far-reaching changes to the way that they are being run, if they are to fulfil their full potential to make life better for their members. In some countries, SHEs are expanding rapidly, while in others some traditional types of SHEs are in decline. Meanwhile, new types of SHEs are emerging, at the same time as the more conventional SHEs are evolving to meet current and future challenges.

The scope for developing both existing and new SHEs is almost boundless; it's only the capacity, tenacity and creativity of their leaders, that limits them. To increase their effectiveness, leaders need to get to know the 'self-help model of enterprise', and develop their knowledge of their markets, the techniques, and systems required to run successful SHEs.

## Simple but not simplistic

The concept of commercial business is straightforward and rudimentary because in profit-driven enterprises people invest their money in a business with the aim of making yet more money. People can choose to run a business themselves, pay other people to run it, or invest money in a company run by others. When investing money in a business, investors rely on others to run them; it doesn't really matter what it does or how they run it, so long as it's legal, makes money and isn't careless about their investment. This isn't a political statement but a reality.

The idea behind self-help enterprise is also simple yet ingenious. SHEs are started when a group of people gets together to form an enterprise in response to their dissatisfaction with whatever the current players in a specific market provide, or in some cases don't offer. Members have got to have a clear perception of what they want to change in the market and how they are going to achieve these changes. Members have to agree upon their common purpose, their market intervention strategy, the design of their organization, and the systems needed to run their enterprise.

## Why are self-help enterprises different?

Those looking for quick fixes and simplistic approaches to running SHEs are only heading for disappointment. It's incredibly naive to believe that SHEs can achieve much of value unless they deploy the systems essential to running a flourishing enterprise of this form.

If people are to be prepared so that they can set-up, run and develop SHEs, it's imperative that they acquire a thorough understanding of the true nature of enterprises rooted in self-help and mutual action. SHEs are not commercial businesses, and they are not charities, they are in fact associations of equal persons seeking to improve their members' position within a specific market. These unique features separate them from investor-owned companies, which are associations of finance (capital) with the purpose of making money for their owners.

Compared to all other forms of enterprise, SHEs have their own purposes and a particular function. These features mean they need to be run differently, need to utilise a specific kind of organization, and be supported by specifically designed systems: all of which are essential if they are to remain bona-fide self-help enterprises.

The term 'function', as used in this book, means 'what the organization does to achieve its purpose'. This is highlighted because to properly understand this form of enterprise it's necessary to know that SHEs have the function of intervening in the market in the best interest of their members. It's imperative to be clear as to the function of an organization because it's only likely to succeed when those running the organization focus on this.

## What is a bona-fide self-help enterprise?
Genuine SHEs are democratically-controlled by their members and unequivocally run for their mutual benefit. They operate using unique systems of organization, association, economics and management, and may be identified by their adherence to a specific set of foundation practices.

### Critical differences
SHEs have to be viable, solvent, maintain their liquidity and be run based on generating enough margin to cover all costs and foreseeable risks. They typically reinvest the bulk of any 'operating surplus' they may generate into improving the quality and value of the services and other benefits supplied to their members. The main task of their managers is to achieve the purpose set by the members, while concurrently optimising all the resources deployed. This

13

contrasts with the main task of managers of commercial businesses, who are charged with securing 'profit maximisation' for the benefit of the owners of the enterprise.

### Forms of enterprise

Self-help enterprises are one of several forms of enterprise available within an economy. In a market economy, there are also forms of enterprises driven by the 'profit motive', these range from 'sole traders' to large public companies. All the diverse types of profit-driven enterprises belong to a group referred to as 'commercial businesses. Another group of enterprises are those run to achieve outcomes other than profit, and it's customary to refer to these as 'not-for-profit' enterprises, these are 'outcomes-driven' enterprises, which can, in turn, be subdivided into two distinct forms, which are:

- **Cause-driven enterprises** - motivated by the desire to support a specific cause or project
- **Self-help enterprises** - driven by the aspiration of their members to achieve an agreed purpose by the application of self-help and mutual action.

See *Figure A-1 Forms of enterprise.*

### The competence of leaders

Throughout the book, considerable stress is placed on the importance of SHEs having the right form of organization and appropriate systems in place. This is not in any way intended to distract from the necessity of having leaders who are passionate about getting a 'better deal' and running a better organization for the benefit of their members. However, without the proper organization and systems, it's highly unlikely that even the most enthusiastic leader will make a success of their enterprise. Leaders that don't properly understand their organizations and the systems

14

needed run them are like a worker who doesn't have the tools required to do their job.

## The meaning of success

Success for SHEs means securing improvements to the lives of their members by intervening in specific the markets on their behalf. Achieving such ambitions demands that every system deployed by the enterprise is designed and implemented to ensure that the enterprise achieves a set of planned outcomes that move the enterprise towards achieving its strategic aims.

Good intentions are never enough when it comes to achieving life-changing results by SHEs, nor will the reciting of platitudes bring about any useful improvements. SHEs should deliver real benefits to their members; this typically includes developing their members' individual capacity to lead more prosperous and fulfilling lives. Often this requires that SHEs help members build their resilience to withstand the vagaries of the market and empower them to respond positively to changing conditions. This contrasts with the approach of many commercial businesses that frequently generate their profits by exploiting the weakness of their customers, workers, and suppliers.

## Making a difference

SHEs can address many of the most pressing problems that face the mass of people in most parts of the world today. For example, by countering deep-rooted social issues such as where:

- Credit unions or authentic cooperative banks provide members with a real alternative to exorbitant rates of interest, irresponsible lending and financial exclusion.
- Building societies or savings and credit associations provide responsible mortgages at fair interest rates, thus promoting home ownership.

- Mutual insurance providers offer fair and equitable cover for all manner of risks, which, if not adequately covered, could be disastrous for people of limited means.
- Housing co-ops provide services to tenants allowing them to have greater control over their living conditions.
- Providing health and care services that allow patients to take more responsibility for the own well-being.
- Eliminating extreme poverty when producers gain a fairer share of the gross value of their produce.
- Worker co-ops provide rewarding and fulfilling livelihoods.
- Consumer co-ops supply healthy food as an alternative to over-processed or noxious foods.

## A national imperative

SHEs have a valuable role to play in every market economy by responding to market failure, curbing the excesses of dominant businesses and by helping secure positive social transformation within society. When SHEs work correctly, they have the power to make a significant contribution in the national interest, by furnishing the means of increasing international competitiveness, improving national productivity and by counteracting the rise of corporatocracy.

Many governments are now struggling to control their national debt, causing them to follow austerity programmes, which leads to the curtailment of public services. When the State's provision of essential services is inadequate citizens often turn to self-help solutions, but their efforts will only achieve beneficial outcomes when their leaders accept the necessity of focusing on the real needs of their members.

With the prospect of so many positives, it's essential to tackle head-on the weaknesses that hold back so many SHEs. If this form of enterprise is to expand its role in the economy, SHEs have to become much more effective at delivering life-changing benefits to members.

### *Summing up*

*Enterprises that Change Lives* recalls that just a few generations ago, a quiet revolution swept throughout Europe and soon after this expanded to many other parts of the world. The mass of people discovered that they could help themselves to improve their lives by taking mutual action using self-help enterprises. By the beginning of the 20th century, it seemed that self-help enterprises were unstoppable and would take on an ever-increasing role in national economies.

Much has changed since that time; most obviously the enormous advances in science and technology and the globalisation of markets. Even more significant, has been the decline in the influence of the 'self-help mindset' - the conviction that people can take more control over their lives, which now seems to have been replaced by increased dependency on international mega-businesses and on a more pervasive and controlling State. Even though, there are still millions of people throughout the world, who use self-help enterprises to provide goods, services and livelihoods that improve their members' daily lives.

Although the ways of operating SHEs in the 19th and 20th centuries were ground-breaking in their day, they have not sufficiently advanced to equip SHEs to work in today's conditions. The result is that many SHEs are not ready to challenge many of the big businesses that now dominate markets, constrain our freedom and limit our creativity. What's more, the mass of people seems to be condemned to a life of drudgery unless they can rediscover the self-help mindset and make their enterprises work more effectively on their behalf.

This book advocates a logical approach to running SHEs and encourages leaders to learn what they need to know if their enterprises are to achieve their full potential. This calls for leaders to: rediscover the self-help mindset, learn how to make markets work for the benefit of their members, understand the significance of having a clear-cut and holistic purpose and function, knowing the kind of organization and the model of enterprise required. Besides, learning how to: develop a market intervention strategy, create the right organizational culture, grow their enterprises, develop the leaders needed and debunk many of the myths and mindtraps that hold back the advancement of SHEs. All of which are essential if SHEs are to bring real change to the lives of their members. This requires that their leaders realise that if the outcomes desired are to be achieved, the systems indispensable to running genuinely successful SHEs need to be in place. This book explains the power of systems and their role in running successful enterprises and details the practices that underlie these systems. It concludes with an assessment of what needs to be done to empower people to help themselves; including, what actions leaders can initiate jointly and the public policy framework necessary to expand the role of SHEs in the economy.

## *Figure A-1. Forms of enterprise*

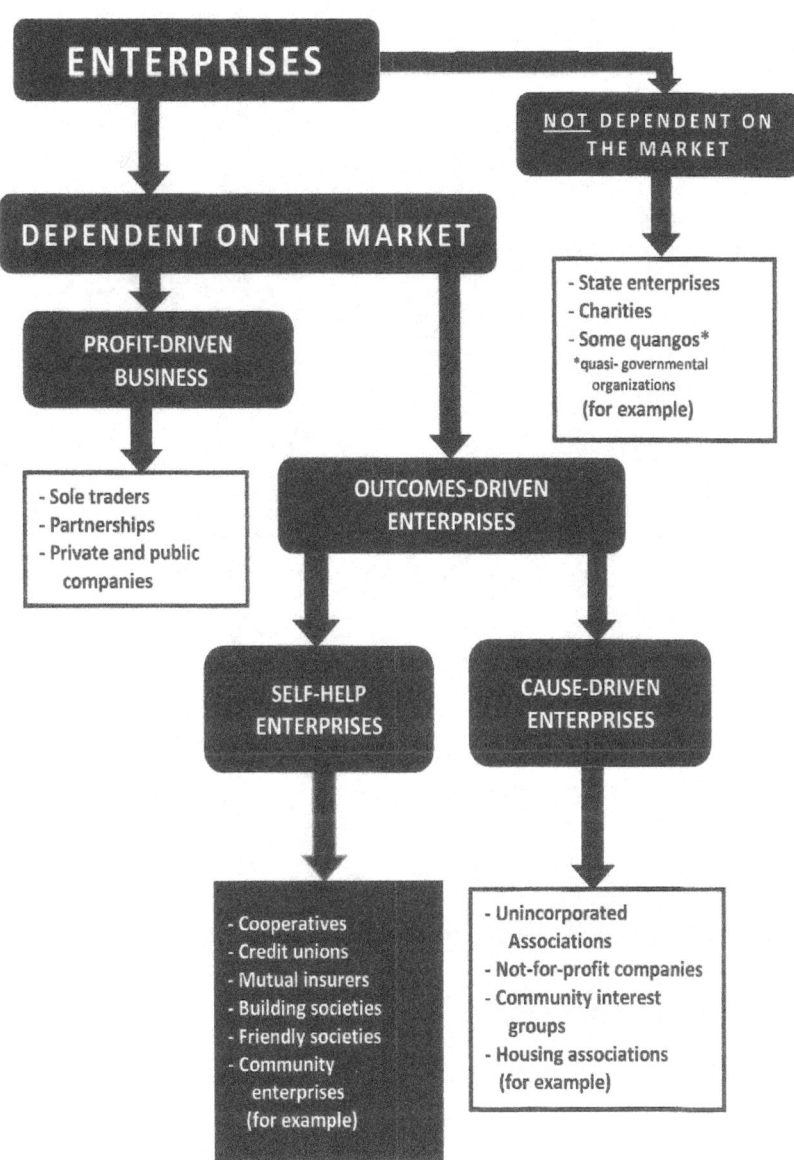

# 2. MEANINGS ARE IN PEOPLE

## Using the correct terminology
The use of accurate terminology is essential to gaining an accurate understanding of self-help enterprises. Without the self-discipline required to use the correct terminology, only confusion will prevail, rendering it most difficult to grasp the essential facts about this form of enterprise. All worthwhile learning can be demanding, but the devotion of both time and energy in upgrading our knowledge and skills is an essential investment. This process may also include 'unlearning' some of the fictions that imprison our imagination and limits our capacity to see the opportunities open to both ourselves and our enterprises.

## Dictionary definitions are not enough
It's not unusual to hear people involved with SHEs complaining about the fact that 'the public', and likewise members, do not fully understand cooperatives, credit unions and other types of SHEs. The same people then go on to refer to SHEs as 'businesses', while simultaneously insisting that they are 'social enterprises. They sometimes talk about 'sharing profits with members' while concurrently telling people that SHEs are 'not-for-profit enterprises. In these circumstances, is it any wonder that so many people become confused when it comes to understanding SHEs?

Examine any good dictionary, and it will quickly reveal that many of the words used in everyday conversation have more than one meaning, which means that it's difficult to know with certainty that both the speaker and listener attribute the same meaning to the same word. This kind of confusion is common, for example when people attach meanings to words in popular parlance, which are often incorrect. In addition, many words are emotive and can arouse intense feelings in some individuals, which can result in them jumping to wrong conclusions, often curtailing any rational discussion of the topic. It's imperative to realise that the meanings of words rest with both the speaker and the listener, this confirms the necessity of remembering that 'meanings are in the minds of people'—not in dictionaries.

### *When there are no words for it*

When I first started working outside of the UK, I discovered that many languages had no equivalent words for many terms used in the day-to-day operations of self-help enterprises. For example, it was commonplace to find that words such as 'enterprise plan', 'marketing', and 'margin' had no equivalent in local languages. I found this even more pronounced when I began working in post-communist countries. Often, people would speak in their own language, for example, Russian or Polish, and then interject English words into their conversation, which could sound quite incongruous to the expatriate listener. However, this highlighted the need for local people to be sure, in their own minds, as to the shared-meaning of such words and phrases.

When the first cooperatives, friendly societies, and building societies were set up in Britain, similar misunderstandings arose, because the people starting-up the enterprises hadn't yet developed a vocabulary to describe the concepts essential to running such enterprises. Consequently, people simply used terms that had become established in the joint-stock companies of the day, such as 'profit', 'shares' and 'shareholding'.

**Emotive words**

Anyone old enough to remember the derogatory words previously in everyday use to describe a person's race, ethnicity, or sexual orientation, will appreciate the negative impact that inappropriate words can have upon relationships — both between people and within the culture of an organization. Choosing the right words to communicate effectively with everyone involved is a vital skill because clarity and shared understanding are essential to ensure that both the reader or listener share the same meaning. Embedded in this practice is an understanding that:

- Unless there is a mutual perception about the meaning of the words used, it's very difficult to communicate our thoughts.

- The words used can have a profound impact on the pervading culture within an organization.

- It's about putting into practice the shared understandings about SHEs, including about how they are best set up and run.

- This is a precondition to establishing a more scientific approach towards creating more effective SHEs.

*Annex II* contains a list of terms and what they mean in the context of this book. This is intended to help the process of communicating ideas about SHEs. Initially, it may be sufficient to 'scan read' this list and then consult it whenever there is a need to clarify the meaning of any of the terms listed.

# 3. CHANGING LIVES IN A CHANGING WORLD

**The world today and tomorrow**

In recent decades, rapid advancement in science and technology, accompanied by the globalisation of markets, have brought about massive changes to the ways that most of us live our lives. Despite all the advancements, throughout the world masses of people continue to be seriously disadvantaged in the markets where they try to survive and prosper. Major social upheavals are taking place in many parts of the world, creating new relationships between family members and people now organize their lives in different ways. The root causes of such social changes are found not only in the impact of recent technologies and globalisation but in the growing power of multinational companies and the loss of many traditional livelihoods.

Although overall living conditions may have improved, the lives of the mass of people are still far from satisfactory. This is most obvious in developing economies and where those who govern routinely exploit those they rule. Even in many richer nations, bleak living conditions prevail in marginalised communities that co-exist with those living comfortable lives. In short, despite the magnitude of the changes made during the past half-century, these have not delivered significant gains to much of the world's population, and daily-life remains a constant struggle for millions worldwide.

The effects of global warming on our environment and the failure of governments to cope with the climate shifts predicted are going to produce even more challenging conditions for future generations.

### The limits of the State

When governments try to intervene within markets, such interventions have rarely worked well in practice, and have often made things even worse over the long-run. The lives of those who feel powerless are made considerably more difficult when the State and many of its institutions are enmeshed in various kinds of corruption, and when multinationals wield such power that even honest governments are unable to control them; see *Chapter 5*.

### Crucial issues

Several issues are causing serious obstacles to the development of SHEs in many parts of the world. These shortcomings are preventing SHEs from reaching their true potential and are all addressed in this book. They include that:

- The people running SHEs often lack clarity about their true purpose and function. Many seem to believe that SHEs are just another kind of 'business' — one that just happens to be nominally-owned by members.

- Increasingly, SHEs are mutating into enterprises that are no longer authentic, with many changing into organizations that primarily serve the interests of those who run them on a day-to-day basis.

- There is no widely accepted workable enterprise model. The model required is one that includes all the practices and systems necessary to sustain fully effective SHEs.

- The failure of SHEs, both individually and collectively, to invest sufficiently in developing the abilities of the leaders necessary to run dynamic SHEs.

- Politicians and policy-makers typically don't recognise the importance of fostering self-help as an essential means of developing and empowering citizens.

- National educational institutions, in most countries, pay scant attention to the self-help form of enterprise within their core curriculum. Even when SHEs do feature in the programme of study, the subject matter is frequently nothing short of dogma and misinformation.

- The prevalence of myths and misunderstandings about SHEs abound. This requires concerted action to refute such errors and untruths; otherwise, the people involved in them (let alone the wider public) will never properly comprehend the true nature of this form of enterprise; see *Chapter 14.*

## The significance of culture

Even where all of the other necessary systems are in place, these alone will not guarantee success; this can only come about when the right kind of 'culture' prevails within the enterprise. The culture required is one where everybody involved in running the enterprise is committed to achieving their enterprise's purpose - and serving their members. Sustaining the 'right kind of culture' entails using a system that ensures that this happens; see *Chapter 11.*

## The challenges facing leaders

Change is a continuous, accelerating and inevitable process, so wherever the methods and systems of an enterprise are not sufficiently resilient to cope with new realities, it's bound to face big problems. In the case of SHEs, if they are incapable of responding to such changes, it means that they soon become unable to help members to tackle the big challenges they as individuals and communities are facing.

The experience of SHEs since their inception, informs us that whenever the real needs of members are being met, SHEs grow and prosper. Unfortunately, where leaders lose sight of the real purpose of their enterprise, and/or if they forget that they exist to serve their members, they will inevitably either go into decline or be hijacked by self-serving cliques. In other cases, SHEs fail to keep pace with the significant changes taking place in their markets or fail to develop the kind of systems that are critical to their continuing to operate as genuine SHEs.

Wherever leaders of SHEs don't secure the changes needed, their enterprises will often, by default, convert into a type of commercial business. In other cases, leaders have attempted to re-brand their enterprise as a so-called 'social enterprise'. The reality is, that if SHEs are to remain or revert to being genuine SHEs, their leaders need to embrace the fact a well-defined and practical enterprise model is essential. The first challenge for leaders is to accept the reality of the situation and to invest the time and energy needed to grasp the essentials of this model.

### Inadequate education

Many otherwise highly educated people are likely to subscribe to fictions about SHEs, often simply because their education has not included coverage of the self-help form of enterprise. Very often, the education system doesn't place sufficient value on practical experience or provide sufficient awareness about the needs and concerns of ordinary people. Those who are constrained by such learning omissions often seem unable to envisage an enterprise, other than a charity, that is run 'not-for-profit' and is tasked with achieving other goals. There are also those who pretend not to know the true nature of SHEs, because to admit the truth is not in their own interests.

### Protecting SHEs and their members

In many SHEs, the indispensable drivers of self-help and mutual action have either been forgotten or deliberately neglected.

28

Members and leaders of SHEs need to see that if they vote into office or hire people to run their enterprises who are not committed to the purpose of their enterprise, then it will inevitably fail. Predictably, such appointees endeavour to convert the members' enterprise into what becomes 'just another commercial business', with such interlopers becoming the main beneficiaries of their activities. This kind of situation generally arises due to the weaknesses of leaders and failings in their organization and governance, especially in the absence of an effective system of oversight. This typically occurs when the protection given by the legislation covering SHEs is defective because it doesn't adequately safeguard the interests of grassroots members.

The reality is that most professional managers are trained to operate only within commercial businesses; and ordinarily, they will have no credible understanding of the self-help model of enterprise unless and until they are provided with the kind of training that prepares them for a management role in SHEs. This presents a major problem for SHEs because managers who have not acquired a proper grasp of this form of enterprise will inevitably revert to the practices with which they are familiar. Often, these will be practices that are entirely inappropriate for use within SHEs. Leaders should be aware that running SHEs is radically different from running other forms of enterprise.

**Mutant enterprises**
Many enterprises bearing names that imply that they are bona-fide SHEs, may not, in fact, be authentic. In some countries, businesses can get away with calling themselves, for example, 'cooperatives' or 'building' societies, when they are not by any stretch of the imagination truly SHEs'. Numerous previously genuine SHEs have become enterprises that primarily serve the interest of those who

run them rather than the members that own them. So, it's not unusual to find that, in many countries, some of the names of certain types of SHEs have been damaged by their misuse, this results in the public no longer have any confidence in SHEs. It's the same situation in those countries where the State has appropriated SHEs.

In cases where governments have failed to regulate the use of the specific names that ought to be reserved for use by genuine SHEs, they are not only being hijacked by self-serving cliques but very often being demutualised where the law allows. This has been the fate of many building societies in the UK and of agricultural co-ops in many countries.

### *Ten large UK buildings societies demutualised*

Between 1987 and 2000, ten large UK buildings societies demutualised. This decimation of SHEs occurred and included Northern Rock, Bradford & Bingley and Abbey national, building societies. This flurry of demutualisation activity took place with the tacit encouragement of the government of the day. The fate of these former Building Societies offers a stark warning of the dangers of following strategies that are high-risk; typically, borrowing money using international capital markets to bankroll rapid expansion. The motivation behind such demutualisation seemed to be that it offered a pathway for their directors and top managers to secure huge personal benefit packages.

Most frequently, SHEs are taken over by a self-interested clique of members and or by their senior managers. While in other cases SHEs have been taken over by investors who have been allowed to secure a controlling interest. SHEs are not only at risk from internal takeovers but likely to be at risk of being infiltrated by political opportunists and, in some countries, they have been subject to takeover by the apparatus of the State.

In some SHEs, their *de-facto* purpose has changed to protect the jobs and lifestyles of top managers and the positions of officeholders. As a result, they are often generating short-term gains that are used to pay bonuses to top managers. Worryingly, many of the people involved with SHEs don't appear to know how and why previously highly effective SHEs have either ceased operating or have mutated into organizations that are no longer authentic self-help enterprises.

### Incompatible practices

If SHEs are to improve the lives of their members, their leaders have to grasp that many of the systems used by other forms of enterprise are incompatible with the purposes of SHEs. For example, **in commercial businesses**:

- **The strategic planning system** is built on the premise that the organization is paramount because it makes money for its owners; while in SHEs, the planning process needs to be founded on the premise of 'how best to meet the future needs of members'.

- **They are looking for a marketing strategy** that maximises profit from a specific market; while in SHEs, they need to find a market intervention strategy that works in the best interest of their members.

- **The methods of financing the enterprise** can be any means that will result in maximising profit; while in SHEs, the methods of financing have to be limited to those that protect their enterprise from the avarice of predatory investors.

- **Their economic system** needs to facilitate profit maximisation; while in SHEs, their system must be fitting for an enterprise motivated by the desire to meet the needs of its members while optimising the resources deployed in the process.

- **Their methods of accounting and control** are designed to account for finance and profit primarily; while in SHEs, the accounting and control system needs to be designed to measure progress toward the strategic aims and outcomes that members want, and on securing the productive use of all resources deployed.

- **Their means of rewarding people** are designed to encourage profit maximization; while in SHEs, people need to be rewarded based on their achieving the purpose of the enterprise and for optimising the resources deployed.

- **Their approach to obtaining the people required** to run their enterprise is based on finding the individuals needed both internally and externally from the large pool of people who are familiar with operating commercial businesses; while in SHEs, they need to invest in preparing the best available people for all essential roles within the enterprise, including both those in elected roles and those holding managerial positions.

### *Rural infrastructure*

A notable example of how self-help enterprises can solve problems (that are often beyond the capacity of the State to resolve) is provided by the rural communities in the UK that have maintained important services in their villages. Over the last ten years, more than 350 village shops and 46 public houses have been formed as SHEs, all providing services in their own communities. These enterprises have helped to put the brakes on the decline of rural communities across the country. These developments continue to be backed by advice and support from the Plunkett Foundation working in support of rural communities

In rural areas, access to the Internet is holding back the prosperity of communities. For example, in Sweden SHEs are helping to secure full-speed broadband to all areas of Sweden. Self-help solutions have been the driving force behind the spread of connections in rural areas. Today, co-ops cover approximately 20% of the infrastructure of broadband in Sweden, which has supplied the solution for many thousands of households that previously lacked access to the Internet.

# 4. REDISCOVERING SELF-HELP

## *Self-help enterprises — the first wave*

The 19th century was a period of social change. Slavery was largely abolished, and the second Industrial Revolution led to massive urbanisation. Often, early attempts to set up SHEs ended in failure, but by the second half of the century, SHEs developed sets of practices that became the basis for the rapid expansion of several types of this form of enterprise. Sets of practices were pioneered by visionaries, developed and subsequently taken up worldwide, resulting in SHEs becoming major players in the economies in very many countries.

Although approaches to running SHEs worked well enough for more than a century, this was a time when activities were local, and most leaders were well-known in their communities. However, the earlier methods of operating such enterprises proved to be insufficiently vigorous or durable when used in the larger, geographically dispersed, organizations. Those SHEs that failed to modify the way they were organized were beginning to go into decline, which in many cases ended in their demise or mutation.

The future of SHEs now lies in the hands of those leading a new wave of enterprises, both new ventures and resurgent enterprises, which are led by people willing and able to adopt a much stronger and sustainable approach to running their organizations.

This will involve adopting practices and systems that will keep people focused on their purpose.

Each new generation has to find improved ways of running their enterprises that are in tune with their times. However, if the mistakes of the past are to be avoided by new generations of leaders, it's essential that they appreciate the reasons why SHEs so often failed to adapt to the changes taking place in their markets, locally, nationally and globally. If new leaders of SHEs don't learn from past mistakes and adopt better ways of running their enterprises, they are highly likely to repeat the same errors as their predecessors.

At the time I started working in my local consumer co-op, in 1953, retail cooperatives still held a significant share of the UK retail market, offering a complete range of services covering both food and non-food sectors; and ran funeral services, footwear repairs factories, bakeries, dairies and abattoirs. Building societies, which supplied home loans and saving facilities, were present on most high streets, as were trustee savings banks, which sought to create thrifty habits amongst small savers who were then outside the market served by commercial banks. Many of these savings banks were later taken over by the government. Mutual insurers were significant, as were friendly societies, which were the main providers of sickness benefits and medical insurance until the birth of the National Health Service. In rural areas, agricultural co-ops were very important suppliers of farming requisites. Many of the very large enterprises had already begun to decline, having reached their peak of economic and social influence around the 1930s.

## Self-help and mutual action

Throughout life everyone has choices to make, he or she can accept their unfortunate lives, or they can seek to change whatever is prevents them from getting what they want out of life. People begin to take control of their lives whenever they identify what they need to change, and then find ways of achieving such change.

When the goods or services needed are not available, or when people are being cheated, taken advantage of, or ripped off in a variety of ways, their frustration will frequently result in the sense of anger. However, this anger needs to be controlled and positively directed. Otherwise, nothing will change for the better. In such circumstances, people adopting the self-help mindset will react by taking positive action. SHEs emerge when people are no longer willing to accept being exploited or poorly served.

Self-help calls for self-belief, self-discipline and self-control, but it's never the easy choice, which is to wait for someone else to do something. Any decision to do nothing usually means remaining dependent upon others and their choices. Often, it's necessary to unlearn helplessness; this is a process that can become much easier when individuals join with others to take mutual action.

## The self-help mindset

A crucial step towards properly understanding SHEs is to acknowledge that the self-help mindset should drive them. Where leaders forget about the necessity of supporting the self-help mindset their enterprises are imperilled.

SHEs are the product of peoples' desire to improve their lives, to secure a better future for themselves, their families and their communities. When people want to achieve major improvements in their lives, self-help and mutual action is often the only realistic way of bringing about improvements in the daily lives of people that don't own and control substantial resources. SHEs are founded when people decide to take greater control over their lives and to stop letting others take the most significant decisions about their lives.

## The origins of SHEs

In the 18th century, the exploited common people in various parts of the world began to realise that they could not rely upon others to improve their lives and that nobody but themselves would make the sweeping changes necessary to enrich their lives. Groups of people began to set-up enterprises that could help them combat the power of the powerful and unscrupulous elites. Many different approaches were tried, including self-supporting communities in which the members sought to insulate themselves against the reality of markets in which they had no power. However, very few of their ventures made any significant impact, and most efforts to change lives by this means were often short-lived.

It was not until the 19th century that fully effective self-help enterprises began to be developed when systematic approaches were formulated and widely copied. These included consumer, farmer and worker co-ops, friendly societies and building societies, as well as mutual insurers and several types of credit institutions. Soon the concepts of self-help and mutual action began to spread like wildfire throughout many parts of the world, first in Europe, and then worldwide. SHEs were set up to meet the needs of groups of buyers and sellers in every situation where markets exist, soon becoming one of the main mechanisms for improving the daily lives of ordinary people.

## Meeting real needs

Consumers who wanted unadulterated foodstuffs, honest weights and measures, and reasonable prices set up retail cooperatives.

Agricultural producers set up cooperatives to get a better deal for their produce and to obtain farm inputs of decent quality at a reasonable price. Workers wanting a just price for their labour and better working conditions set up worker cooperatives, and people requiring insurance formed mutual insurers. People seeking protection from the risks of sickness and unemployment set up friendly societies to make available sickness benefits and to gain access to healthcare services.

Friendly societies and retail cooperatives often offered facilities for small-scale savings to those who had no access to banks. People who wanted better homes started housing cooperatives of several types; as well as building societies that at first helped people to build decent homes, and later got members to save for deposits and supplied loans to buy their own homes. People that are seeking credit on acceptable terms set up farmers' banks, credit societies, and later credit unions. These were the most renowned examples, but in addition, many other types of SHEs were set up, all with the intention of achieving a better deal for their members. Following these early pioneers, all manner of self-help ventures became a worldwide phenomenon, embraced by millions as being the best means of improving their lot in life. *Annex I* – provides a list of many of the diverse types and activities of SHEs.

**Dependency**
People were beginning to grasp that the fight against poverty and gross inequality cannot be won until its underlying causes are confronted. Chief among these causes is the passive acceptance of dependency. People become dependent upon those who exploit their weaknesses, and fuel their addictions, ranging from drugs, alcohol, gambling, consumer goods (whether for the latest fashion

or gadget), or the debts they incur when borrowing money to feed their addictions.

In the political sphere, dependency arises whenever people come to rely on elites that often gain control over governments, or when an electorate is convinced that only by bowing to a political elite will they secure services from the State. A harmful dependency arises when people become reliant on the largess of those who control charities or non-governmental organizations. The self-help mindset causes people to reject all kinds of dependency, including if this arises when members become over-dependent upon their professional managers and then surrender the members right to control them democratically. This often happens when managers devise over-complex organizations that members are unable to understand, let alone control.

The self-help mindset converts into action when people reject dependency, and instead decide to work together with others to rid themselves of their reliance upon those people and organizations that are taking advantage of them.

**The errors of 'do-gooders.'**
Charity is often more about the people dispensing it than those receiving it. Would-be benefactors are often driven by a desire for recognition and redemption, and often end-up satisfying their own needs rather than meeting the real needs of the people they are supposed to be aiding. Well-intentioned people are often diverted into dispensing the kind of charity that holds back self-help. Helping people to help themselves is, in many circumstances, by far the best way to put sincere compassion into effect. Charities ought to guard against fuelling dependency and instead work to promote self-help initiatives if they truly want to help people develop lasting solutions to their problems.

Even in SHEs, those running them sometimes hold the mistaken belief that they should be handing out donations to the less fortunate, while others seem to muddle up SHEs with charities. It needs to be clear that any benefits arising from their activities belong to the individual members that own them so, it's up to members to decide how their money is spent, money should never be spent on creating dependency.

## Short-termism

People lose control over their lives when they opt for the short-term fix, instead of taking the long-term view – in other words, they need to be making provident decisions. Being 'provident' means showing wise foresight about the future or events that pose a risk to their wellbeing, exercising stewardship in the management of their own affairs and resources. The term 'provident societies 'was originally used by the British to describe the self-help societies that were committed to improving their members' lives. Those setting-up such societies understood that they had to make future-focused decisions if their lives were ever to improve.

People need to grasp the fact that to enhance their economic position this calls for a strong commitment to making better decisions, which normally means making decisions based upon securing longer-term outcomes. The avoidance of speculation-for-profit is a very important practice forming part of the self-help economic system. Only the very rich can afford to gamble with the future of their families; ordinary folk have to be much more prudent and risk-averse. The very rich know that when they hold most of the tickets in the lottery of life, they are almost bound to win.

People of limited means often do not think or plan long-term, either because any money they have is spent on simply surviving, or because they are too easily persuaded to spend what little they've got. For example, the imprudent person who receives a windfall tends to consume it rather than set it aside for a rainy day or put it to productive use. When people work together, they can make provision for the longer term; this again is a key element of the self-help economic system.

**Taking control**

The poorest people are among those who have little or no control over the factors that can have a devastating impact upon their lives; for example, naturally occurring events such as the weather, earthquakes, and volcanic eruptions. Other kinds of events can have a ruinous impact on poor people's lives, such as the pace of technological advances and social change. SHEs have the capacity to help their members cope with the negative impact of the dramatic changes that inevitably come into their lives.

Even if the events themselves cannot be controlled, it's possible to control how to respond to them. It's feasible to build up resilience in the face of such events, for example, by longer-term decision-making, such as arranging mutual insurance cover or setting money aside to use only when unexpected events occur. Members can build up the institutional strength of their enterprises in similar ways.

**Self-help decision-making**

People can only take control of their lives when they are determined to make good their weaknesses, decide to curb their addictions and take a longer term approach to the way they live their lives. Members of SHEs take the long view, securing a balance between benefits today and benefits tomorrow, they cannot have all the jam today, leaving tomorrow to look after itself. The first step towards people changing their lives involves changing their habits and replacing those habits that undermine the practice of self-help.

People committed to self-help make their decisions using a habitual process that is both logical and designed to ensure that they are achieving longer-term outcomes. Better decision-making helps people avoid the usual consequences of opting for short-term fixes and unethical actions – decisions that perpetuate a cycle of disappointing results and that lead a person down a road into poverty.

The self-help decision-making process involves:

- Carefully considering any reasonable alternative courses of action available. Then, and only then, making a decision that will support the achievement of their objectives.

- Setting clear goals and desired outcomes, this following a careful review of all the available evidence.

This process involves securing the best evidence and advice available, making our own decisions, and taking responsibility for the outcomes that arise. The process of evidence-based decision-making works well for both individuals and for SHEs. Within enterprises, some added steps in the process are necessary, with decisions that take account of the context of the organization, its policies and precedents.

Another key element of the self-help mindset is the realisation that everything has its price, and that nothing is ever truly 'free'. This means understanding that there is no such thing as a 'free lunch'; in other words, if someone appears to be giving something for nothing, invariably they will be expecting something in return.

**What works**

Another dimension to the kind of decision-making so essential to the self-help mindset is the process of seeking out and employing 'best-practice'. This should ensure that people aren't continually chasing the latest theory, fad, or fashion, and it means not rushing into 'hare-brained' schemes, and where everyone else feels they have to jump on the latest bandwagon. Neither does it mean over-investing energy in debating theory, when ideas can be tested in real situations and valuable experience drawn from others. The self-help mindset steers members through a habitual logical process, requiring them to examine their decisions rigorously and to discover whether there is evidence that any proposed action can achieve the desired result.

Best-practice is arrived at as the result of a disciplined and continuous approach to figuring out what works and what doesn't. It calls for research about the outcomes of the practices adopted by others, and which have proven workable and have produced the desired results. This approach also helps in formulating a raft of sound practices to support achieving the outcomes desired.

Substantial resources should not be committed until proper research has been undertaken, shared, and tested against the actual experience of others working in similar conditions. The self-help mindset leads us to be aware that there is such a thing as 'the wisdom of crowds', which means that many people with the same problem collectively stand a better chance of finding the best solution than any individual or organization has on its own. Such an approach doesn't exclude innovation and experimentation; on the contrary, it requires that all innovative ideas be judged by the evidence of their effectiveness, having been tested in a pragmatic and measured way. This means not committing significant resources all at once; that is, not until the validity and viability of any new approach are proven.

## Mutual support

SHEs can be the facilitator that helps people change their lives.

In the same way that many people are brainwashed into believing they cannot do things, such as mathematics or read financial statements, many people find it difficult to believe that self-help and mutual-action is a possibility for them. In these situations, the value of mutual action deserves recognition, because people working together and supporting each other can achieve things that would otherwise seem impossible.

Once it has been proven that people like themselves have achieved their aims, their own ambitions become more achievable. The main benefit of joint action through a self-help enterprise is that individuals can exercise collective power. People develop inner strength by building their personal capacity to respond positively to events that threaten their standard of living and by responding collectively to prepare for such eventualities.

Many people spend their lives repeating the same mistakes, often until they reach a point where they lose confidence in their ability to make essential adjustments in the way they live. In many cases, they need the help and support of others, expressly those experiencing the same desire to alter their lives. Mutual action offers the route out of inertia. SHEs should help members develop the capacity to stand on their own feet by increasing their power to withstand the vagaries of the market and the misfortunes of life; and by empowering them to respond positively to changing circumstances with resilience.

## Working together

Mutual action means members are working together to achieve a common purpose – in other words; they 'cooperate'. Cooperation entails balancing the needs of the individual with those of the group and becomes the means of creating added-value. It allows the individual to keep their independence while combining with other to use self-help and mutual action in the best interest of all involved.

Cooperation is not an alternative to competition; it's the alternative to acting in isolation. In practice, people often cooperate to compete. Based on their own experiences, most people will realise how humans behave when they experience certain conditions; they will know that some kinds of behaviour foster and sustain cooperation, while others will destroy it. Effective cooperation requires following a complete set of practices, which are set out in *Chapter 24.*

## Self-development and empowerment

One of the chief benefits of SHE membership is the opportunities it provides for self-development. Members can gain confidence when they do things for themselves and take steps to increase their control over their own lives. 'Education' is a nebulous term, often used in the context of SHEs when the term 'empowerment' would be more appropriate. People become empowered when they recognise their own ability to bring real and lasting change in their lives by working with others. It's when they discover that it involves improving their knowledge, skills, and competence by practical application. For example, many developing countries struggle to offer adequate basic education for the mass of people, so SHEs often become involved with efforts to improve the literacy and numeracy of their members and their families.

In most situations, SHEs play a substantive role in empowering their members, employees, and other stakeholders. This can mean helping people to figure out how to make democratic organizations work effectively, how to keep control over their SHEs, how to manage both their personal and joint finances. Most importantly, understanding the dynamics of the markets in which they and their enterprises need to operate. In many countries, members need to be empowered by developing the skills necessary to use computers and communications devices, both as members and in everyday life.

### Questioning the unquestionable

The self-help mindset includes having a healthy distrust of those who constantly tell others about their belief in so-called 'values'. Instead, they should wait to be convinced of the integrity by the actions of these self-proclaiming paragons of virtue. It's extremely naive to believe that merely uttering platitudes or claiming a commitment to high-minded values will bring about change in peoples' behaviour. Talk alone rarely ever changes anything.

Effective mutual action, along with true cooperative behaviour, can make a real difference in the lives of the members of SHEs. Expounding a set of values but having no guiding strategy for their implementation can only result in cynicism, which can, in turn, destroy cooperation and eventually their enterprise.

### Self-help solutions

When SHEs prosper, they do so not because of their different method of ownership or any theoretical advantages that may be cited. They flourish when they are providing people with what they want – a better deal, a better organization and a better future. Here it's essential to stress again that a better deal doesn't mean 'better' solely in financial terms, it means better as measured against any criteria that reflect the outcomes that members consider to be of value to themselves. Often, it's also about members and their leaders having the courage to resist the social pressures aimed at influencing people to become dependent upon big companies, big government and other kinds of patronage. It needs to be understood that when individuals give up their right to choose, then someone else will choose for them.

## Collective amnesia

As a species, humans seem to have a remarkable capacity to forget even the most important lessons that they and their forebearers should have learned from past experiences. It's not only individuals who lose important memories; many organizations appear to have no institutional memory. Nations, too, often have no reliable recall of critical events, the vacuum being filled by myths promoted by those either holding power or by those with a dogma to peddle. All this suggests that it's easy to forget the most important lessons that should have been learned over the centuries. Using experience as a guide and routinely referencing it, should help us make better decisions about our future. When people don't remember and learn, they are likely to repeat the same mistakes all over again

Current generations seem to ignore the role played by self-help enterprise in lifting several generations out of deprivations caused by extreme poverty. In the UK, for example, consumer cooperatives gave the mass of people an alternative to accepting adulterated food, perpetual debt, and many other exploitative practices used by dishonest traders. Friendly societies offered access to health care, unemployment, and sickness benefits; while building societies offered the means of escaping the grasp of unscrupulous landlords and the support to become homeowners. Meanwhile, farmers could source their supplies, chiefly seeds, that could be relied upon.

Throughout the world, there are comparable examples of the benefits achieved by self-help ventures, and in many countries' similar achievements by SHEs, which are still expanding. In many countries, recent statistics relating to the increases in average household debt, much of it acquired using credit cards that attract usurious levels of interest, and the growing number of families now living below the poverty line, are just two indicators of the need for a major resurgence of SHEs.

The populace seems to have forgotten why and how self-help and mutual action can best be made to work in practice and forgotten the true meanings and importance of words such as 'provident', 'societies', 'membership' and 'surplus'. In many cases, SHEs have been financed from sources, such as the international financial markets, which has so often led to members losing control of their enterprises.

### Concern for the community
Self-help, not selfish-help, should be at the heart of SHEs, so it not surprising that SHEs often make donations to support the less fortunate in their local communities. However, such benevolence should always favour supporting self-help initiatives, because only self-help offers long-term benefits, while 'handouts' are likely to perpetuate dependency. In many cases a significant portion of any surplus arising from the activities of the enterprise stays in the enterprise, to be reinvested within the community and to improve the quality and value of the services offered to members.

Commercial businesses usually make charitable or cultural donations as a means of securing public goodwill, and often as a means of counteracting public anxiety about the impact of their business activities within a community. The self-help form of enterprise is different because they should not exploit any of their stakeholders, nor to be persuaded to believe it should compete with commercial businesses by increasing the extent of their charitable giving. Instead, lasting, more equal, and fairer relationships should be developed with all other stakeholders, including the communities in which they work. SHEs need to engage with their community and communicate the fact that they champion self-help and mutual action.

### The self-help mindset drives SHEs

In SHEs where the self-help mindset is no longer present, and leaders have become complacent, such SHEs are soon reduced to organizations that no longer serve their members. Where SHEs have been hijacked, at least the same passion that surrounded their birth is called for to restore control of the enterprise to its rightful owners – its members.

Securing peoples' continuing commitment to mutual action depends on their leaders running enterprises that truly deliver tangible benefits to their members. In this context, 'tangible benefit' means not only financial gains but anything that members' value. The *theoretical* advantages of mutual action are not enough to motivate ordinary people, in fact very few are interested in the abstract act of 'cooperating' and will not respond to appeals for support simply because 'self-help' is thought to be inherently 'a good thing'.

Given the challenges facing humanity and the contribution that self-help and mutual action can make towards improving peoples' lives, now is the time to rediscover, reassess and reengineer SHEs.

# 5. MAKING MARKETS WORK FOR PEOPLE

## The market

Put simply, 'the market' is any situation where buyers and sellers conduct trade and where goods and services change hands for money or some other means of exchange. The fundamental forces are supply and demand, and the two main groups of players are buyers and sellers. Markets vary in size, range, geographic scale, type, and location, as well as the types of goods and services traded – and since the advent of cyber-markets, they don't even have a specific geographic location. Markets enable trade, the distribution and allocation of resources in a society, and allow any tradeable commodity, including information, to be valued and priced. They may be formed deliberately or emerge spontaneously to enable the exchange of rights of ownership.

## The alternative to conflict

When a primitive man wanted the possessions of others, he simply took them by force, and this is still happening in places where enforcement of the rule of law is weak or the powerful reign unchecked. The advancement of peaceful civilisation started when people began trading goods and services, first by barter and then by the use of money as the basis of exchange.

Marketplaces, where people meet to trade, were progressively set up but were often dominated by the rich and powerful and where traders ready to cheat or trade unfairly had free rein. Over time, governments, and other bodies, local, national, and international, introduced regulations to curb the worst excesses of those seeking to exploit markets to their own advantage.

Nevertheless, the regulation of markets is still often weak or non-existent, and most are imperfect because either buyers or sellers occupy a more dominant position, and as a result become exploitative. Typically, this occurs when some participants have a monopoly, or near monopoly or the market is distorted by some other means.

## Disadvantaged by the market

Some sections of the population are often disadvantaged in a market because they are unable to exercise enough power within them. People lack power for a variety of reasons, though most often it's because they do not control enough resources to compete effectively, for example, when they lack enough finance to run the production or processing facilities needed to add value to commodities such as food crops and livestock. In other cases, they are exploited when cartels, criminals, cheats or dominant participants, distort or control a market.

In some cases, 'sellers' may dominate markets, while in others 'buyers' exercise disproportionate power, but in either case, some people are at a disadvantage because of their lack of power in a specific market. In many cases, there are those who are disadvantaged in a market because they don't have a proper understanding of its workings or don't have the knowledge (market intelligence) or the skills necessary to compete effectively against the other participants; this is generally the situation in the case of individuals and small-scale players. However, when the smaller players in the market take mutual action, they not only increase their direct power but (by enabling them to make better-informed decisions) they empower their members both as individuals and as a joint enterprise.

All decision-makers in SHEs need to have a good understanding of how the market works and more specifically know about those markets where the enterprise is involved. Member-leaders and professional managers, at all levels, should be equipped to carry out their tasks, this includes the key responsibility for helping their members to understand the markets in which they have to operate. Prior to taking up any decision-making role within SHEs, all would-be leaders ought to be able to demonstrate that they have such awareness.

## Speculation and its impact on 'real' markets

It's essential to separate real markets for goods and services from the contrived or speculative markets used by those seeking to speculate (gamble) upon price movements within a market. The fact that enormous amounts of money can be made from speculation often completely distorts the real markets for goods and services. Frequently, investors are not looking for returns from investments in the 'real' economy, by investing in efficient and profitable enterprises, but instead, are chasing super-profits generated by speculating upon the movements in share and commodity prices.

The dichotomy between real and speculative markets is one of the greatest challenges to democracy and is one of the root causes of the current levels of inequality between the rich and the poor. Democratic governments worldwide have to confront this issue before any progress towards achieving a fairer society can take place. Transactions designed to cover risk, such as the authentic trading in the 'futures' of real commodities, can be entirely legitimate and have a place in the operation of real markets, but pure speculation for profit needs to be shunned.

## Exploiting the market

Problems arise for consumers when businesses seek to exploit their customers or to achieve 'super-profits' by dominating a market, distorting competition, and preventing market access to would-be competitors. The fact is that the bulk of shareholders in many big businesses gain relatively small benefits from their investment when compared to the share of benefits that go to the top managers and directors running them. The investments of many company shareholders are held, via their pension funds and insurance policies, without any real control from the bulk of their actual owners. Instead, they are typically run conscience-free, by directors and senior managers, who often appropriate the lion's share of the benefits arising from the business.

Even in long-standing democracies, where laws are implemented that exert some control over corruption, many of the largest and most scrutinised companies still try to cheat consumers and other stakeholders. They do this by colluding with other businesses to manipulate markets, by taking secret commissions (bribes), and by misselling and other dubious marketing practices. In the poorer countries of the world, embezzlement, monopolistic behaviour, and many other forms of cheating are often endemic. Dictatorial rulers dole out entire industries to their friends, who then find ways of diverting money into their own pockets via offshore bank accounts.

Undermining competition does not always mean a crime has been committed; often it's the work of a government that franchises a legal monopoly, thereby sanctioning protectionism by allowing only one or two companies to participate in a market.

## Malfunctioning markets

While some denounce the market as the source of inequality, others insist that only a completely free-market can offer prosperity. Both conflicting points of view arise from several popular misconceptions about the market. The ability to trade goods and services within open and fair markets is, in fact, fundamental to the proper operation of a democratic State. Those who advocate a completely unregulated market are often the same people who have little or no interest in running an open and fair market, and who seek the right to secure a position in the market that will allow them to make excessive profits.

Attempts to replace markets with bureaucratic arrangements have failed the world over. In many countries, the State attempts to regulate a market by undertaking just enough oversight to ensure that no player can outrageously exploit its dominant position. However, in most States competition laws and regulatory bodies do little to ensure that new entrants can enter markets that are not working as they should. Often this is simply because enormous amounts of finance are required by any enterprise that seeks to challenge the dominance of large national and international companies.

Some speak of SHEs as if they are an alternative to the market, but this cannot be right because SHEs only work properly in an open market. SHEs are an alternative to profit-driven businesses not an alternative to the market. The original rules of the Rochdale Society of Equitable Pioneers (a British consumer cooperative set up in 1844) included the requirement to 'sell at market prices' — so they certainly envisaged operating within the framework of the market. There are countless examples of failures in the market, but to date, the alternative models have inevitably resulted in even greater unfairness, as anyone who has seen at first-hand the results of attempts to replace the market with a command-economy will doubtless confirm.

## Smart markets

Markets in which buying or selling decisions are based not solely upon price but consider such features as 'fair trade', environmental sustainability and an assessment of the health risks and benefits can be described as 'smart markets'. Most buyers and sellers are only prepared to moderate their decisions within certain limits and accept to pay what they consider to be a reasonable price for such values-based benefits. Well-run SHEs can, and often do, set standards when they intervene within a market, converting it into a smart market. Commercial businesses will normally respond by moderating their behaviour when faced with competitors that operate to higher ethical standards as well as giving a better deal in financial terms.

## Sharing the added-value

Except in times of abnormal scarcity, most primary producers, (for example, dairy farmers, coffee or olive growers, small-scale entrepreneurs and low or semi-skilled workers) will find it difficult to make a decent living. This because they wield very little power in the markets where they sell their products and services, they regularly find that those holding power depress the producers' share of the selling price achieved in its final market (the ultimate consumer). When their product enters a processing or marketing chain, someone else typically takes the value-added of their product. This occurs, for example, when raw milk becomes butter, cheese, yoghurt, or other processed products, or is sold in packs through a large retail chain.

The fact is that in many cases it is the investors in the processing, production, and marketing channels which take the major share of the value-added to produce, or to the products of the labour and skills of other people. Unless primary producers of all types unite to set-up enterprises that secure a fairer share of the added value, they will not be able to secure a decent living for themselves and their families.

## Sustaining small and medium-sized enterprises

Thousands of SHEs worldwide are helping member-businesses raise their capacity to withstand the vagaries of the market and increase their power to compete and prosper. These SHEs range from those offering common services to small businesses right up to very large-scale enterprises marketing their members' products internationally. In a world dominated by multinationals, most sole traders, partnerships, artisans, tradespersons, family farms, and many other small to medium enterprises (SMEs) can derive significant benefits from using SHEs to intervene in the market on their behalf. Although these enterprises help increase the profitability of their members' businesses, it is not the role of SHEs to generate profits for the enterprise as a mutual entity.

### *Supporting producers*

Relatively small-scale producers are routinely ruthlessly exploited by middlemen and food-processing companies because producers working on their own have very little power in their respective markets. Today, some of the world's most effective SHEs are those formed by farmers and growers. In the UK, and in some its former dominions and colonies, producers were late in coming to realise the benefits of forming SHEs. This being due to political support for State-sponsored marketing boards, which mainly operated between the 1930s up to about the end of the 20th Century. In those countries that successfully organized SHEs, they have significantly increased their international competitiveness and the prosperity of their members.

Many countries have some very successful SHEs organized by producers, notable examples include New Zealand's Fonterra, Australia's Bulk Handling Co-op, in Scandinavia, Arla Foods and Columbia's National Federation of Coffee Growers. Producers also benefit their joint purchasing of farming inputs, for example in India IFFCO. In the USA, the majority of America's two million farmers and ranchers belong to one or more farmer cooperatives. Fishermen/women also form SHEs.

## The scale of a market

The globalisation of markets is not a new phenomenon – it began many centuries ago when sailing ships offered the means of trading goods between far-flung countries. Most ordinary people were unaffected by globalisation, and this stayed the case until the growth of speedy, low-cost communications and transport methods brought products from the world to their doorstep. Earlier, the scale of these markets was normally limited to a small geographic area, sometimes as small as a village, but typically to market towns, cities, or further afield. Today, however, most production is influenced by the national, regional, and global markets for both products and services. Although some markets stay small, for instance, a village shop or a local public house, a broader market still influences these sub-markets. For example, if the prices charged in the village shop are too high, then the people able to do so will travel to a more distant shop or supermarket offering lower prices.

## Marketing and its cost

'Marketing' combines the process of finding the products or services that may be of interest to customers with the strategies for sales, communications, and the development of the enterprise. Enterprises build customer relationships and create value for their customers and themselves through this integrated process that starts with market research and follows on through market segmentation, enterprise planning and execution, and ends with pre-sale and post-sale promotional activities. However, marketing in the context of a self-help enterprise has a different character, because its members are, in the first place, the owners of the enterprise – not just prospective customers or 'a market' just waiting to be exploited.

One of the main benefits of SHEs is the prospect of reducing the cost structure in a sector of the market; this is because they should not be resorting to employing expensive marketing techniques, which can significantly add to the costs of many products and services. If there is a direct and productive relationship between the members and the management of their enterprise, then marketing costs can be lower, which should result in increased member benefits. In commercial businesses, many managers are convinced that the only way to increase growth is to spend vast amounts on marketing and branding, which is ordinarily not in the best interest of consumers. SHEs often do not tap into one of their inherent advantages – their members – who, when properly engaged, should become the real experts in the markets where they are directly involved.

## The importance of focus

SHEs need to focus on a specific market, or on several closely related markets and intervene within specific markets in ways that benefit their members. The scale of their operations should allow them to follow an intervention strategy that offers tangible advantages to members. This often means that the enterprise needs to work to reduce costs, compared to those of current players in the market, which invariably means lower unit labour and other costs.

There are several reasons for concentrating each self-help enterprise on specific markets, perhaps most important is that members engage with their enterprises when they have an active interest and involvement in that market. Members representatives, most essentially directors, need to have a thorough understanding of how these specific markets work in practice, which is unlikely to be the case if SHEs become conglomerates; see *Chapter 10*.

### Changing markets
One of the most significant facts about the market is that it's constantly changing. In earlier times, changes in the market were typically slow and more predictable, these days most markets alter both faster and more often. Now, often in response to developing technology and to the social changes that alter peoples' lifestyles. Any enterprise that doesn't have an inbuilt capacity to respond to such modifications cannot have a long-term future. This means that those running enterprises keep their organizations lean and fit, so that when change does occur, they can respond quickly and appropriately. In SHEs, the method of democratic control and the practices in place to support it should be designed to help, not inhibit future improvement.

When a market changes, for whatever reason, it often signals that a modification to the market-intervention strategy will be necessary, and many SHEs have declined as a direct result of not adapting their strategy when faced with such change. In recent times, most of the things influencing markets have arisen from technological advances, increasing globalisation or because of significant social changes.

When many of the early types of SHEs were started, their market or catchment area was limited in geographical terms. Typically, many towns were little more than expanded villages, and cities a conglomeration of villages or small towns, and established 'market towns' acted as the hub or the centre of that market. The enterprises that served the population in each market competed within an area that was constrained by the limits of the people's mobility.

When new means of transport were developed, in the first place it was canals, after this railways and then arterial road networks. Followed by international sea lanes and air transport. These advances in transport were matched by equally significant developments in communications, which combined to bring vast changes to the size and scale of many markets. Markets often expanded from being very local to become global. This is not to say that there aren't still many thriving local markets. Nevertheless, markets have tended to become more specialised and geographically diverse. Specialisation shouldn't be thought of only in terms of products or commodities, but by the methods of distribution, an example of which is the growth of internet retailers such as Amazon and eBay. Sadly, many SHEs do not appreciate what is happening in their markets because their enterprises have not been designed to respond rapidly to change. It needs to be appreciated, that when a self-help enterprise enters any specific market, this should generate change within that market. Therefore, almost as soon as the enterprise starts trading its market intervention strategy will need to be reviewed.

## Markets in transition

There is often a vital role for SHEs when markets are in a state of flux before they make a transition in response to major changes in market conditions. For example, when there are major advances in technologies that cause the market to change, or where changes take place in a specific market, or when significant social change is taking place. The nature of such changes can be many and varied. Recent changes include the globalisation of markets, the increasing mechanisation and scale of farming, the wider acceptance of gender equality and its impact on the labour market, and the changes in technology that have affected so many trades and industries.

When such major changes do take place, SHEs can help reduce some of the most damaging effects of such change and often help accelerate their positive impact. Very often it's the most vulnerable participant in the market who endure the most negative aspects of such change.

## Self-help in cyber-markets

Cyber-markets are operating for almost anything and everything, these markets offer new opportunities for both buyers and sellers of all manner of goods and services, including SHEs. Trading online is now commonplace in much of the world, and cyber-markets have become fundamental to cross-border and global trade. Online information and search tools help consumers find and compare alternative offers, while various online devices, forums, and electronic payment methods help e-commerce. As well as improving consumer choice and empowerment, these developments have the capacity to generate increased competition and economic growth. They offer a platform to support new entrants in many markets, particularly by innovators who can challenge traditional enterprises.

Cyber-markets can work more efficiently for the benefit of both buyers and sellers, enabling better-targeted spending and greater optimisation of resources. Most consumers no longer differentiate between online and offline transactions, and the line between them is increasingly blurred. Some shoppers start by searching the 'real' world on the high street and then go online to comparison shop before making their purchase; others shop the other way around. For sellers, online activity enables all forms of enterprise to be more responsive to consumer demand, leading to a broader range of products and services and more personalised offers. Eventually, all types of SHE will engage with their related cyber-markets if they are to survive.

As with any market, cyber-markets are open to abuse, and self-help and mutual action will be essential for helping both buyers and sellers achieve a better deal. Alongside the huge benefits that the internet offers by way of improved information and choice, new sources of consumer exploitation are emerging, such as fake reviews, undisclosed commercial blogging, complex tariff structures, misleading or skewed search results, and 'drip pricing' (adding taxes, payment-card charges, or other extras to make the total price far higher than the one originally quoted). In addition, practices such as 'concealed recurring payments' and 'complex bundling' can both harm consumer interests and distort competition. The negative effects can be even worse in markets characterised by information irregularities, consumer biases, inertia selling or where vulnerable people are being targeted.

Too much choice can create problems that can, in effect, lead to no choice at all, as people get swamped with too much information and just shut down. The shabby or illegal online practices of some commercial business and individuals create both an elevated risk in cyber-markets and an opportunity for SHEs to offer a trustworthy alternative. The dubious trading practices of many players within cyber-markets are fundamentally anti-competitive and cry out for the intervention of effective SHEs.

## Challenging current platform owners

The advent of all manner of newer players in the market, based on their use of innovative approaches to 'doing business' over the internet, are transforming all manner of sectors. Organizations such as Amazon, E-bay, Gumtree, Uber, Airbnb, to name but a few, all have the potential to exercise power in the market that can become exploitive.

The operators of 'price comparison websites', while ostensibly benefiting the interests of consumers, often only add costs to transactions by means of securing commissions from goods and services providers. In addition, despite strong denials by site-owners, the recommendations provided may often be biased towards those suppliers that offer them commissions or introduction fees. If people want to get truly independent advice, SHEs are best placed to supply this. However, members will need to be prepared to cover the operating costs of providing authentic independent advice.

The digital marketing platforms (an umbrella term for the marketing of products or services using digital technologies) can seriously disadvantage those people who depend on these platforms for their livelihood. In many cases workers and small business owners are being exploited by the owners of such platforms, undoubtedly there are opportunities for SHEs to be organized to mount a challenge to the domination of the market by current platform-owners; also, for SHEs that formulate new platforms that have the potential to bring real benefits to their members.

### Enter the State – exit the State

Following the 1917 revolution in Russia, many people, all over the world, switched from believing in self-help to believing that they could rely upon the State to deliver the changes they yearned for. In several countries the provision of services by the State became the favoured way, although the extent of State involvement varied from a fully Soviet-style planned economy to more specific interventions, including the nationalisation of key industries and services, the introduction of marketing boards for agricultural products, and establishment of public trusts (for example, the BBC in the UK).

In Britain nationalisation was the chosen way for several industries, State marketing boards were favoured over agricultural cooperatives, and local authority schemes (and later housing associations) were supported instead of housing cooperatives. Recent decades have seen a decline in most methods of direct State intervention because in most cases the results were far from satisfactory. If the State is to intervene in markets in the best interest of its citizens, then this is best done by means of providing the conditions needed to encourage the growth of genuine SHEs. The old models of State intervention that rely on politicians and their appointees to run State enterprises are hardly likely to be more successful than earlier efforts to operate nationalised industries. This is not to say that there is not the possibility of developing transitional models of enterprise, so long as they are set on a clear pathway towards becoming bona-fide self-help enterprises within a specified time-frame.

### Where there is no market

Whenever the market is not working properly, this can bring untold suffering - and usually disproportionately impacts the most vulnerable sections of society. I saw this first-hand in 1980 when I worked with fishing co-ops in Madagascar. At that time the government had attempted to control the cereals market with the result that farmers simply stopped planting grains. Madagascar went from being a net exporter to a position of extreme shortages of food grains. Even worse, were the situations I found in Poland and Russia, immediately following the collapse of their communist regimes. I was there to assess what could be done to prepare for the emergence of a market economy and to see what could be done to revive self-help enterprises.

**The overall market system**

If markets are to be made to work, so they operate for the benefit of ordinary citizens, then governments need to provide SHEs with fully effective and supportive laws, as well as a positive public policy environment. Well-run, truly effective SHEs can in so many different situations eliminate the problems caused by malfunctioning markets. Usually, being more effective over the long-term, and without incurring the high cost to taxpayers when yet more layers of market regulation are added. The intervention of SHEs being preferable to taking on the high-risk of unintended consequences that accompany most schemes involving direct State intervention.

### Cooperative banks in Finland

In Finland, (2015) there were over 229 locally owned cooperative banks networked to provide a nationwide service through the OP-Pohjola Group. In addition, the

Finnish local cooperative bank group consists of 42 independent banks each operating in its own region. This group was established in 1997 to enable the member banks to continue operating independently as the other cooperative bank group in Finland believed it was too centrally administered. The method of organization used in Finland contrasts with the form used in some other countries, where their cooperative banks started out as a kind of development bank.

In the case of the UK, their cooperative banks were originally a department of their central organizations that provided a service for the deposit of surplus funds from their member consumer co-ops. Both the English and Scottish cooperative banks offered no direct individual membership rights to their banking customers when in later developments they changed into retail banks. Most of the experience of having co-op banks as an adjunct to other services has not proved to be positive. For example, the former Scottish Co-op bank, the UK's Co-op Bank (see *Chapter 23* - The wrong type of finance), Australia's Co-op bank and the Botswana Co-op bank, all used this form of organization, which resulted in their failure as self-help enterprises.

# 6. PURPOSE AND FUNCTION

## The importance of purpose and function

SHEs exist to achieve their common purpose, which can be whatever the founding members and their successors agree it is; provided it's legal and permitted by the SHE's rules. This chapter looks at the vital role that a clear-cut holistic purpose and function play in running effective SHEs. Members, in particular, their leaders, need to know how to go about establishing their purpose as well as everything else they have to do to achieve it.

Whenever there is no *clear* purpose there is nothing to unite the membership; and, most damaging, is when the vacuum created is filled by one that is set by a self-serving clique. The leaders of SHEs have got to help their members to set a purpose that will unify the members, binding them together to take mutual action. Where people (members and all other significant stakeholders) are committed to an unambiguous, purpose, this empowers them to succeed in their endeavours and concentrates the efforts of all those involved. This purpose is often referred to as the 'common purpose'; however, in this book, this term will only be used when it's necessary for the sake of clarity, in all other cases the word 'purpose' is used.

The undisciplined pursuit of countless opportunities as they arise, with increased options and chances, only leads to the dissipation of effort and results in the available energy and resources being spread thinner over diverse activities. Whenever people do not purposefully and deliberately choose where to concentrate their energies and time, they soon lose sight of everything that is truly important. So, it's essential that all concerned cut-down on distractions, simplify, and concentrate on what is most critical.

## Why people set up and join SHEs

When a person becomes a member of a self-help enterprise, they are normally motivated to join because they wish to enjoy the benefits, they believe the enterprise will provide. People join and remain members of SHEs when they accept the total membership package, which includes, the rights, responsibilities and commitment to the purpose that unites members. it's being committed to achieving the common purpose that qualifies a person to be considered to be accepted as a member of any specific self-help enterprise.

## Defining the purpose

When people join SHEs, they are normally expecting more than access to whatever services the enterprise provides; typically, they expect to access a better deal in specified markets, than they would otherwise get, an organization that they can trust and a continuing relationship that helps them to improve their future. This means that they need a 'holistic purpose' that encompass all the different facets that it comprises; see *Figure B -6 A holistic purpose.*

The purpose of SHEs need to be both visionary and pragmatic, not simply dreaming about a better life; but actually, changing lives for the better. This ordinarily means improving their members' position in the markets they engage with and satisfying their joint needs that should be both concrete and realistic. For example, it's naïve and pointless to set out a purpose that implies that the enterprise intends to 'change the world'. Typically, the main thrust of the purpose will be to remedy specific deficiencies in a specific market, meeting the specific needs of members should be the driving force motivating all the people involved in the enterprise.

## Avoiding confusion

Setting the purpose of a self-help enterprise ought not to be confused with the kind of practices often followed by commercial businesses. They often adopt so-called 'mission statements' that usually only present 'pseudo-purposes' - for example: 'to become the market leader' in a specific market. Often, seeking to obscure their true intent, which is to make money for their owners.

Mission statements', usually only record 'intentions' about how they seek to maximise profitability, and which can be changed whenever it suits them. Many organizations produce extravagant mission statements that are generally nothing more than a meaningless fudge; this is not what SHEs need. On the other hand, SHEs are mainly about finding practical solutions to everyday problems and helping members to meet the challenges faced by members in their daily lives. The strategic aims, intermediate objectives and the immediate priorities of the enterprise all need to be agreed, all, reflecting what members want from their enterprise

## The core of the purpose

When a group of people decide to set up an enterprise, they will normally have a very clear idea about what they want to change in a market and the benefits that they seek to bring to members. The most immediate outcomes that members want will form the core of the purpose. For example, in a:

- Farmers' marketing enterprise – getting fairer terms and reaching new markets for their produce.

- Consumer food co-op – supplying healthy and sustainable foodstuffs at fair prices.

- Credit union – providing ethical financial services including savings and loans at both fair and reasonable rates.

71

- Rural community co-op - securing access to important services, such as a local shop, transport, or banking facilities.

- Worker co-op – providing jobs that give self-fulfilment, fair rewards, more lifestyle choices and good working conditions.

- Tenant housing co-op - to secure better living conditions, get fair rents, reliable maintenance and a supportive community.

- Care co-op - to secure high standards of care that meet the real needs of individuals, at a fair and reasonable cost.

(Please note - these are broad examples, all SHEs need to tailor their core purpose to fit their own situation)

Of course, members will expect their leaders to get down to the detail of how to achieve the outcomes they want, which will involve developing a market intervention strategy; *see Chapter 10.*

**Organizational development**
A critical part of the overall intent of a self-help enterprise is the creation of an organization that has the capacity to deliver the purpose of the enterprise. To do this requires building an organization that members can trust, this is not something that can be left to chance, such improvements have to be planned.

The intention to create and sustain a 'better organization' needs to be part of the enterprise's purpose. Consequently, it has to be reflected in the plans of the enterprise. Specific objectives and outcomes have to be set so that the organization progresses towards being the kind of organization that it needs to become. This will involve - developing people in all roles throughout the enterprise, changing the organization's structure and associated practices; especially, the organizational culture. In particular, should equip members to be more resilient in the face of changes in the market, and helping members to improve the quality of their decisions when facing choices offered by the market.

## Strategic aims

The strategic aims of the enterprise may be separated into longer-term aim that provides the general direction of travel, and medium-term aims that are much more specific. When setting-out these aims, it can be helpful to elicit answers to the following questions:

- What's the nature of the better deal that the enterprise aims to secure for its members?

- What will the enterprise do to ensure it always acts in the best interest of its members and how will the enterprise help member's, as individuals, improve their capacity to operate in the market?

- How will the enterprise help to safeguard the members' future within the market?


All of these elements should be built into a strategic plan. The plan will set out when and how the strategic aims should be achieved, alongside the specific outcomes to be achieved.

Prior to embarking on settling on more specific aims, it's normal to undertake research and consultations, internally and more widely, to arrive at a view on what will happen in the future, especially in the next 5-10 years. Only then will it be possible to make reasonable forecasts about the direction the market is taking and what other factors are likely to influence the way the enterprise will need to respond.

Setting or updating the core purpose of the enterprise is the first step in the operational planning process, just as setting or updating the strategic aims of the enterprise is the first step in the strategic planning process (as outlined in the management system; see *Chapter 20.*).

### How function provides focus

Any form of organization will struggle to achieve its purpose unless it has a very clear function, and all involved in the enterprise understand what this is. The function provides focus as this limits its activities to those that are in line with its purpose. In most commercial businesses their purpose and function are one and the same, which is to make money for their owners. Although, in many family-owned businesses it's more about securing a livelihood and a particular lifestyle

Where the function of an organization is not clear; or where the people running the organization do not concentrate on this, they are prone to become distracted. The meaning of concentrate in this context is the same as when using a pair of binoculars or a telescope. This does not mean fixating on something to the total exclusion of everything that is going on around them. Instead, it means constantly adjusting and adapting the field of vision to what is being seen.

SHEs invariably get into trouble when they don't stick to their proper function and instead seek to become involved in other tasks such as social engineering, promoting a religion, a political dogma, or other partisan causes, none of which directly further the purpose of the enterprise.

When SHEs exercise their collective power in a market, they are often challenging powerful elites or those reaping large profits from markets that are neither free nor fair. When responding to the reaction of those dominating markets, members often discover that to secure wider social and political change requires support from politicians. For example, where it's justifiable to lobby governments and other institutions to secure changes to conditions that disadvantage members in the market. However, to directly support partisan politicians is an entirely different matter. This is not to say that individual members don't pursue their own beliefs, which may or may not be shared with other members. However, separate and independent organizations, having other functions, are needed.to them carry out.

When SHEs do become involved in extraneous activities, this can only damage the essential equivalence that needs to exist between members, because to support any specific set of partisan beliefs means discriminating against those members that do not support these. When the focus is lost, there is a failure to concentrate on what is essential, and most significantly, such distractions destroy the essential singularity of purpose. Organizations that undertake multiple functions usually prove to be poor performers in all functions. Expecting a single organization to carry out more than one function is like trying to ride two or more horses at the same time.

**Ownership and survival aren't purposes**
Ownership itself brings very little benefit to members, significant benefits only arise when the enterprise acts to intervene within a market on behalf of its members. Simply setting-up and running an enterprise that operates in the same way as any commercial business brings few benefits to grassroots members. Although, this may provide jobs and a good living to those running it. The continued survival of an organization is not in itself a valid purpose.

A 'sense of ownership' can be a powerful thing but only if this is accompanied by other benefits arising from its activities. Also, members need to fully understand that ownership in the context of a self-help enterprise is fundamentally different from the meaning that people often attach to the word 'ownership'. In SHEs, it means 'beneficial, mutual' ownership, which means that the current members have use of the assets of the enterprise and benefit from their use. Current members are in effect trustees, holding assets on behalf of both current and future members.

SHEs don't always have to own much in the way of assets to effectively intervene within some markets. For example, farmers can sometimes jointly hire an agent or employ people to combine their crops and market it jointly. Another example is where individuals simply bulk their purchasing power to get a better deal

### Economic and social purposes

The benefits SHEs secure on behalf of their members cannot be rigidly separated between economic and social benefits; all the benefits from membership are part of a complete package, which needs to be fully integrated with the holistic purpose.

Many people jump to the conclusion that because SHEs can play an influential role in creating social change, then they also believe that SHEs should have separate social objectives. Many noteworthy social changes occurring in the 19th and 20th centuries were as a result of socio-economic changes that were sometimes led by SHEs. Significant changes occurred in the balance of power within markets, which often occurs when SHEs intervened on behalf of their members. However, this does not mean that SHEs should embark upon disparate programmes with the intention of creating social change.

When SHEs put more disposable income into the hands of their members, it is they who decide how to save or spend their own money. For example, most members make rational choices when it comes to prioritising their expenditure. There are also millions of poor people in those countries that have inadequate healthcare and pitiable education systems, who realise that getting access to such services for their children is their priority.

SHEs can help their members by giving advice and increase their capacity to change many aspects of their lives, but it is not the role of leaders to spend their members' money on charitable programmes, no matter how well-intentioned. The fact is that all the objectives of SHEs need to be integrated and are in truth all socio-economic.

## The role of members in setting the purpose

The membership should agree on the purpose of their enterprise, in the first place at its conception, and thereafter review it regularly to ensure that it continues to be fully relevant. The involvement of external facilitators to aid the process may be helpful, but the agreed purpose must be owned by the membership and expressed in terms that grassroots members understand; most definitely this should *not* be written in 'management-speak'.

The highest level of contribution towards the achievement of the purpose can only be assured when all the necessary systems are in place as these will make executing the intentions and plans of the enterprise as effortless as possible. Having a clear overarching intent enables people to check regularly and to evaluate their activities and the behaviour of all the people involved.

Leaders can be trained in communication techniques, how to foster teamwork, and engage in endless feedback sessions, but if an organization does not have clarity of goals and roles, it will not succeed

Whatever the purpose of an enterprise is today, it will one day become necessary to change or redefine it. Change becomes necessary when the market and the needs of members change; so, it's important that it be reviewed on a regular basis. Whilst the purpose of an enterprise may change over time the function remains the same.

## Put it in writing

Typically, SHEs start in a small way and grow over time into large-scale enterprises. When first set up, the numbers of people involved are normally quite small and their organization simple. Often the purpose of these SHEs will have seemed so obvious to those involved that it never occurred to their leaders to set it down in writing. As an enterprise grows in scale and the membership increases, eventually there comes a time when it becomes critical to state its purpose in writing, and for this to be formally adopted by the membership, it needs to be readily understood by members and earn their commitment. Unless this is documented, the organization can easily drift away from it and in its place follow a different agenda, which is often no longer based on serving its grassroots members.

Statements of purpose that sound grandiose and are too wide-ranging are usually ignored by those involved in the day-to-day running of the enterprise. When all that is offered is a set of vague values or loose idealism, these are typically too bland and generic to inspire any passion and will never be worthwhile. Where this is all that is offered, people will revert to prioritising shorter-term objectives, paying attention only to tactics, which are often in direct conflict with achieving the strategic aims of the enterprise.

## Meeting resistance

In SHEs that have been operating without a clearly defined purpose, its managers may be reluctant to see the situation change to one where the enterprise is purposely managed. They may prefer to run the enterprise as though it were a commercial business. In these circumstances, any dissenters need to be offered a re-education programme. Hopefully, if the education provided is well planned and delivered, such managers will be able to adjust to the new reality; if not, then there is no alternative but to replace them.

## Measuring success

The success or failure of a commercial business is relatively easy to measure because it can be easily calculated in terms of how much money it makes for its owners. The main issue for commercial businesses is the balance between short-term gains and gains secured over the longer-term.

The performance of SHEs needs to be measured by comparing the outcomes achieved by the enterprise with the outcomes set out in the plans of the enterprise. The measure of their attainment is the extent to which they are achieving their agreed goals. Of course, all SHEs need to remain viable, solvent, and liquid, otherwise they have no chance of achieving their purpose. Unless people are clear about what is they are measuring and how they are going to measure this, there will be no way of measuring how successful SHEs are.

The media, including some purporting to support SHEs, often report the results of SHEs as though the only measure of their achievements is those expressed in terms profits and financial returns, completely ignoring their *real* achievements or lack of them.

Most senior managers of SHEs realise that a self-help enterprise cannot afford to pay them higher salaries if they do not produce the wherewithal, which to them normally means creating a 'disposable surplus'. If left to their own devices and without adequate oversight, many senior managers don't concentrate on achieving the goals set by their members; instead, the *de facto* purpose becomes profit maximization.

## The importance of oversight

Universally, all kinds of incorporated enterprises are at risk from those that may misappropriate their funds and assets. Several types of audit systems, both internal and external, can be designed to prevent this occurring. In past times, the main concern was that employees might steal the petty cash. Nowadays, it's not unprecedented for senior managers to try stealing the entire enterprise, an outcome often achieved by the demutualisation of SHEs. Financial audit systems are, of course, crucial. but then again in SHEs, oversight should go far beyond this. A well-conceived system of oversight has to be in place to ensure that the enterprise stays committed to its purpose and function; see *Chapter 22* for more details on how to do this.

## Some essential practices

The practices that underpin system for sustaining the purpose needs to include:

- Conducting a process, fully involving members, for the establishment and regular review of the enterprise's strategic aims and the current operating objectives

- Ensuring that all directors, managers and staff are made fully aware, and are committed to, the enterprise's purpose by means of providing induction and refresher training programmes. The fundamentals of such programmes need to be communicated all the above groups and members, on a regular basis.

- As an integral part of the management system, the top key result areas (KRAs) need to be identified. These must be measurable and cover all aspects of the enterprise's purpose.

Also, the key result indicators (KRIs) need to be set in respect of each KRA.

- Ensuring that all rewards and incentive offered are directly related to the achievement of the purpose

- Maintain a vigorous system of oversight of purpose delivery, involving direct reporting to members

- Ensuring that the qualifications criteria for membership include having a commitment to the enterprise's purpose

- Ensuring that the accounting and reporting systems are designed to provide members with not only financial information but all the facts necessary to allow them to judge how well the enterprise is achieving its purpose.

### *Loss of purpose: European consumer co-ops*

When chasing growth becomes the purpose of an enterprise (replacing its original intent) it will inevitably fail. This is what caused the downfall of major consumer co-ops in many countries in Europe. For example, Coop Dortmund started in 1902 with 349 members, one shop and two employees. Following mergers, it became Dortmund-Kassel, an enterprise with 500,000 members, 350 supermarkets, 16 department stores and 74 business centres, employing 15,000 staff; with a total turnover of DM 2.5 billion. In 1989 about DM 45 million was invested in shop modernisation, 31 new shops were opened with a surface of 25.000 sq. m. and 12 shops were expanded. In 1998 Coop Dortmund-Kassel collapsed and was eventually liquidated.

The reasons for this failure are attributed to the management seeking to follow approaches and techniques developed for investor-driven organizations, for example, the exclusion of members from goal setting and policy decisions, giving total autonomy to a professional board, measuring success by growth of market share, profit growth and shareholder value; and applying company-style methods of fundraising to attract investor-members - by promising high return on invested capital in the form of dividends. The outcome of this strategy was to reduce members to simple shareholders and also to treat them merely as 'customers.

Similarly, in 1995 Konsum Austria became bankrupt. It had slipped from being known as the 'Red Giant' on the retail scene and having 25% of the Austrian population as members. In 1978 the process of merging all of Austria's consumer co-operatives commenced, resulting in national society. Unfortunately, the management was left to run the new 'super-co-op', which began chasing market share with little regard for its position as a member-owned and controlled enterprise.

## Figure B-6. A holistic purpose

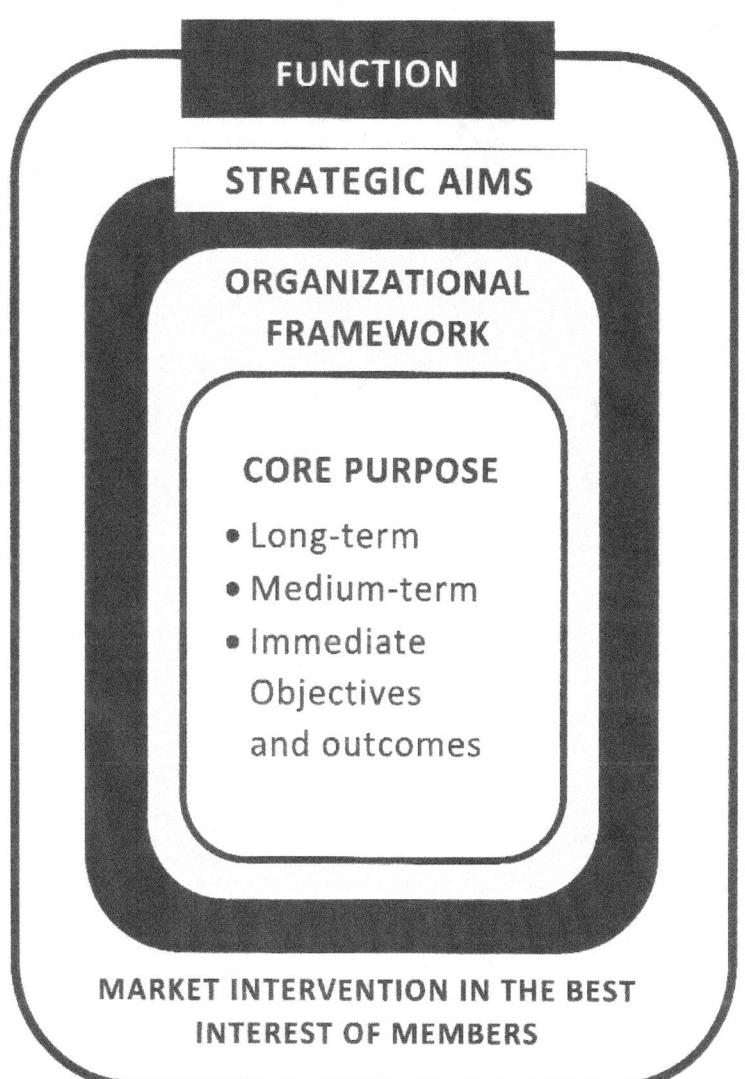

# 7. REENGINEERING ORGANIZATIONS

### Reengineering – what it means

'Reengineering' means the practice of rethinking and redesigning the way organizations work so that they better support their purpose, function and the efficiency of the process. In the context of SHEs, this involves redesigning organizations to improve their capacity to achieve their purpose and to serve their members better.

### Organizations are tools

Organizations are the tools people use whenever they want to achieve agreed objectives in association with others. As with all tools, the more specifically designed the tool the more effective it will be. From the smallest group, through to the most complex multinational enterprise, the same components underlie all forms of organization, these are the 'task' (the purpose), the 'team' (or teams) and the 'individuals' that make up the teams. The 'organization' supplies the framework within which both teams and individuals work and inter-relate.

The first question to ask about any organization is – 'What is its purpose?' The next is 'what is its function?' It may be difficult to believe, but it's not unusual to find that many of the people who are supposed to be directing organizations, let alone those that own them and those that work in them, are often unable to provide any rational answer to either of these vital questions.

## Organizational hazards

There are several hazards that threaten all forms of organization. These are threats that need to be kept in mind when designing and running organizations, and include when:

- **Their true purpose becomes lost** due to the conflicting motives of the people involved in running its day-to-day operations. The energy going into achieving the organization's aims does not match the energy directed into the pursuit of personal concerns, such as office politics, ego trips by decision-makers, and a variety of other diversions.

- **They prioritise the interests of those who run them** on a day-to-day basis, above delivering benefits to their rightful owners. It's not unusual to find that the driving force in organizations becomes the enhancement of the lifestyle of their senior managers, defending their jobs and privileges. Especially when changes are to be made when such considerations will often trump all others. If permitted, those exercising powers within an organization will use all available means to hold on to their power and positions.

- **They emphasise short-term benefits** and do not give enough time and resources to building the organization so that it's prepared to meet the future. When short-termism is predominant, the enterprise will eventually fall behind, becoming irrelevant within the market.

- **Those running the organization resist essential change** because they have no real incentive to support change. Change needs to be driven by the *owners* of the enterprise and mechanisms that routinely provide the capacity and the right incentives to make essential changes. This requires that those affected adversely by the process of change be treated fairly and with compassion.

- **They cease to be 'learning' organizations** when to prosper they need to be constantly responding to the environment in which they operate. When organizations stop learning, they start dying. As they grow, they often lose their capacity to learn. As a result, both the structures and the thinking of the individuals involved, become more rigid. When problems arise, the proposed solutions often turn out to be short-term fixes, with the result that the same problems re-emerge in the future. In many situations, real and lasting change only occurs when the underlying systems are changed.

- **Cultural collapse occurs** - Organizations can rapidly move from a position of delivering on their purpose to one where they are struggling to survive, this happens when leaders do not live-out the required culture. This often occurs when there is a change of leadership without adequate preparation for the transition. Culture is an important factor in creating success in all organization, but in SHEs, it's absolutely crucial.

- **The electoral cycle causes elected leaders to focus on results** that will impress their electorate, chiefly in the run-up to elections and political expediency often replaces the long view

- **Conflicts of interest occur** - The owners of many organizations often appear to be blind to the conflicts of interest that exist in their organizations. The owners sometimes allow the introduction of rewards systems that encourage senior managers to pursue goals that are contrary to the real interest of its owners. Often allowing them to embark upon growth strategies that primarily promote the interests of managers concerned about expanding their personal wealth. It's essential that member-leaders uncover all conflicts of interest within their enterprise and resolve them.

- **Egos and obsessions prevail** – The most profound threats to organizations arise when those controlling them are ruled by their egos and their obsessions, including when people become addicted to power. Whenever organizations are controlled by those who seek to satisfy their inflated egos - - - often pushing their enterprise to become bigger, grander, and a monument to their vanity.

## Specific threats to self-help enterprises

SHEs are open to many of the same hazards that can endanger all forms of organization but, in addition, they face some very particular risks. Members, and above all their leaders, ought to fully appreciate the specific hazards facing this form of enterprise and learn how these risks can be managed. Among such threats are those arising from the fact that SHEs need to be democratically controlled. Where members are not engaged with their enterprise and are neither properly informed nor empowered, their enterprise is wide-open to both internal and external hijack, often resulting in a *de facto* change in the ownership.

## Organizational design

Organizations, including SHEs, all need to be designed so that they can deal effectively with those human weaknesses that affect them all. Organizations can be likened to ships, neither can travel in two different directions simultaneously. If SHEs are to perform as they should, they need a very specific system of organization.

If leaders are to acquire the capacity to design and develop effective organizations, they must face up to some very important truths about how, in practice, people in organizations typically behave. In addition, they need to be aware of and understand the foundations of organizations.

Weaknesses in the design of an organization can result in them becoming 'unfit for purpose'. Such flaws often arise when those involved in their design simply follow practices with which they are familiar, rather than seeking to discover the most suitable system of organization needed to meet the specific requirements of SHEs. For example, there is a tendency to merely copy those practices used in local government, trade unions, churches; and, as is most prevalent, those used in commercial businesses - all of which are inappropriate for use in SHEs. The system adopted should, of course, meet the requirements of the relevant legislation and be rooted in the self-help enterprise model.

**Retaining control**
There are always predators, both within and without an organization, who will seize any opportunity to take control away from the membership. Humans can be very adept at concealing their weaknesses, including their addictions, so systematically checking on how people are behaving within our organizations is vital.

Without adequate legislation and effective oversight, most organizations will predictably default to a position where they prioritise the interests of those running them day-to-day. In other cases, SHEs transform to being run in the interest of those who provide their finance. In either case, whenever this kind of change happens, the outcome is that the interests of their true owners are side-lined. Those who have in effect 'stolen' the enterprise from its rightful owners inevitably also resort to exploiting of their disenfranchised members. This kind of scenario can happen in all manner of organization, including investor-owned companies, cause-driven enterprises, as well as in SHEs.

There are many public companies that are not being run in the best interest of their shareholders. Instead, they are often being run primarily in the interest of their top managers. In such cases, the benefits that should go to their shareholders are often creamed-off by their senior managers. The investors involved, typically also include lots of ordinary people who have their pension funds invested in these companies. It sometimes seems that the company executives involved feel that they are entitled to live their lives as though they are part of medieval royalty. Most damaging, the same situation often prevails in countries where the government, which should serve its citizens, instead only serves the interests of a political elite that in reality runs the country.

### The foundations of organizations

Ensuring that organizations both serve the people that own them and achieve their purposes, has to be the priority for all leaders. This means that they know and are committed to, the foundation on which their organizations are built. Understanding what these foundations are, and how they differ in distinct forms of organization, provide both the key to designing them and a framework for understanding them. These foundations are:

**Motivation** - what drives the enterprise; for example, is to generate wealth for its owners or to achieve other objectives?

**Purpose** - what is the purpose of the organization and what exactly is it intended to achieve?

**Function** - what is it that the organization will actually do?

**The basis of association** – for example, is it an association of equal persons, or is it hierarchical, or is it an association of finance?

**The basis of relationships** - for example, are relationships to be exploitative or equitable?

**The method of control** - for example, is the enterprise controlled by significant providers of finance, or is control exercised by benefactors or trustees, or is the enterprise subject to democratic control?

**The economic basis** - for example, is the organization self-sustaining or dependent upon benefactors or sponsors; is the organization driven by profit maximization or by resource optimisation?

**The basis of ownership** - who owns the organization and on what basis (for example in proportion to shareholding, held in trust, or mutually owned)?

**Sovereignty** or lack of it - is the organization truly independent or is it subject to external direction; for example, by the State, a political organization, or by those providing finance?

**It's time perspective** - is the organization driven by short-term expediency, does it have a limited lifespan, or is it committed to a long-term outlook?

The answers to the above questions should help people to reach a good understanding of the true nature of each form of enterprise and determine the system of organization needed to achieve the purpose of the enterprise; See *Figure C-7 The foundations of organizations*.

## The life-cycle of enterprises

In general, all forms of enterprise appear to follow a life-cycle that starts at their inception. At their start-up, they are normally led by an entrepreneur or an outstanding leader who provides the driving force necessary to establish the enterprise. Where it's a joint enterprise, with more than a single individual at the helm, then the leadership role is shared by a group of like-minded persons.

The next stage in the development of an enterprise will usually require a generation of leaders who have the foresight to build the enterprise, this by means of developing longer-term strategies and introducing the practices and systems necessary to expand and strengthen the enterprise. Alternatively, they may choose not to expand, in which case they inevitably stagnate and overtaken by the changes in their market.

Finally, most enterprises reach a stage in their life-cycle that leads to their decline and demise. During this terminal stage, the people controlling the enterprise are no longer motivated by a passionate commitment to growing the enterprise. Instead, control passes into the hands of those motivated by a desire to enjoy the wealth generated by the enterprise, along with the prestige and lifestyle they can obtain from the enterprise. This sort of pattern of events seems to apply equally in all forms of enterprise. However, the usual conclusion in commercial business is that it is sold-off, subject to take-over, or files for bankruptcy. In SHEs, the third stage of this cycle is manifested in the mutation of the enterprise into one that only serves a clique of members and/or top managers.

All types of SHEs need to take steps to prevent the onset of the terminal phase of the enterprise life-cycle. Such preventative measures include:

- Preparing in advance, a pool of leaders with the capacity and commitment to run genuine SHEs. This means ensuring that there are enough people that have a very clear vision of what they need to achieve and have an unshakable commitment to improving the lives of their members.

- Having appropriate systems in place to ensure that the organization follows a 'built-in' process of renewal.

- Devising a robust system of oversight, which is necessary to ensure that each new generation pursues their enterprise's purpose and adheres to the 'foundation practices'.

- Maintaining practices, rules and policies that will prevent their enterprise from being hijacked by self-serving individuals.

- Investing in developing 'authentic' member-leaders and fully-trained managers, who provide the continuity of kind of creative leadership needed to ensure the resilience of the enterprise.

## *Figure C-7 The foundations of organizations*

NOTE: The foundations of organizations are set out in the diagram below, this seeks to illustrate how these foundations are a complete set of practices that are required to implement each element of the overall system. Different forms of organization call for different sets of practices to create the form necessary to achieve their different purposes and functions.

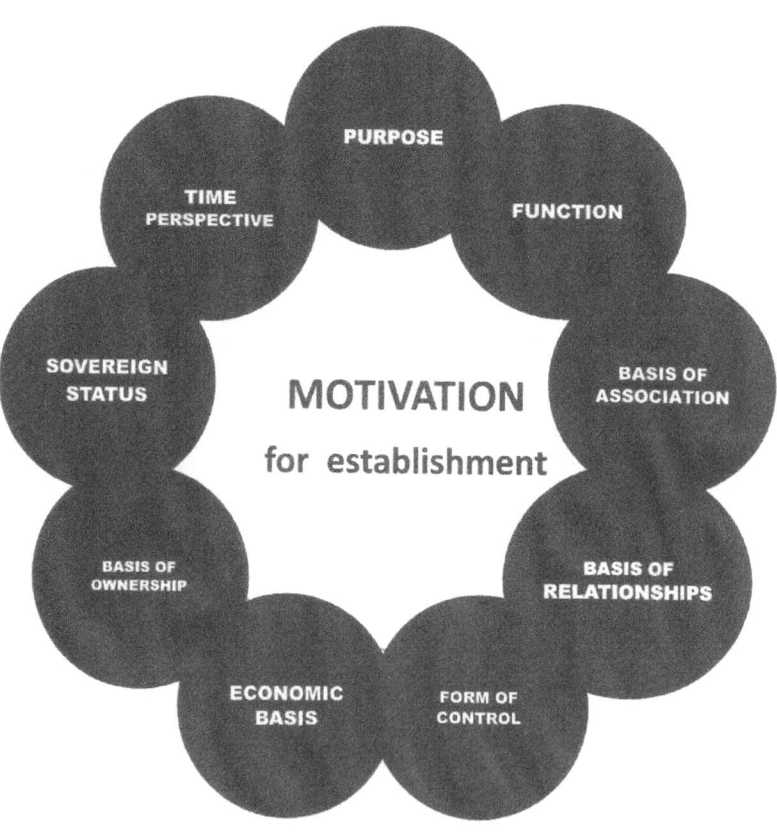

# 8. FORMS AND MODELS OF ENTERPRISE

## Forms of enterprise

Individuals and groups will have different motives for setting-up enterprises, so they require different forms of organization to match their differing intentions. Each specific form of enterprise has to be designed to enable its owners to achieve their aims and fulfil the proper function of the enterprise.

People seeking to set up an enterprise can choose from the available forms and types provided within the body of laws in their specific country. Most will often only choose from the forms and type of enterprise offered by those advising them, although often adapting this to their specific needs, within the limits of the existing laws. The availability of tried and tested forms and types of enterprises helps to shorten the process of founding a new enterprise and reduce the risk of their failure.

The various forms of enterprise include sole traders, partnerships, and investor-owned companies. Companies may be either private companies or public companies; the latter trade their shares using a stock exchange. The other main form of enterprises is those commonly called 'not-for-profit' enterprises, which can be further divided into two distinct groups. First, there are 'cause-driven' enterprises, which are motivated by the desire to further a specific cause. Second, there are enterprises driven by the desire of members to achieve their specific mutual purposes, these are called 'self-help' enterprises.

One *form* of enterprise may be the basis of several distinct *types* of each form; for example, the investor-owned company supplies the basis for both private and public companies. The self-help form of enterprise supplies the basis for many distinct types of SHEs. These include for example, cooperatives, credit unions, community enterprises, building societies and friendly societies; and all of the other types as listed in *Annex I*. The foundations of each form of enterprise are built around the motivation that drives them, here it will be helpful to again refer to *Figure A-1 Forms of enterprise*.

**Comparing forms of enterprise**

If people are to understand something properly, it's usually helpful to compare it with other similar things. Here, the comparison is made between the self-help form of enterprise and other forms of enterprise. In the first place, it helps to discover the relative position of each in relation to the other available forms.

The various forms of enterprise working within the market all have one shared feature, which is that they all need to survive within the market. This means that they do not rely on subsidies or donations for their survival. The foundations of each form of enterprise are markedly different; these are compared in *Figure D-8 Identifying forms of enterprise*.

**Buyers and sellers**

There are two classes of SHEs; there are those serving sellers and those serving buyers in the market. SHEs of sellers include worker cooperatives, those selling their labour, skills, and knowledge, producer enterprises that market products and other goods on behalf of their members, and service cooperatives that provide joint-services mainly to small and medium-sized enterprises (SMEs). While consumer-owned enterprises act for their members by buying and/or negotiating to secure goods and services on their behalf; these are consumer-owned enterprises and include consumer co-ops, building societies, mutual insurers, credit unions, community co-ops; they all offer goods and services to their members, in their capacity as consumers.

SHEs of both sellers and buyers, and SHEs working in separate markets can very advantageously collaborate to set-up federal enterprises that offer all manner of joint services. A 'federal' means an organization formed by several SHEs coming together to run a separate entity that can act on behalf of its member enterprises. For example, when several retail cooperatives set-up a federal to jointly buy goods for sale in their shops, or when a grouping of credit unions establish an enterprise that can offer more services, such as insurance products, for their members. These are services that they would be unable to sustain as an individual enterprise, or to secure benefits of scale by forming an enterprise in which the members are other SHEs; for more about federals see *Chapter 12*.

**Legal frameworks**
The State will normally offer specific legal frameworks for the different forms of enterprise - for example, a Companies Act, a Charities law, a Cooperative law, etc. Sometimes, special laws cover specific types of a form of enterprise, typically this applies to financial services, for example, banking, insurance, and pensions. Although some types of self-help enterprise can only register using specific legislation, in other cases the founders of the enterprise may be able to choose from various other options for incorporating their enterprise. It's crucial that groups of people wishing to set-up SHEs avail themselves of the best advice, which is customarily from specialist support or national organizations, rather than relying upon the services of a general legal practitioner.

The forms of enterprises include individual/sole traders and partnerships, which do not normally register under any legislation. On the other hand, corporate entities (those having a legal personality separate from the individuals involved in them) are required to register under specific laws. For example, in the UK, the Companies Acts or the Co-operative and Community Benefit Societies Act. All SHEs, once registered (incorporated) under any of the available options, become corporate entities registered companies, societies, and associations, all acquire a corporate identity, that is separate from the individuals that own the enterprise; and, most notably, the capacity to sue and be sued as a corporate body. Governments make legal provision for various forms of organization, including enterprises, to become incorporated; this enables them to act as corporate entities, and gives the protection afforded by having limited liability, which means that the liability of its owners is limited to the extent of the shares, or other classes of equity investments that they hold in their enterprise.

## The diversity of forms

As previously explained, there are many different forms and types of enterprise, and in the interest of progress, such diversity is to be welcomed. Enterprise's set-up by benefactors that remains under patron or trustee-control can't be accepted as genuine SHEs if ultimate control of the enterprise rests with any persons that aren't, members. This is because they are not subject to democratic control, so these are not a bona-fide self-help enterprise. This is not to say that such enterprises cannot make an important contribution to their national economies, and often have many shared characteristics, but this does not mean that they are in fact SHEs. For example, in the UK, - The John Lewis Partnership, and in Switzerland - the country's largest retailer, Migros, both provide benefits to their workers and customers, but they aren't SHEs.

Internationally, there are several notable enterprises that are in practice externally controlled due to their financial dependence on other bodies, many make use of a name that implies that they are SHEs, but because they are not democratically-controlled by their members, these are not genuine SHEs. Sometimes, such enterprises are referred to as 'multi-stakeholder' enterprises, apparently because different stakeholders (e.g. consumers, workers, investors) are represented on what is a kind of consultative or advisory board. In such enterprises, when it truly matters, important decisions are often made by the individuals or organizations that control their finances. See *Chapter 14* for more on this issue.

## Models of enterprise

An enterprise model provides an outline of a form of enterprise, including its foundations, along with other essential systems and practices, which are required to sustain them. A model of enterprise ought to set out the essential practices that support the implementation of the foundations of the organization, as well as identifying the most important systems required to implement the model. An enterprise model should explain the overall system and supply guidance to decision-makers throughout the enterprise.

It's essential to differentiate between a 'business model' and a 'model of enterprise'. A business model may be defined as 'the plan implemented by a business to generate revenue and make a profit from its operations'; on the other hand, a model of enterprise outlines a specific *form* of enterprise, laying down its foundation practices along with the full raft of other practices critical to the overall system. An enterprise model should explain its underlying logic, and crucially, it needs to provide leaders with a clear-cut framework to guide them in the day-to-day running of their enterprises.

# Figure D-8 Identifying forms of enterprise (1)

| GROUPS: | PROFIT-DRIVEN | | OUTCOMES-DRIVEN | |
|---|---|---|---|---|
| **FORM OF ENTERPRISE** ➡ | **SOLE TRADER/ PARTNERSHIPS** | **SHAREHOLDER COMPANIES** | **NOT-FOR-PROFIT COMPANIES** | **SELF-HELP ENTERPRISES** |
| **FOUNDATIONS** | ⬇ | ⬇ | ⬇ | ⬇ |
| **1. MOTIVATION** | Personal wealth generation | Personal wealth generation | Altruism, or a belief system | mutual action to improve the members' position in a market |
| **2. PURPOSE** | Personal ambitions | Increasing shareholder value | Specific outcomes | common purpose as decided by members |
| **3. FUNCTION** | Profit generation | Profit generation | Furthering 'the cause' | Market intervention in the best interest of members |
| **4. BASIS OF ASSOCIATION** | Individual ownership or partnership | Shareholding (an association of capital) | Trusteeship or an association of persons | An association of persons |
| **5. FORM OF CONTROL** | Individual or partners | Dominant shareholders | Appointees who may or not be elected | Democratic control by members |

*Continued...*

# *Figure D-8 Identifying forms of enterprise (2)*

| GROUP: | PROFIT-DRIVEN | | OUTCOMES-DRIVEN | |
|---|---|---|---|---|
| **FORM OF ENTERPRISE** ➡ | **SOLE TRADER/ PARTNERSHIPS** | **SHAREHOLDER COMPANIES** | **NOT-FOR-PROFIT COMPANIES** | **SELF-HELP ENTERPRISES** |
| FOUNDATIONS ⬇ | ⬇ | ⬇ | ⬇ | ⬇ |
| 6. ECONOMIC BASIS | Self-sustaining via Profit maximization | Self-sustaining via Profit maximisation | Self-sustaining via Resource optimization or Profit maximization | The self-help economic system |
| 7. OWNERSHIP BASIS | Individuals | Shareholding | Stewardship/ trusteeship | Beneficial mutual ownership |
| 8. SOVEREIGNTY | Independent, but often under control of financiers | Subservient to major shareholders | Independent or tied to power of benefactors | Independent and self-governing |
| 9. BASIS OF RELATIONS | Individuals | Dominance of major shareholders | Can be equitable but often linked to the power of patronage | Equitable |
| 10. TIME PERSPECTIVE | Dependent upon individual commitment | Most commonly short-termism | Depends upon sustaining commitment to 'the cause' | Long-termism |

# 9. THE SELF-HELP ENTERPRISE MODEL

## The significance of the self-help enterprise model

Leaders of SHEs need to have a handle on the true character of their organizations, and what it takes to make them work effectively. People need frameworks to help them better understand their organizations, and an enterprise model offers such a framework. The model explains the underlying logic for both the design and operation of SHEs. It's designed to ensure that SHEs achieve their purpose and continuously serve their members.

The model is particularly valuable when starting up a new self-help enterprise, but it's equally essential during their day-to-day operation and invaluable when an enterprise is undergoing any significant change. Leaders of SHEs need to acquire a thorough appreciation of the model because it will help them to release the latent power of their membership, to get their people to work together cooperatively, and to reap the benefits of following the self-help economic system. It offers enterprises a set of practices that will generate the necessary pressure to perform and supplies a spur to both innovation and renewal.

People not conversant with the model often struggle to grasp the essentials, because many of their most critical practices may seem to fly-in-the-face of everything that they have previously learned about enterprises; even more so where their training and experience has been limited to commercial business. However, people may well be even more confused if they have only had experience of working in mutant SHEs.

## Critical differences

In themselves SHEs aren't intended to be profit-centres, all of the benefits that SHEs generate for their members belong to their members; and, any surplus remaining after the process of providing any services to their members also belongs to the members. It is the members (in a general meeting) who decide how any surplus is to be used or distributed. Again, it's worth remembering that the benefits generated by SHEs, are not by any means limited only to those that are measured in financial terms.

Where the members are individual consumers, the benefits created by mutual action should be distributed by members, by whatever means they have agreed. Where the members are businesses (such as tradesmen/women, family farms, or small to medium-sized enterprises), SHEs can help their members to increase their individual profitability, but it's *not* the task of a self-help enterprise to generate profits for SHEs as corporate entities. SHEs need to operate with such margin that covers all costs and provides cover for foreseeable risks, but any remaining surplus belongs to its members.

Many of the practices and systems that are essential to make SHEs work properly are fundamentally different from those followed in all other forms of enterprise. The most important of these practices are the foundation practices that underpin their enterprise model.

## Foundation practices

SHEs rely upon their foundation practices, which are central to the self-help form of enterprise, these are as follows:

1.  **Motivation** - Motivated to achieve a common purpose by means of mutual action.

2. **Purpose** - Dedicated to achieving their purpose as mutually set by their members which ought to result in improving the lives of its members, see *Chapter 6*.

3. **Function** - Their function is market intervention in the best interest of their members.

4. **The basis of association** – SHEs are voluntary associations of equal persons.

5. **The basis of relationships** - Based on equitable relationships, this means being committed to treating all its members equally. The practice of equivalence needs to prevail in all dealings with members of a self-help enterprise, meaning that all have equal: votes, voice, chances, responsibilities, access to the best deals and being equally valued as a human being. It means being obligated to be fair and honest in all its dealings.

6. **Method of control** – SHEs need to be democratically controlled by their members, using a system of control based upon equivalence and everyone having equal rights. This means that each member only has the power of one vote, see *Chapter 21*.

7. **Economic basis** – SHEs have to be economically self-sustaining and run in accord with the self-help economic system. This means that the enterprise has to be viable, solvent, and have adequate liquidity. Finance has to be the servant of the enterprise, not its master, and resource optimisation is the driver, not profit maximization. A complete set of economic practices that together make up the self-help economic system is set out in *Chapter 19*.

8. **The basis of ownership** – SHEs are owned by their members on a beneficial and mutual basis. This means

that the current members have use of the assets of the enterprise and benefit from their use, also that current members are in effect trustees, holding the assets on behalf of both current and future members. Members own their personal investments in the enterprise but have no automatic claim upon the enterprise in respect of any increase in the value of the assets held by the enterprise. The assets the enterprise owns are mutually-owned on behalf of its members.

9. **Sovereign status** – SHEs need to be independent and in control of their destiny, which means that SHEs need to be sovereign entities. Otherwise, they will not be able to act in the best interest of their members. This means being free from the control of the State, free from political interference, and free from control by investors, patrons, and/or cliques, of any kind. SHEs should not be overly dependent upon their senior managers or on any benefactors or patrons.

10. **Time perspective** – SHEs should be committed to the long-term, this means exercising foresight and stewardship in the management of their affairs, and in the use of their resources. Planning to meet not only the current needs of their members but also providing for longer-term future needs. This calls for responsible planning and management of their resources, supporting the concepts of sustainability and of beneficial mutual ownership.

The above foundations are an important part of the self-help enterprise model, and the rules of all bona-fide SHEs should incorporate all of them. These foundations need to be supported and sustained by all the systems that make up the totality of the model. Universally, the major reason for the failure or mutation of SHEs is that they do not sustain their foundation. Only the membership, using predetermined procedures, should have the power to change any policies relating to any application of the foundation practices; see *Figure E-9 The foundations of SHEs*.

## An overview of the self-help enterprise model
The following are the main components of the model:

**Motivated** by the desire to meet a shared need using self-help and mutual action.

**The purpose** of the enterprise is to secure a better deal – a better organization – a better future for members, forming a holistic purpose; see *Chapter 6*.

**Function-focused** – concentrated upon market intervention in the best interest of its members, which involves the formulation and the implementation of a workable market intervention strategy.

**A set of dynamic and complete systems** are necessary to secure the achievement of the enterprise's purpose. These will include the systems of organization, association, economics, and management.

**All systems are subject to regular review** and revised to make them fully relevant to the current needs of members.

See *Figure F – 9 The self-help enterprise model.*

The components of the enterprise model are also present in the system of organization, which are elaborated in *Chapter 17*.

## The process

Implanting the self-help enterprise model is a process best started during the early planning of a venture because this offers the framework for developing the enterprise. Established enterprises can introduce the model to bring about its reform. The process starts when the members affirm or reaffirm their commitment to the self-help mindset, fix upon their overall purpose, define their market intervention strategy, develop the essential systems, and building this into all systems including a renewal process.

## The legislative framework for SHEs

When considering the available options for incorporation or registration, leaders should consider the longer-term needs of their enterprise, rather than taking the route of expediency. Sometimes, for example, by seeking to secure finance by means of grants, soft loans, or other methods of finance that may be available only to bodies that are charities. Leaders should not allow their enterprise to adopt a method of organization that is inappropriate for achieving their purpose. It's understandable that leaders look for ways of getting any benefits that may arise from securing charitable status or by qualifying for government support schemes; nevertheless, they should never lose sight of the fact that they are *not* running a charity. Charities dispense benevolence, unlike self-help enterprises, which are run for the benefit of their members who are people that seek the help themselves. The main problem for many new or budding SHEs is that the law follows behind the current requirements of such enterprises.

Although some types of self-help enterprise can only register using specific legislation, in other cases the founders of the enterprise may choose from distinct options when incorporating their enterprise. For example, in the United Kingdom, credit unions can only be registered using the Credit Unions Act. Although most SHEs choose to register using the Co-operative and Benefit Societies Acts 2014, some make use of the Companies Acts, registering as a conventional company, as a community interest company; or as a company limited by guarantee, where the liability of its owners is limited to a fixed sum of money.

The legal framework necessary to foster thriving SHEs should support and sustain all their essential features. In many countries, senior managers are setting the agenda for legislative change. In other cases, people with a very narrow political agenda are setting it. Often, the main aim of those calling for changes in the law is to make SHEs more like investor-owned companies and less accountable to their members. This situation is confounded by the scarcity of law-makers that have an adequate understanding of the kind of laws needed to support genuine SHEs.

In many countries, the legislative framework for SHEs is underdeveloped. Generally, this is because they have not always enjoyed the degree of attention from educators and legislators that they deserve. Powerful companies often see SHEs as a threat to their unbridled dominance of profitable markets, so they consistently lobby against measures that can help the expansion of SHEs.

### Anomalies within laws relating to SHEs

People in Britain, even today, are dealing with the legacy of deficiencies in the earliest of laws. The current legislation still includes some of the terms that are inappropriate for use in SHEs. For example, the Co-operative and Community Benefit Societies Act 2014 continues to make use of the wording in the Industrial and Provident Societies Act 1893, such as: 'the application of profits', when to be consistent with the intentions of the Act the word 'surplus' ought to have been used. This was perpetuated in the Industrial and Provident Societies Act 1965 and into the current legislation. In both the 1893 and 1965 Acts this wording appeared only in schedules to the act, but it has now been included in the body of the 2014 Act.

### Registration/incorporation

In some countries, it's possible to register SHEs under a variety of different laws, contrasting with the situation in other countries where there is very specific legislation under which various types of SHEs are registered. Where SHEs can be registered under a variety of different laws, as for example is the position in the United Kingdom, this can result in considerable confusion about what is and what is not a self-help enterprise. Some enterprises that started out as genuine SHEs have since drifted away from their original purpose. Often continue using terms such as 'cooperative', 'mutual', or other names that imply they are genuine SHEs, even though they are no longer under member-control. Conversely, there are some organizations not registered under any law that labels them as being SHEs, but in practice, they operate under member-control and have all of the same characteristics as self-help enterprises.

The basic framework for the organization should be set out within its rules. Such a founding document is necessary to complete registration under whichever is the proper body of law (here, the term 'rules' is used to include all the available different types of founding documents). In many cases, model rules are used by SHEs; these are an off-the-peg governing document available from specialist support or national organizations of SHEs. Regardless of the format of the rules, it should always be remembered that SHEs need to be run by, and for, the benefit of the people that make up its membership. Therefore, grassroots members need to grasp the true nature of their organization and how it ought to work in practice.

## Achieving major changes

Significant change rarely happens overnight, it calls for a carefully crafted plan, so leaders have to develop these plans that supply a roadmap for their implementation. The transition to a more effective organization cannot be simply imposed upon members; this requires that they are involved every step of the way.

## *Figure E-9 The foundations of SHEs*

The foundations of self-help enterprises are set out in the diagram below; this illustrates the system of organization required in SHEs. All the systems and subsystems necessary to run flourishing SHEs need to be rooted in these foundations. Together, they supply the overall system needed to achieve the purpose of the enterprise.

# *Figure F-9 The self-help enterprise model*

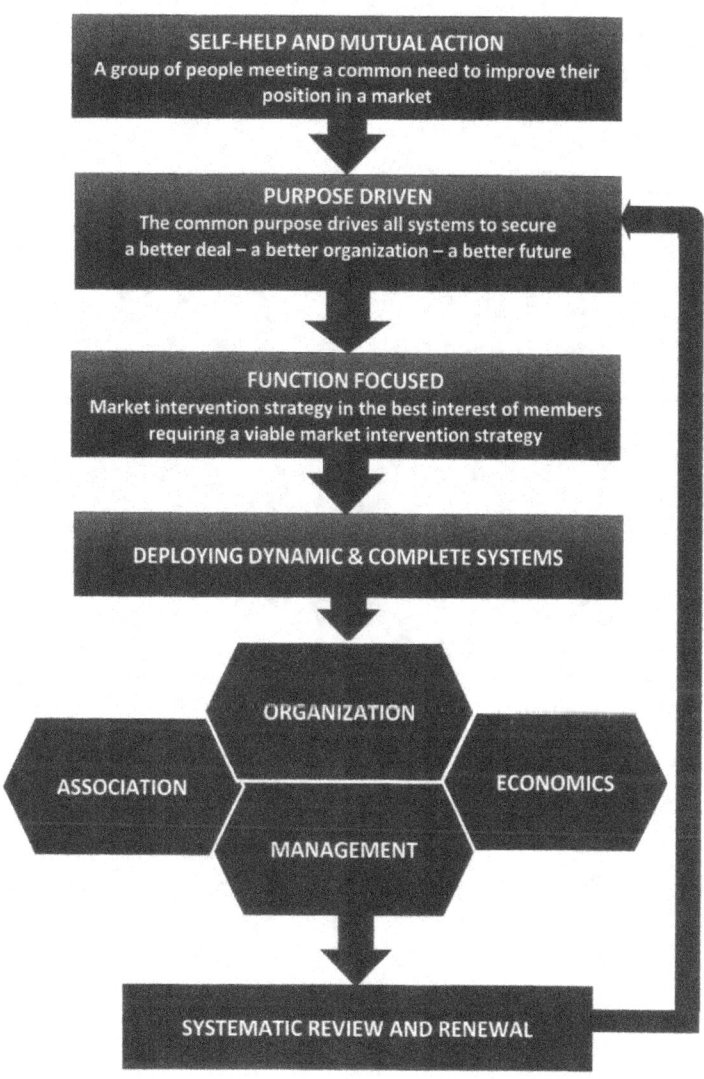

# 10. MARKET INTERVENTION STRATEGIES

**Market intervention**

The way the enterprise will change the position of members in a specific market needs to be defined, and this needs to be set out in a market intervention strategy. This strategy, of course, has to be viable; and, will frequently involve finding an innovative approach to intervening in the targeted market. Merely copying what current players in the market already do will often be unlikely to provide the basis for a viable strategy. The strategy selected should set out how, in practice, the enterprise will intervene within a market to secure a better deal for their members. The chosen strategy becomes the primary driver in founding and sustaining the enterprise. The strategy has to be regularly reviewed and updated to ensure that it continues to be the right approach in current and future conditions. Also, to maintain the enterprise's continuing relevance in the lives of members.

**Market intervention v marketing**

Commercial businesses become successful when they come up with a unique selling proposition (USP), which can put them ahead of the competition, they then typically invest heavily in advertising and marketing aimed at persuading people to buy their products or services. Notwithstanding that their USP, may offer no tangible benefits to their customers. This approach to the market can lead people involved in SHEs to jump to the conclusion that their enterprise should do the same. Some managers appear to see everything through the prism of a marketing and branding strategy, which is often inappropriate for SHEs. As an alternative,

SHEs need a market intervention strategy, driven not by profit maximisation, but by a commitment to achieving the changes in the market that their members need.

In all types of consumer-based SHEs, members ought never to be regarded as merely a market to be exploited. Instead, the members, who are the owners of the enterprise, are the people that SHEs need to serve. Members need their SHEs to follow a market intervention strategy that works for them. They most certainly don't need inertia selling, trickery, misselling, or any of the many other practices that are designed to get them to buy things that they do not need. SHEs need to be communicating with, and engaging their members, making it clear that they are genuinely working in the best interest of their members.

**Developing a strategy**
When designing an intervention strategy, leaders first need to specify what is wrong with the current situation in the market. This could be that the current players in the market are exploiting people, are dishonest, incompetent, or just not offering what people need. In the case of worker and producer-based enterprises, they are not able to gain access to a market, share in the value-added to their products, or to get an equitable price or terms.

Once the nature of the failings in the market is identified, the next task is to work out exactly how their enterprise is going to change things by exercising their members' joint-power within the market. The process of developing a market intervention strategy is one that needs to be repeated on a rolling basis so that the strategy can be improved, updated, or replaced, as conditions alter. There needs to be a real commitment from leaders to keeping this strategy in-step with any changes occurring within the market, and in social and economic conditions that will impact their enterprise.

Unlike commercial businesses, SHEs are not to be managed merely to compete with other players in the market, the task for those managing SHEs is to *get the best possible deal* for their members. SHEs need to act on behalf of their members as their agent and should be hunting-down any operational inefficiencies that prevent them from offering a better deal to their members. SHEs need to be constantly seeking innovative ways of improving the deal available to members. Again, it needs to be stressed, that 'a better deal' has to be evaluated by reference to the entire package offered to members, inclusive of both financial and other benefits. There is never any room for complacency in SHEs, because only by continually responding to changes in the market can they ensure that they are always working in the best interest of their members.

A 'market intervention strategy', is not the same thing as a 'marketing strategy'. In commercial businesses, a marketing strategy will be designed to maximise profitability for the benefit of the owners of the enterprise.

In producer-owned and worker-owned SHEs, their market intervention strategy sets out how the enterprise will deliver benefits to members as the result of such intervention. As sellers within a market, their enterprise will also have a marketing strategy, but because SHEs need to be committed to building long-term relationships with their customers, this should not be based upon exploiting the weaknesses of their customers for short-term gain.

**What members need from the market**
Leaders should be clear as to what it is that their enterprise brings to the market or wants from the market. Workers and producers bring their labour, skills, knowledge, and in the case of producers, their control over the means of production (for example, farmers

have their land, artisans their tools). While in the case of consumers the seek the satisfaction of their needs.

Just continuing to do what has always been done, is rarely going to satisfy members' needs, even though they may often start out thinking that it is. For example, if it becomes clear that workers or producers will not be able to achieve a decent living from their current activities, even if they were to gain a greater share of the added-value from their produce. In such circumstances, their SHEs may need to help members to make the transition to an alternative way of deploying their knowledge, skills, and personal assets.

Likewise, consumers may start out thinking that they merely want to get lower prices for what they already buy, but often this is not the most crucial factor. Members may want their enterprise to help them to source something that offers a better way of meeting their needs. For example, members of a consumer food co-op may provide life-changing benefits if they sourced healthier, locally produced foodstuffs. Another example may be a group of farmers who currently use their enterprise to negotiate lower purchase prices for their farm machinery, but who may be better served if they were helped to set up a machinery ring (a machinery sharing cooperative).

## Building on the foundation practices

Every market intervention strategy should be built upon the foundation practices of SHEs, which will include their commitment to honest trading, building long-term relationships with all other stakeholders, and the strength and resilience that should be provided by a committed membership. The advantages of SHEs, compared with other players in a market, should be clear enough for members to understand. For example, the overall cost of finance in SHEs ought to be lower compared to an investor-controlled business, because their finance should come from members, ethical investors and the retention of surpluses. SHEs should avoid short-termism, profit maximisation, and speculation, which in turn means that SHEs provide their members with a sustainable future. These practices are all part of the self-help economic system; as set out in *Chapter 19.*

The development of an intervention strategy involves finding better ways of doing things, with the aim of providing members with benefits that are not now available in the market. This can be a better price, but this alone is rarely enough to sustain any enterprise over the long-term. In the case of SHEs serving consumers (buyers), part of the overall intervention strategy will inevitably include offering goods or services that provide better value and/or other benefits sought by members. In the case of SHEs that serve sellers (producers and workers), the market intervention strategy needs to offer not only a better deal for the members but tangible benefits to their customers. In all types of SHEs, an essential element of the strategy will be the maintenance of a high level of trust in their enterprise. Members need to believe that their enterprise will always act in their best interests, this means being a 'better organization' when compared to other market participants.

Yet another element of the strategy involves finding ways of cutting down or eliminating costs, by finding more efficient ways of doing things. Just mimicking the practices of other players in the market will rarely be enough to change the market. In most cases, SHEs require deliberate strategies that keep their costs down or adds value to what they provide. SHEs need to find ways of cutting out the costs of corporate waste and those arising from the excesses of those managing the enterprise, which is so often prevalent in investor-owned companies and that should have no place in SHEs.

## Building the capacity of members

Another significant element of any strategy often involves developing the ability of members to improve their individual position in the market. In the case of consumers, this means expanding their understanding of the market, for example by learning how to spot the tricks, marketing ruses, and other forms of deceit, which are often employed by other players in the market. In credit unions and different types of financial service SHEs, members should be helped to improve their capacity to manage their own finances. In the case of workers, it will typically involve them enhancing their knowledge and skills, so advancing the market value of their members' labour, knowledge and skills. In the case of producers, helping them to fathom the demands of the market in which they work, and how, as producers, they can meet these demands both in the current market and into the future.

## Creativity

The driving force behind the establishment of many SHEs has been the desire to solve a problem that confronts the group. Driven by necessity, the groups' joint resources, will include their collective experience, which will often help to supply the solution to their problem. SHEs need to be innovative; there is little point in merely attempting to imitate others already in the market. SHEs should offer benefits that are superior to those of other enterprises, and this usually means doing things differently.

All the most significant types of SHEs were set up to achieve goals in a different and better way than the businesses already in the market. For example, credit cooperatives offering collective guarantees to secure loans not available to individuals, and consumer co-ops selling only pure, unadulterated foods and sharing surpluses in the form of a dividend in relation to their members' purchases. Both examples illustrate that SHEs that offer something different succeed; they cannot be enterprises that only provide the same tired approaches used by commercial businesses.

## *Worker co-ops*

Worldwide, there are many examples of successful worker co-ops, perhaps the most well-known are Spain's Mondragon co-ops. In the UK, worker cooperatives pioneered the introduction of many innovative technologies, and the promotion of whole and organic foods. Although SHEs are invariably innovators in their chosen markets when first set up, over time they need to continually reinvent themselves in response to changing circumstances and the evolving needs of their members. Put bluntly, SHEs that do not continually adapt and remain creative soon outlive their usefulness.

The real risks for any enterprise arise from doing what they did last year and the year before while waiting for someone else to innovate. This is not to suggest that SHEs should follow every novel or hare-brained scheme that comes along, instead, they should know what is happening in the market, which calls for careful research, analysis, and testing before any widespread application of change. If member-leaders simply wait for their managers to come up with innovative ideas that will help the membership, they may well be disappointed. Managers, especially those only knowledgeable about traditional commercial businesses, are often creatively blinkered, and just follow the industry market-leaders like sheep.

### Uniting around a single strategy

Choosing a strategy is all about making choices. It takes courage, insight, and foresight to see which activities and efforts will add up to the best approach in any specific market. It demands meticulous research, asking tough questions, and making sound trade-offs, exercising severe discipline to cut out the competing priorities that can distract from their true intentions. There is often a danger of making unwise compromises, opting to go for a straddling strategy, which means trying to keep a current approach intact while simultaneously trying to adopt the strategy of another player in the market. For example, in trying to offer a low cost, cash & carry service while at the same time keeping maintaining a costly personal home delivery service, and/or also offering expensive free extended credit options.

In some situations, one group of members ends-up subsidising another group of members because the costs of providing extra services mean that those members (who don't require them) share these additional costs. This it is not a strategy that can work in the long-term. Extra services always mean extra costs, so members need to be ready to pay for what they get, rather than relying on other members to subsidise them.

### Game-changing strategies

Creative thinking by the members of pioneering SHEs has often resulted in the development of game-changing market intervention strategies. The founders of early SHEs first gained a clear understanding of the failings within a defined market and then responded to the problems identified by developing bold and original solutions. Such novel approaches allowed their SHEs to transform the position of their members within the market.

Here are a few examples of the ambitious ideas behind the market intervention strategies of successful SHEs:

- Building societies, in the late 18th century, at first organized their members to build houses for themselves, but later evolved into societies that helped members to save for a deposit, while their society provided a mortgage to buy their home.

- The Rochdale method of consumer cooperation, in the UK – for more details see the end of this chapter.

- The Raiffeisen method for agricultural credit.

- The Caisse Populaire de Lévis in Quebec, Canada.

- The cooperative creamery model promoted by Horace Plunkett, in Ireland.

- The credit union model of mutual saving and borrowing.

- The Amul dairy cooperative, based at Anand, in the State of Gujarat, India.

There have been, and continue to be, many more game-changing interventions strategies, developed by SHEs all over the world. The fact is that most flourishing SHEs have adopted a ground-breaking strategy. It needs to be recognised that no approach is sufficiently robust to last forever. Therefore, all market intervention strategies need to be regularly reviewed. Following such review, plans have to be developed, updated, or discarded, as and when market and social conditions alter.

**The role of members**
An effective market intervention strategy requires the commitment of members and their engagement with their enterprise. The higher the level of member commitment achieved, the higher is the resulting member-benefits. In all cases, a financial commitment by the member is needed to cement their engagement with their SHEs. Making an investment or placing at least some of their savings into their own enterprise, helps demonstrate their commitment.

Members should appreciate the basics of the strategy, and their leaders, senior managers, and key employees all need to understand the basis of the strategy and have at the very least an appreciation of the dynamics of the market in which they are working. The aims and the outcomes of the approach have to be clear. The best way of gaining an understanding of the requirements for a valid market intervention strategy is to check out the examples supplied by successful SHEs everywhere.

Whatever the intervention strategy pursued, it's essential that this is supported by a complete package of systems, which are needed to ensure its proper implementation, and the realisation of the strategy. One critical practice is to regularly. review and adjust the approach, at least annually Such a review needs to be undertaken with complete honesty and be driven by the desire to meet both the current and future needs of members. Otherwise, any review can just become an exercise in protecting jobs and positions.

**More singers than songwriters**
Most market intervention strategies once developed and proven to work by one self-help enterprise, are quickly adopted and replicated by new groups in other locations. There will always be more singers than songwriters. The creative pioneers who came up with the ground-breaking strategies enabled SHEs to give exceptional benefits to their members. They supplied the seeds that grew into many new SHEs, so it's important to support those who are ready to test innovative approaches and to help the dissemination process once such new concepts are tested and shown to work in practice. The widespread proliferation of SHEs, based on shared market intervention strategies are abundant. There are many examples of SHEs developing effective new approaches that are then replicated by other groups that also set-up similar

enterprises elsewhere, and this same form of expansion of SHEs continues to this day.

Others wishing to replicate the accomplishments of pioneering enterprises need to implement the complete package of the successful enterprise that they want to copy. Often a kind of self-help enterprise system of licencing can ease the propagation of new market intervention strategies, which is a means of supplying new SHEs with a complete package of systems and set-up support. This has been the basis of the approach to developing credit unions, where they have spread nationwide in many countries, which has also been the essence of the support supplied by the Plunkett Foundation, for the development of community-owned retail shops and pubs in the UK.

### Redundant strategies

A familiar predicament for many SHEs is that their leaders remain wedded to a specific market intervention strategy, this even though conditions within the market have changed significantly. With the result that their enterprise becomes irrelevant to the lives of their members. The root cause of this problem is the failure of leaders to keep abreast with the events taking place in their markets. SHEs have to be flexible enough to respond whenever this occurs.

### Copying mega-businesses

Often people allow themselves to be over-influenced by the mega-businesses that control our lives in so many ways. Finding ourselves accepting the idea that only large enterprises are worthwhile; and, because many SHEs are run by people who think that they need to be even more like such businesses, they allow themselves to be persuaded to accept approaches that should have no place in SHEs. Often thoughtlessly adopting alien practices, such as:

- Using the same kind of marketing tricks as those used in many businesses that exploit members, and which are unacceptable in SHEs.

- Spending vast sums on managing the 'brand', believing that this is more important than simply always telling the truth about their organizations.

- Believing that increasing the scale of operations is more important than designing organizations that can deliver what their members genuinely need.

**Conglomerates**

A conglomerate means a large business that consists of several companies or departments that deal with a variety of very different enterprises, manufacturing, or commercial activities. In the 1960s, ambitious senior managers of international companies constructed huge conglomerates made up of dozens or even hundreds of often-unrelated activities. The rationale was to insulate investors against the fluctuations in any one industry by diversifying across several sectors. The end results were typically disappointing, this because the individual enterprises were often disadvantaged, rather than helped, by their unified management that often had no in-depth knowledge of the new markets they were entering. Also, senior managers often used the more profitable parts of the combined business to subsidise other parts that were unprofitable. Their priority, it seemed, was not so much to make a profit for investors, but rather to keep their own empires intact. The result, in many cases, was that within a few decades most of these conglomerates crumbled or were dissolved.

A conglomerate is not an appropriate format for a self-help enterprise; because this approach to securing growth will generally take it outside of the fields of competence of member-directors who ultimately control the enterprise. Further to this, their members are unlikely to have the capacity to exercise control over such enterprises or to become fully engaged by them.

The active control of a conglomerate is only possible by employing the same financial controls and management practices as used by investor-controlled businesses. The use of such methods can be damaging to the self-help mindset, and regularly results in the adoption of the same kind of culture prevalent in commercial businesses.

The better arrangement is to have separate SHEs, with their own members, each working in different markets. Market-specific SHEs, are much better placed to engage their members actively, and for their representatives to be able to control them properly. Internationally, the most effective large-scale SHEs concentrate on clearly-defined markets or a group of closely related markets. Carefully thought-out plans need to be constructed by the leaders of those SHEs that have blundered into becoming conglomerates. Reversing such conglomeration calls for careful plans to be prepared for the necessary transition into separate enterprises.

**Embracing the change process**
As soon as a self-help enterprise enters the market, this event changes the market, and their intervention will trigger a reaction from the other players within the market. It's essential that leaders of SHEs are fully aware of the changes taking place in their markets; and, most important, what is driving such events. The gathering of market intelligence is a critical task, but this is different from it is within a commercial business. This is because it's the way the changes in their markets are affecting their members that need to drive their response, and this should be the driver of any new market intervention strategy.

## The impact of globalisation

Many SHEs were set up when the markets in which they worked were under-developed, over time the market becomes more sophisticated, subject to the effect of globalisation, or change driven by modern technologies. One problem for SHEs is that the kind of investment needed to challenge significant players in the market can be hard to come by. The answer to this often requires a response that is both creative and radical. SHEs need to review their market intervention strategy systematically. Otherwise, when adjustments take place in their markets, they may be too slow to respond, which in turn can result in their marginalisation. SHEs need to re-evaluate their market intervention strategy constantly; this task has to be integral to the strategic planning process.

Leaders of SHEs should ensure that their strategic planning practices, supported by effective policies, enables people throughout their enterprise to be fully aware of what is happening in the markets in which they are involved and that they are ready to change their intervention strategy when the market demands a response. This means keeping their organization lean and agile so that there are fewer barriers to change whenever this becomes necessary.

## Market intervention - key practices

Establishing the key practices that are needed to develop and sustain an effective market intervention strategy should be combined into the overall management system. The following are some of the critical practices required:

- Members are fully involved in setting all strategy. There is no room for arrogance on the part of leaders or managers. Members are not always the most articulate people, but when the time is given to listening, it will often be discovered that they do understand a lot about the markets that they are involved with. There is a need to reach out to all members, who are often just busy surviving in a challenging world.

- Leaders need to be aware of the danger of allowing the agenda to be set by a vocal minority of activists who often inhabit a very different reality from most grassroots members.

- The formation and review of the intervention strategy are undertaken as a precursor to the planning process.

- The collection and review of market intelligence need to be a continuous process, which feeds into the process of strategy formation.

- Systematically combating the misinformation and trickery or dishonesty that often allows those holding power to exploit those disadvantaged within a market.

- Help by building the capacity of members to improve their position in the market.

## Early market intervention strategies

When the Rochdale Society of Equitable Pioneers was set up in 1844, their market intervention strategy, although not named as such, was included in a document called 'Law the First'. This statement set out a very ambitious strategy, but was replaced in 1860, and set out within a statement published in the Society's Almanack. Only items numbered 3 to 6 in this document were part of the market intervention strategy, which by this time was concentrated upon retailing, the remaining points confirmed important practices that became accepted 'foundation practices' in many self-help enterprises; these two documents are reproduced below.

## The Rochdale Society of Equitable Pioneers
**– Law and Objects 1844**

The objects and plans of this Society are to form arrangements for the pecuniary benefit of the social and domestic conditions of its members, by raising a sufficient amount of capital in shares of one pound each, to bring into operation the following plans and arrangements:

1. Establishing a store for the sale of provisions, clothing etc.

2. The building, purchasing or erecting a number of houses in which those members desiring to assist each other in improving their domestic and social conditions may reside.

3. To commence the manufacture of such articles as the Society may determine upon, for the employment of such members as may be without employment or who may be suffering in consequence of the repeated reduction in their wages.

4. As a further benefit and security to the members of this Society, the Society shall purchase or rent an estate or estates of land, which shall be cultivated by the members who may be out of employment, or whose labour may be badly remunerated.

5. That, as soon as practicable, the Society shall proceed to arrange the powers of production, distribution, education, and government or in other words, to establish a self-supporting colony of united interests or assist other societies in establishing such colonies.

6. That for the promotion of sobriety. A temperance hotel be opened in one of the society's houses as soon as convenient.

## The Rochdale Society of Equitable Pioneers
### A Statement made in the society's almanack of 1860

The present Co-operative Movement does not intend to meddle with the various religious or political differences which now exist in society, but by a common bond, namely, that of self-interest, to join together the means, the energies, and the talents of all for the common benefit of each.

1. That capital should be of their own providing and bear a fixed rate of interest
2. That only the purest provisions procurable should be supplied to members
3. That full weight and measure should be given
4. That market prices should be charged, and no credit is given or asked
5. That profits should be divided pro rata upon the amount of purchases made by each member
6. That the principle of 'one member one vote' should obtain in government and the equality of the sexes in membership
7. That the management should be in the hands of officers and committee elected periodically
8. That a definite percentage of profits be allotted to education
9. That frequent statements and balance sheets should be presented to members.

### Some lessons from cooperative banking

Leaders of cooperative banks need to know what kind of bank they are running on behalf of their members. There are mainly three types of banks these are:

- **Retail banks** - *Retail banking, also known as consumer banking, is the conventional mass-market banking in which individual customers use local branches of larger commercial banks. Services offered include savings and checking accounts, mortgages, personal loans, debit/credit cards and certificates of deposit. In retail banking, the focus is on the individual consumer.*

- **Investment banks** - *full-service investment banks usually provide both advisory and financing banking services to their clients, often undertaking research covering a broad array of financial products, including equities, credit, foreign currency, commodities, and their derivatives.*

- **Development banks** – *a financial institution designed to provide medium- and long-term capital for productive investment, often accompanied by technical assistance.*

Most of the world's cooperative banks started as local banks where their members are individuals or small businesses – such as farming businesses. These local banks are owned by their customers and continue to operate at the foundations of their banking system. Some have expanded into investment banking. For example, Crédit Agricole, Rabobank, Desjardins Bank.

# 11. CULTURE IS CRUCIAL

**What is meant by culture?**

The culture of an organization is revealed in the collective behaviour of the people who are part of the organization, and in the meanings that people attach to their actions. Culture includes its standards of behaviour, its vision of its purpose and function; and in the norms, working language, systems, beliefs, and habits, prevailing throughout the organization.

In practice, the culture is, a set of shared assumptions that guide interpretation and action in an organization, and these define appropriate behaviour for people involved in the day-to-day activities. The culture affects the way that people interact with each other, including with members, clients, and all other stakeholders. Although an organization may have an overarching culture, in larger enterprises there are sometimes conflicting cultures within various parts of the same organization. In SHEs, it's critical that the prevailing culture reflects their status as a self-help enterprise.

The right culture doesn't come about by accident, but by design, this requires that the right practices are in place throughout the organization. The process of embedding the right culture starts when the expected standards of behaviour are set-out unambiguously. These standards need to become 'the norm' throughout the enterprise and are accepted as the *only* acceptable standards of behaviour. This includes, for example, that the culture is reflected in recruitment practices, the training and empowerment processes, the rewards system; and provides the basis of relationships with all stakeholders.

## Creating the 'right' culture

This chapter deals with the system needed to support the development and maintenance of an appropriate culture in a self-help enterprise. The aim of the system is to ensure the prevailing culture positively contributes towards achieving the purpose of the enterprise.

There are many organizations that appear to have sound policies in place and yet don't deliver the kind of services that they were set-up to provide. They often do not achieve what they should, simply because the pervading culture is at odds with its declared aims. Notorious examples of this kind of situation have been revealed in those health and care facilities where a defective culture has permeated the organization, leading to the extreme mistreatment of patients by those who should be giving compassionate care. This kind of situation can arise in all manner of bodies, where the necessary culture is not in place. In many SHEs, similar deficiencies of culture often prevail because the people running the enterprise have lost sight of the fact that they exist to serve their members.

## Mutual trust

Mutual trust between the enterprise and individual members, and between members, is essential to the effectiveness of SHEs. Securing mutual trust within any organization is highly dependent upon having in place a proper and well-established culture. Members should be able to trust their leaders to run their enterprise in the best interest of members. Trust has to be earned and is only secured when all are committed to a set of systems that ensures the integrity of the enterprise. This requires that everyone involved knows the standards of behaviour that are expected from them, and that all deviations from the required standards be challenged at once, whenever they occur. In the absence of a clear purpose embedded within the culture, the organization invariably switches to working to gain more wealth and greater glory for those running it.

## Changing the culture

To achieve significant cultural change involves the adoption of clear practices that ensure the desired culture is sustained throughout the organization. This calls for the adoption of revised practices, clear-cut policies that are well understood, and are implemented with commitment and determination. Cultural change involves changing the behaviour of people, and, in most cases, the process of change only begins when the language now used is changed to meet the required standard. This means changing the language from one that reinforces the old culture to one that embeds the new culture.

There is little point in reciting so-called 'values', even when these sincerely believed, or any other list of platitudes, as though these could somehow provide a mantra that will change the behaviour of the people running the enterprise. What is needed, is the constant implementation of all the foundation practices, which need to be supported by a full set of foundation policies.

Where SHEs have become something other than a bona-fide self-help enterprise, then before they can return to being legitimate, a massive cultural-shift will be needed. If SHEs are to be enterprises that truly help to change the lives of their members, such profound change needs a fundamental change of mindset. Such changes can only be started and driven by their member-leaders, who need to be well prepared, courageous, and fully committed to achieving the rehabilitation of their enterprises.

## A culture of equivalence

Members should be convinced that they will share all benefits among themselves fairly and that they will have a real say in the running of their venture. All members need to be treated equally, not just in theory but in everyday practice. In enterprises run by workers or producers, all members should believe that they will be treated equitably. There can be no room for any practices that favour any particular class of members.

In many consumer-owned enterprises, it seems that everybody else gets a better deal than the grassroots members, who are often missed-out or are side-lined. Employees and directors get discounts applied to their purchases; senior managers get all manner of perquisites; staff, students, and other groups get exclusive deals. Meanwhile, the ordinary members, who own the enterprise, are treated as no more than third-rate customers. Their so-called 'leaders' make speeches about their commitment to the values of fairness and equality; in these circumstances is it any wonder that their members are neither committed to or feel in any way engaged by, their enterprise?

## Hypocrisy - the great demotivator

Some people in SHEs are fond of talking about 'values' and 'principles', but this can become extremely damaging to any enterprise if these are shown to be mere platitudes. Values are worthless unless they become the standard for actual behaviour, and if backed up by effective systems built on practices that support the implementation of values in practice.

If any policy is to have any meaning, proper sanctions and rewards are needed to support it. Hypocrisy is the great demotivator because when members' leaders and senior managers work to double standards, the only result is cynicism. This causes the destruction of goodwill and a lack of commitment to the enterprise, disaffecting members, employees, and other stakeholders alike. Hypocrisy is like a plague, if an organization does not have in place the 'hygiene factors' to prevent its spread, it can end up killing it. These factors are a set of practices that ensure that hypocrites are outed as soon as ever they reveal themselves. A code of cultural practice, an agreed acceptable terminology and prohibiting the use of platitudes and meaningless statements, can all help to put an end to hypocrisy.

## Talking about members

Members of SHEs have a profoundly different role to that of a customer. Producers and workers have customers, but all types of consumer and community-controlled enterprises should only have 'members' and 'prospective members. Worker cooperatives should only have members and prospective members, not employees. Without this basic distinction, reflecting the importance of members, the essential culture within such enterprises will not be achieved. Customers of worker and producer-owned enterprises should never be regarded as people who can be tricked into buying goods or services. Customers of these types of SHEs are the very people and organizations that they have to build long-term relationships.

The broad acceptance of the importance of the self-help mindset will deeply influence the culture of the enterprise. Many commercial businesses seek to create dependency on the part of their customers, employees, and suppliers; however, the presence of the self-help mindset means that relationships between the organization and its members should be of a different order. Relationships are forged with members built on strengthening the capacity of the individual to deal with situations arising that threaten their wellbeing and helping them to respond positively by taking mutual action to deal with their problems.

**Language embodies the culture**
The words used within an organization, often define the relationships between people, and these relationships are critical when seeking the cooperation of others. Cooperation is easily undermined where the people involved do not choose their words thoughtfully. This is not a matter of being 'politically correct', but it is instead a question of whether what people say fosters cooperation or destroys it. People involved in SHEs have to be careful to use the correct terminology, using only words that reflect the true character of their enterprise.

Our words need to reinforce what has to be true, which is that the organization is, in fact, a self-help enterprise. Codes of practice can play an important role in supporting the right culture, but most important is the complete commitment of its leaders to the spirit of the code. Leaders should prove their commitment by their personal example, or to put this another way, leaders at all levels must always 'walk the talk'.

**Dislodging fixations**
Most ordinary people, when they hear an organization described as 'a business' will at once assume that it is a commercial business, run with the objective of making a profit. What most people actually mean when they describe a self-help enterprise as a 'business' is that it's run in a business-like manner. To talk about SHEs as being a 'businesses' can only cause confusion. Senior managers frequently like to call their organizations 'businesses', because when they think of the enterprise as a business, this appears to give them a licence to behave in a certain way, encouraging them to think that their members are nothing more than a market to be exploited.

The desire of some managers to call self-help enterprises 'a business', often has a lot to do with the way that they see themselves and how they think their colleagues and peers in other enterprises perceive them. Some being more interested in impressing their peers and 'pals at the golf club', or in other circles in which they move, than in delivering what their members need.

At the other end of the spectrum of misinformation, there are those that talk about their enterprise as being a 'social enterprise', which to many people means an enterprise with benevolent intent; and, for some the kind of body that they would like to be associated. This, while spending their members' money so that they can bask in the reflected glory arising from such benevolence.

Sustaining the 'right' culture in SHEs involves *not* using the kind of language that is only associated with commercial businesses, which is not appropriate in SHEs. For example, people need to be reminded that often when people talk about 'profit' what they really mean is 'margin', which is the difference between all costs and the price realised for any product or service.

**The practices required**
A full set of interdependent practices are to be followed by SHEs if they are to are to build the kind of culture that needs to prevail. These practices include the following:

- Members are *always* put first.
- Nobody gets a better deal than a member.
- All members have equal access to all deals.
- Transparency in all dealings with members is the norm.
- Induction training and updating are routinely provided to all those dealing with members. This is to ensure that all

involved in the enterprise know how a self-help enterprise needs to operate.

-   Honest communication needs to replace all the 'spin', misleading practices and management-speak, which is so often the currency in commercial businesses.

-   Everyone, throughout the organization, should realise that a different mindset is required in SHEs. This means always working in the best interest of members, not exploiting their weaknesses.

-   Education to empower is an essential element in all SHEs. Leaders must always be conscious of the fact that many of the people that need to change their attitudes often have a personal stake in safeguarding their present positions and livelihoods. This can cause people to resist much-needed change and can block the pathway to realigning the individual's interest with the purpose of the enterprise, so this awareness has to be integrated within the enterprise's people development system; see *Chapter 20*.

# 12. GROWING SELF-HELP ENTERPRISES

## The meaning of growth

Self-help enterprises often need to become bigger to secure the economies of scale necessary to help SHEs secure even better deals in the market. In many cases, federal or networked enterprises can best achieve such economies, while keeping close engagement with their members. The best scale for SHEs is one that balances economies of scale with the framework needed to support a democratically controlled enterprise.

When seeking to grow SHEs, it's necessary to assess how best to develop the services and benefits delivered to members, while maintaining members' commitment to their enterprise. This can be achieved by thinking about how the benefits arising from the mutual action can be extended to many more of those who can benefit from the activities of this form of enterprise. Decisions about growing SHEs are not be made simply because more prestige is attached to becoming a bigger enterprise, with the prospect of bigger salaries and perks for those who run the enterprise.

## Economies of scale

Economies of scale are the cost advantages that enterprises may obtain due to its size, output, or scale of operation. This is because the cost per unit of output normally decreases when the volume of activity increases and the fixed costs of the activity can be spread over more units of output. Achieving the benefits of scale is often an integral element of the market intervention strategy, and the more members that can combine their purchasing or selling power, the more influence their enterprise will have within any given market. However, in practice, there can be important limitations to the application of this concept, due to the impact that the increased scale of operations has on the relationships between the people involved.

The self-help economic system differs from those used in commercial businesses, and the basis for making many economic decisions is fundamentally different. This is because SHEs have to balance the advantages that can be achieved from securing economies of scale with the need to work in ways that will sustain both positive human relationships and democratic member-control. SHEs need to prove that they can be relied upon to always act in the best interests of their members. So, when increasing the volume of activity, this needs to be matched by the building-up of trust and the level of engagement with members.

## Organic growth

Many SHEs start small and grow organically into large and complex organizations, often outstripping the capacity of their elected leaders and managers, and/or their capacity to finance rapidly expanding operations. The pressure to deliver increased economic benefits to members regularly results in SHEs seeking to achieve economies of scale. Sometimes, economies of scale are sought through the means of mergers between smaller-scale SHEs, or by amalgamation with a larger enterprise. In the process, many of the fundamental characteristics of self-help enterprise are often lost.

Organizations that were once small, local, and based upon direct democracy, often find that they need to transform into using a more advanced type of democracy. To achieve this transformation successfully calls for both committed leaders of the highest calibre, and the full involvement of the membership. The unintended outcome of expansion is often the alienation of the membership. Transition to an enterprise that properly balances securing economies of scale against the downside of big organizations calls for creative approaches if these drawbacks are to be avoided. This may include looking at the idea of well-managed, franchise-like operations, federals, and the use of 'umbrella' cooperatives.

## *The dangers of buying businesses*

Sometimes SHEs get the opportunity to purchase businesses, and their leaders may think that this is an easy way of expanding the scale of their operations. However, there are many pitfalls involved in buying an established concern, and such acquisitions have often caused the downfall of otherwise successful SHEs. The main problems are normally caused by the fact that the previous customers or owners of the business may not readily accept becoming members of the enterprise. Typically, there will be a completely different culture within the business being purchased. If it is a substantial concern, it may well overwhelm the original enterprise. Even when a self-help enterprise is merged or transferred into another SHE, there are often many obstacles to unifying two different enterprises. Clearly, 'organic growth' provides a sounder basis for developing SHEs than by acquiring existing businesses.

### Umbrella cooperatives

SHEs can usually achieve economies of scale by means of spreading administrative and other costs while maintaining separate enterprises operating in different specific markets. This can be achieved by working together with other SHEs to provide central services. For example, UK farmers producing grain crops (such as wheat, barley, and oats) have developed a method of using separate cooperatives for marketing crops, offering storage facilities, and for trading in futures (fixing prices for future delivery). Farmers join those specific cooperatives that are relevant to their needs. Each of the separate cooperatives is a member of a central service cooperative that supplies all the administrative, accounting, and logistical support needed by his or her primary level cooperatives.

In many situations, there are opportunities to develop umbrella or 'hub' cooperatives that provide all central services (often including shared top level management) in a specific region. This approach can create the basis for developing and expanding all forms of self-help enterprises in their region.

## Scaling-up organizations

Small-scale SHEs are vitally important, and there are a great many more opportunities for their further application in a wide variety of situations. One of the main constraints to the advancement of a self-help enterprise has often been the failure to modify the organizational model for effective application to larger-scale operations. When SHEs grow to any significant size - measured by their number of members and/or their turnover, then multiple problems often beset them, especially where they lose sight of their 'reason for being' and become irrelevant to the lives of their members.

SHEs work well on a scale that reflects the need for human relationships to develop, and when the people involved know each other, and appreciate their fellow members based on existing relationships. However, by using modern-day communications methods, provided there exists a strong commitment to a common purpose in the context of a specific market (or a group of closely related markets) then an increased scale and geographical coverage ought not to become a disadvantage.

## Conflicting motivations

Senior managers often want to pursue growth to the detriment of the enterprise's long-term effectiveness, because such growth can bring much bigger rewards for themselves. SHEs should be both nimble and straightforward so that they can quickly change in response to new conditions in the market. Senior managers often want to move beyond their present markets because expanding into new areas could increase their wealth and power. A new market needs a different enterprise led by people that fully understand the dynamics of that new market.

In order that the members of SHEs can secure the benefits of scale often needed to make enough impact in the markets in which they work, large numbers of members working together are sometimes necessary. Separate SHEs can combine their power in the market by working with other similar enterprises, all working in defined markets.

There is often considerable confusion about the effect of size and scale upon the effectiveness of SHEs. Plainly, small SHEs are simpler to manage, and it's easier to keep members engaged when there are fewer of them. The right size for a self-help enterprise depends entirely upon the size of the market in which it needs to work. For example, if a self-help enterprise is running a village store serving a village, which in itself is a distinct market, then it ought to prosper. On the other hand, mainstream retailing needs to work as a national, or at least a regional basis to succeed. Some markets are international, for example, the market for processed milk, and in these circumstances, the scale of operations may have to be international.

## Networking and federals

Federal enterprises may be formed to move to the next stage in the market chain, or to run new services for their members when a wider market base is needed to challenge the businesses already trading in a market. Federals may be set up to carry out representational or lobbying work. Federals with trading activities need the full commitment of the senior managers in all member SHEs, so there is a sound case for including them within the governance arrangements.

Federals that try to operate based on only cooperating when the self-interest of all the members of the group is maximised are almost bound to fail. Managers and staff involved in the day-to-day activities often require formal contracts to guide them as to the division of tasks between the federal and the local enterprise. Federals need to continuously deliver real and obvious benefits to their member organizations and stay committed to their purpose. Where the board have allowed their management to pursue their own aims, and this results in the federal not being devoted to increasing benefits to its members, then steps have to be taken to change this situation.

The level of understanding needed for cooperation and mutual ownership to work in major enterprises, especially within federals (SHEs of SHEs) has often not kept pace with the realities of the modern world. Change is needed in many federal enterprises, especially with respect to their democratic processes and governance arrangements; Also, their methods of financing their operations. The way that federals develop and support their leaders often needs to be changed too. Current practices are often perpetuated, even though they were developed in a bygone age, and were designed for small-scale, locally based organizations.

## Federal action

It was not very long after the early primary level SHEs started that those involved hit upon the idea that if individuals gained by working together, then groups of SHEs could also work jointly to multiply such gains. SHEs joined with other SHEs to set-up federations undertaking tasks that no single primary SHE could undertake on its own. In practice, cooperating with other similar enterprises often extends their power to get a better deal for their members. It needs to be remembered that, in fact, it's not the organizations that work together, but it's the individuals within them who need to be committed to securing added benefits for their members. The leaders of SHEs and their management teams need to work with others from different enterprises to achieve their respective purposes. Cooperation between SHEs should not be regarded as just a 'good thing' or undertaken because this is what is expected to happen. Such collaboration must yield tangible benefits for the members of all the SHEs involved.

The most productive collaboration usually takes place between SHEs running the same type of enterprise, for example; all the enterprises are consumer SHEs, or all are worker SHEs. All types of SHEs can gain by lobbying to secure more relevant legislation and more favourable public policy for all types of self-help enterprise. Together, they can provide mutual support and combine to building the capacity of their people, by supplying the specific kind of education and training they need. Federals may carry out representational tasks, supply legal services, consultancy services, education, training and advisory services; as well as sharing of the kind of information that allows for benchmarking, which means comparing performance data between member organizations.

Some of the earliest federal SHEs were set-up to move to the next stage in the market chain; for example, to act as a wholesaler to their retail members, to act as bankers to primary credit enterprises, or to run jointly-owned manufacturing or processing plants. Federals are typically set up to supply new services to their member SHEs, such as banking and insurance services, also where new products or services that called for a bigger scale of operations that could be secured by any single primary level enterprise.

## Difficulties with federals

In many parts of the world, up until about the first half of the 20th century, the expansion of the benefits to be achieved as the result of cooperation appeared to be unlimited. The successes achieved by SHEs world-wide were often mainly made as a result of federal activity. As the economic structures of the world changed and all kinds of factors combined to change the market conditions within which SHEs worked, the response of federals has often been inadequate. One of the main factors precipitating this decline in those SHEs has been the failure to make federals work properly. Too often, federals do not serve their members as they should when the 'tail starts to wag the dog'.

Federals involved in trading and commercial activities do not, in practice, work as well as those formed to provide common services such as legal, training and advisory services. The weaknesses of federals can often be traced back to underlying issues, including for example:

- Where the dividing line between the tasks of the federal and the member enterprises have not been set out clearly in advance, which results in conflicts arising between the managers involved.

- Where the system of governance adopted is unfit-for-purpose for as a federal enterprise.

- Where members are a mixture of both corporate bodies and individuals' problems are almost bound to arise.

## Governance in federals

It's not surprising that when a group of primary SHEs decide to set up a secondary level enterprise, they tend to design the governance along the same lines as those in the member primary SHEs when generally this will not be suitable for a federal. Depending upon the geographical extent of the area from which the member SHEs of the federal is drawn, it may be right for the system of governance to allow for regional representation. However, the structure created should not be overly bureaucratic. Otherwise, decision-making will be slow and cumbersome. Once again, it needs to be emphasised that the task of representation needs to be separated from the task of directing a federal.

The necessity for representation at the broad policy-making level is clear, to ensure that the federal serves the interests of all the member SHEs. But, when it comes to selecting those that will make up its board of directors, competence needs to be the criteria for choosing them. The result of using a representative system for appointing board members not only causes the wrong type of person to be appointed but often means that a board is too large to be effective.

There are often differing views about the composition of the boards of federals. In the case of federals primarily concerned with undertaking representational and associated tasks, lay representatives from member societies are normally the best persons to be its directors. Federals that undertake trading need the commitment of the professional managers (of the member SHEs) so managers should be included in their governance arrangements. However, it's best to have a board where its members are drawn from the boards of directors of the member SHEs, and such directors form the majority.

It can also be a sound practice to include some independent, non-member, non-executive directors, which is a priority when the activities of the federal include those that are beyond the experience of those involved in the direction and management of the member SHEs and in which they may have no prior experience. For example, where members SHEs are retail co-ops, and the federal is involved in manufacturing, or where agricultural marketing SHEs combine to reach export markets where member-directors may have had very little experience.

### Voting systems for federals

The governance systems in federals need to be specially designed to achieve the federal's specific goals. In addition, the way that power is shared between member organizations has to be fair and practical. Simply mirroring the voting method used in the member SHEs is rarely suitable. A straightforward 'one-member-one-vote' arrangement will seldom be satisfactory. Instead, voting methods based upon one vote per member, plus added votes distributed based on the number of members of each member organization may be considered appropriate. In federals with trading activities, voting arrangements may be based on one vote per member plus added votes allocated in relation to the volume of trade transacted with the federal by each member SHE. In both cases, limits are usually imposed, for example by setting a limit to the number of votes allowed to be held by any single member; such limits are designed to prevent the federal being totally dominated by its biggest members.

## The foundations of effective federals

The difficulties of making federals work are not limited to SHEs. The conflict between centralised and de-centralised decision-making is always a contentious issue in large-scale organizations of all types. The advantages of designing a method that balances the respective powers of individual states and the federal body are amply demonstrated by successfully federated countries. Experience has been built up over many years; this provides many useful lessons for all types of federals.

It could be argued, that our capacity to federate successfully is one of the main challenges of our time. Better ways of reconciling the need for a larger scale of working has to be combined with the need for local communities to feel that they can influence what happens to them. Federals are simply an extension of cooperation to a level above that taking place between individuals, in fact, cooperation between SHEs involves the use of the very same system of cooperation, as set out in *Chapter 24*.

If the leaders' of SHEs see no reason to make any sacrifice or compromise, unless it's very obviously in the interest of their own enterprises, then they will never gain anything of significance from federal action.

Federals that started well and gave important benefits for their member SHEs sometimes lose their way, and this occurs because their management loses sight of the fact that they exist to serve their member organizations. This happens when the federal is seen to be more important than its members. This kind of situation arises when the federal's directors have allowed its managers to pursue their own goals, and where managers have come to believe that the federal has a duty to protect the livelihoods of its employees.

## Sound practices for federals

Effective federals are dependent upon the leaders of the member SHEs accepting several key concepts. It's essential that those occupying leadership positions fully know, and are committed to the following concepts:

- **Subsidiarity** - which implies reverse delegation, and the constant acknowledgement that only the specific powers that have been willingly delegated to them by a member organization, can be exercised on their behalf. Once powers or tasks have been delegated to the federal, individual SHEs should not seek to take them back unilaterally and to exercise them for themselves. This means that when SHEs feel in any way dissatisfied with the services offered by their joint enterprise, then their representatives have to discuss the issue head-on with the management of the federal and get the matter resolved. They cannot be allowed to unilaterally take back powers they have previously given to the federal. Another important aspect of subsidiarity is that only if there is an overriding advantage to be gained in the mutual interest of the members of the federal are powers to be delegated to it. In other words, decisions should always be made at a local level, unless there are clear advantages from it being taken at the federal centre.

- **Dual loyalty** - which means that all participants, whether part of the management of the federal or of a member SHE, are all expected to exercise a 'dual loyalty'. They are not expected to act solely in the best interest of a member SHE nor to see that their loyalty is due only to the federal, just as it's expected that the citizens of a federal State will be similarly loyal to their country and their State. (For example, a resident of Texas is not expected to choose between giving loyalty to Texas and to the United States of America, as a nation, dual loyalties are essential.

- **Clear division of tasks** - requiring that the tasks that are to be carried out by the federal are explicitly agreed so that there can be no room for any misunderstanding. This avoids the possibility that powers once delegated can be withdrawn either by mistake or design.

- **Practice transparency of dealing** – requiring that there be no misunderstanding about the benefits that are obtained from federal action. If, for example, there are claims that a federal purchasing SHE is not securing the best deal for any specific class of goods then there needs to be complete openness about the ways such deals could be improved, and information obtained by member SHEs ought to be shared with the federal.

- **Zero tolerance of empire-builders and separatists** - this means that, if the above concepts are fully followed there can be no valid reason to tolerate actions that undermine the relationships between the federal and its member SHEs. If individuals are discovered to be pressing their own interests ahead of the joint interest of the federal and its members, then this has to be dealt with without delay, and steps are taken immediately to ensure that such actions cease.

- **Ring-fencing financial activities** - this means not having the same federal undertaking financial services (e.g. banking, insurance, and other similar services) alongside other tasks such as representational or trading activities. It becomes difficult for the management of a federal to keep such

153

activities separate, and when they do become mixed up the result will frequently end in a 'financial scandal'.

- **Contractual relationships need to be formalised** – this requires that relations between SHEs and their federal need be strengthened by formal, legally-binding, contracts. Such contracts spell out the duties and responsibilities of the parties to the agreement; these can often prevent relationships between SHEs and federals going wrong, especially when the federal concerned is undertaking commercial activities. The managers and staff involved in the day-to-day operation of the federal's activities and their counterparts in member SHEs will often have formal contracts to guide them. It's all very well for the directors of both entities to agree how things should be done but unless those who carry out the practical work know how they are expected to work, the federal will never work as it should.

**Business cooperation and federals**

Federalisation appears to come more naturally to consumer-owned SHEs. In enterprises where their members are businesses or entrepreneurs, SHEs often find it more difficult to operate federals, perhaps because of the nature of their base membership, and the fact that economic goals are usually paramount in such enterprises. For these reasons, it's wise only to seek federal solutions when the benefits to be secured are patently clear. The extension of the benefits of business cooperation may be best secured by setting-up a larger-scale joint enterprise. In all cases, it's important that the members of the primary level SHEs are fully involved in the process of deciding the best way forward.

**Subsidiaries**

Sometimes SHEs use subsidiaries as the means of growing the

income and power of an enterprise, but they are only rarely suitable, and should not be employed when changes in governance and financing arrangements are what is in fact needed. Subsidiaries are sometimes used to hide certain aspects of the enterprise's operations from the scrutiny of their members. For example, subsidiaries are sometimes used to avoid the democratic procedures that, if they are ill-designed, can prevent SHEs from being sufficiently responsive to what is happening within the market.

In some cases, when there is a high-level risk, a subsidiary may be useful, but in all cases, decision-makers should first look to reform current structures so that effective management can be undertaken within the framework of an appropriate system of governance. There are only very limited situations when the use of subsidiaries can be justified, for example when producers want to secure a presence in certain markets that could not otherwise be reached.

In other cases, innovative ways of financing SHEs have not been properly developed; instead, subsidiaries are used as a means of accessing outside finance. Those making decisions about setting-up subsidiaries should take care to look down the road to see what will happen if their enterprise can no longer hold the controlling interest in the new venture. There are circumstances when a subsidiary company can be set up to supply the means to separate out activities from SHEs that are no longer relevant to the enterprise's common.

It's worth repeating that subsidiaries should not be used as a means of circumventing organizational and financing problems that ought to be met head-on. In such cases, there is often a need to change the structures of governance and/or to introduce different financing arrangements. SHEs themselves should always be the main vehicle for securing the benefits that members are seeking as the result of their mutual action. Care should be taken not to set up subsidiaries that can rob members of their control over their own enterprise.

**Expanding the role of self-help enterprises**

All leaders of SHEs need to be aware of how the benefits arising from their mutual action can be extended to others not yet involved in SHEs. The more mainstream this form of enterprise becomes, the better it will be for the national economy while helping each individual enterprise to become more established. Some approaches to expanding the role of SHEs in the wider economy are considered in *Chapter 15*.

# 13. LEADERS AND LEADERSHIP

## Leadership

This chapter sets out the requirements for leaders of SHEs and outlines the kind of systems needed to ensure that SHEs get the quality of the leaders they need. The current leaders of SHEs have to tackle some fundamental issues about the methods used to prepare leaders if they are to recruit and prepare the high-quality leaders required. Processes also need to be put in place that will make sure that where leaders are failing, they are promptly replaced.

If the future advancement of SHEs is to be assured, then top-level leaders cannot abdicate their responsibility for growing future leaders, by delegating this task to junior decision-makers or external bodies. The content and quality of programmes for developing both current and future leaders are of such consequence that decisions about them need to be signed-off at board level.

## Leadership in SHEs

In all but the smallest of enterprises, separate sets of people will carry out two different leadership roles within self-help enterprises. First, there are the members' leaders who are chosen by the members to lead the organization on their behalf; these are the directors of the enterprise who set its overall direction. Next, the directors appoint their senior managers who run the enterprise on a day-to-day basis, such professional managers carry out a different leadership role in the enterprise. Managers may or may not be members of the SHEs they manage, depending upon the nature of the enterprise and if they qualify to become members.

The senior managers of the enterprise lead teams of other managers and staff, all tasked with achieving the enterprise's purpose. Senior managers and all other employees should be working within the framework of policies set out by the board of directors, as outlined in *Chapter 22*.

In large-scale SHEs, there will usually be other roles that are directly elected/appointed by the membership as a body, such as representatives or envoys (representatives that act as a 'go-between' grassroots member and the board). All people acting in leadership and representative roles need to work together in unity. All need to work to the same standards set for *all* leaders throughout the enterprise.

**Vision and reality**
SHEs need leaders who have a vision of what is possible, coupled with the competence to turn concepts into reality. SHEs are neither the product of any arcane theory nor a place to experiment with social engineering. Instead, leaders are needed who focus on the practical and positive impact that their enterprises have on the lives of their members.

The best leaders make use of a set of practices that have been refined over time; these practices supply a framework for running specific types of SHEs, which have been freely shared with others who wanted to develop similar enterprises. SHEs often fail their members when their leaders don't make the necessary modifications to these practices in response to the changes taking place in their markets, the economic conditions and the social environment, within which their enterprises operate.

In all kinds of organizations, the presence of dogmatic preconceptions can create blocks to securing essential change. If their leaders choose to ignore those facts that do not support their current beliefs, their failure to make crucial changes frequently results in their demise or in them turning into an enterprise that is no longer a bona-fide self-help enterprise.

## Authentic leadership

The essential task facing leaders is to help their people to see what is staring them in the face and to remind people that working together with others is often the only way that they will ever change their lives for the better.

It's imperative that members of SHEs have the capacity to identify and select leaders who are both dedicated and competent. Democratic elections need to result in the selection of authentic leaders, but this only happens where adequate communication and education is a continuing process. This requires that members and their representatives find and develop leaders who are passionate about getting a better deal, as well as running an organization that will always treat all members fairly, being both fair and honest in their dealings with all stakeholders. Also, understanding that one of their main tasks as a leader is to develop the people that they lead. Good leaders help everyone to work smarter. A set of practices, including those outlined above, will help members find the kind of leaders they need.

SHEs *don't* need people in leadership roles who try to pass themselves off as authentic leaders, but who are in truth, solely driven by self-interest. Such people are often those looking for their main chance, one that will set-them-up for life. Neither do SHEs need people who want nothing more than to make a career out of becoming an elected representative and securing a portfolio of positions that provide them with a livelihood.

Members sometimes discover that they are let-down by leaders who 'sell-out' to those that offer them personal gain and a ladderup to improve their social status. Members need to learn how to recognise this type of 'pseudo-leader'; these are the people who are only motivated by self-interest.

No matter how well-intentioned, it's never enough that leaders are drawn from those whose only qualification is that that they believe that SHEs are 'a good thing'. SHEs cannot afford to tolerate weak-willed leaders, would-be philanthropists making use of their members' money, or those that see SHEs as a mere stepping-stone to political office; or those who set out to exploit the weaknesses of their people in pursuit of their own ambitions. The challenge facing many SHEs is to find ways of attracting people who have the integrity to become authentic leaders and to supply them with the support and the kind of framework that will foster their development

## Qualifying leaders

Knowing in itself is never enough, what is needed is a deep understanding of the self-help form of enterprise if leaders are to be prepared to carry out their tasks. Leaders have to take a logical approach to their role and develop the necessary people skills All of these calls for serious investment in the personal improvement of the people needed to run SHEs, both by the individual and by their enterprises.

It may seem that too much is expected from our leaders, but it should be appreciated that if they are not skilled enough to do the job, then they will become an encumbrance. A situation that SHEs cannot afford to tolerate. Members should look carefully at the way their leaders are respected and rewarded. High-quality people should not constantly feel that they are undervalued; otherwise, they will eventually step back from important leadership roles.

### Elected and appointed leaders

In the case of elected leaders, they have to be prepared for their role by ensuring that they have the competencies needed to carry out their tasks. All elected leaders should be given a complete induction to their role, which ought to include a thorough briefing covering the board's current policy manual.

Managers from commercial businesses cannot be just 'wheeled-in' to SHEs without undergoing a comprehensive induction that provides them with the knowledge and attitudes needed to carry out a management role in this form of enterprise. Crucially, leaders ought to prove by their actions that they are committed to working to the highest standard of integrity in all their dealings.

The priority is to make sure that everyone is clear as to the strategic aims of the enterprise; see *Chapter 6*. Whenever individuals are involved in too many disparate activities, even constructive activities, they can so easily not achieve their essential quest. For when their activities do not work in concert, they do not add up to any meaningful whole. Teams without purpose inevitably drift-off into irrelevant activities or self-serving pursuits. Only when everyone in the team is clear about exactly what it is they are expected to do, can they coordinate their actions and energies and discard the distractions that divert them,

### Preparing member-leaders

In order to recruit people with the capacity to run SHEs, there needs to be a system in place that ensures that candidates for any position are not only competent but are also committed to the purpose of their enterprise. As part of the nomination and recruitment processes, candidates should sign-up to a code of practice, and confirm their credentials by demonstrating their understanding of the market in which the enterprise operates.

The idea that anybody can be picked to help run a self-help enterprise is only true in the sense that no members should be debarred from the opportunity of holding office in the enterprise. However, this must be qualified by the fact that such positions are no place for incompetent or self-serving individuals.

The rules of the enterprise and the procedures relating to the preparation and choice of those 'fit-for-office' have to be clearly defined. 'Education-to-empower' activities should be open to any member aspiring to be a representative or to hold any office. They have to be able to demonstrate their capacity to fulfil the office to which they aspire.

There needs to be a mechanism for attracting and keeping the best people, and for preparing them for office. In many cases, this will be best achieved by working with other SHEs to develop the kind of people that all their organizations are looking for. This will involve developing a cadre of people able to work in SHEs and who are familiar with the markets in which they work. The investment needed in the provision of such programmes, often requires that this task is undertaken by a federal of SHEs. SHEs only get the right leaders when they invest enough time, resources and effort, into both current and prospective leaders, which in many cases will include the appointment of mentors, However, concentrating on developing leaders is only the beginning, for it's equally important to empower members, helping them to choose their leaders wisely; see the 'people development system' and the 'succession planning system' in *Chapter 20.*

## The downside of social mobility

In the 19th. And 20th. Centuries, when SHEs were set up, most of their leaders were drawn from a class of people that had no access to higher education and were not socially mobile. As a result, there were many more people with outstanding leadership skills who were available to lead SHEs, that in today's world are creamed-off from their communities. In current times, the class structure in many countries has been replaced by a kind of 'meritocracy' (based on ability and talent), and who now have access to universities that are now open to a wider spectrum of people from all social classes.

Large businesses and other types of sizable organizations now recruit more people from diverse backgrounds, and those attending universities are supplied with an education that in most cases makes no constructive mention of SHEs. The result is that the most talented from across all social groups are herded towards those concerns that can offer higher incomes, resulting in a reduced pool of talent available to locally operating SHEs.

Communities are often stripped of their leadership talent, leaving communities bereft of leaders, which can become a major obstacle to lifting communities out of poverty in the world's poorer countries. The can cause communities to become deprived areas that are ghettos inhabited by poverty-stricken people.

There are, however, many young people today, who are bright, smart and capable individuals, who are beginning to realise that if changes are to be made for the betterment of their communities, then they will need to take on important leadership roles within them. It's essential to realise why it is that otherwise intelligent people make the choices they make in their personal and professional life, which so often leads them into meaningless lives. The alternative of working in serving their communities can offer so much more to those who have so much more ability than they often choose to utilise. People now running SHEs need to discover how they can help young people make choices that will allow them to tap into their innate potential.

### Rewarding leaders

Complete transparency is essential when it comes to all payments and any other benefits given to member-leaders. There needs to be a mechanism that supports the independent evaluation of member-directors, and if performance is inadequate, then members should be able to dispense with their services. Members have to be fair to their leaders, who will in most cases have their own livelihoods to maintain and dependants to provide for. The contribution that leaders make needs to be recognised and rewarded in a way that allows them to place their full attention on achieving the outcomes beneficial to the membership.

There has been a professionalization of democratic roles in many diverse types of organizations. In SHEs, once they get beyond a very small scale, they discover the necessity of engaging professionals. When people are appointed to run organizations as professionals, there is no need for many layers of committees. Instead, there is a need to find the shortest route to making the right decisions. Democracy within most SHEs means delegating many powers, but always keeping ultimate control in the hands of the members.

The reward system for all kinds of leaders has to be transparent and fair. It's also essential to be fair to volunteers that work in some SHEs. Such volunteers routinely feel that they are being exploited, expressly when senior managers and some member-leaders appear to be excessively rewarded. To encourage people who devote their time and energy to achieving the aims of their enterprises they do need to be rewarded, but only when they consistently contribute to achieving their enterprise's purpose.

### Finding the right managers

All but the smallest SHEs, employ full-time professionals, experts in their own fields; however, at the same time they have to be fully committed to achieving the enterprise's objectives. Mercenaries, who see their enterprise as simply their source of future wealth, have to be weeded out during the recruitment process, and by the systematic review of their performance. Senior managers should be rewarded with salaries and conditions that are competitive with those available in similar organizations; in addition, they should gain the satisfaction of working for enterprises that contribute more to their communities

Rewards and incentives need to be based on the achievement of their enterprise's goals. The comparative differentials in remuneration often need to be limited by a cap being placed on the levels of the top managers pay when compared to the average of all salaries paid to workers throughout the enterprise; always bearing in mind the perception of fairness, as perceived by workers and members.

In investor-controlled companies, failing leadership is usually replaced promptly, either when the company fails in the market or when the investors believe they are not getting an acceptable return on their investment. In profit-driven enterprises, their leaders are either self-appointed (because they are the dominant investors) or appointed by those with a controlling interest in the enterprise. Either way, investors can 'buy-in the leadership and easily remove those leaders who do not produce the results sought by their owners. This contrasts with the position in many SHEs, where top-level leaders need to be home-grown. Profit-driven enterprises generally find it easy to recruit top managers when starting-up new enterprises replacing them when this becomes necessary, which is because such enterprises are the most common form of enterprise and the education system is principally designed to serve their needs.

## Non-performing leaders

The performance of members who are directors of SHEs is crucial to the success of their enterprises. Therefore, there needs to be a regular review of the performance of all office-holding members, and for the removal of non-performing individuals. It's essential that their capacity to carry out the tasks assigned is gauged against measurable outcomes, including the viability, solvency and liquidity of the enterprise they are controlling. It's important that the outcomes required are regularly reviewed during the planning process and are expressed in measurable terms. The assistance of independent external assessors can be useful but only if people can be identified who are familiar with the self-help form of enterprise.

## A checklist for leaders

All people undertaking or aspiring to leadership roles within SHEs should be able to demonstrate that they are:

- Driven by their desire to secure significant positive changes in the lives of their members.

- Knowledgeable about how to run an organization that is fit-for-purpose as a self-help enterprise.

- Aware of the importance of having a viable market intervention strategy.

- Able to set and support standards of behaviour and performance throughout the enterprise.

- Clear as to the necessity of defined systems, based upon proven best practice, designed to sustain the enterprise.

- Committed to acquiring and updating an adequate knowledge and understanding of the markets in which the

SHE works, the self-help enterprise model, and the legal framework within which they operate.

- Focused on the future, current leaders are in effect trustees acting on behalf of future generations of members.

- Ready to lead by personal example, above all in respect to their integrity.

- Devoted to ensuring that those running the enterprise are always working in the best interest of all members.

## Leadership development

The leadership development system within SHEs needs to cater to member-leaders and manager-leaders. Although there are bound to be differences in some of the technical aspects of each role, and in some cases the depth of knowledge and the level of skills needed by each group of leaders, both groups ought to follow the same core syllabus. This is indispensable if the enterprise is to achieve the unity of purpose that is key to the proper working of self-help enterprises.

A system is required to ensure that the enterprise will have the high-quality leaders needed will include:

- **Job descriptions** have to be prepared for all roles and subject to regular review, with reports on performance for all roles being at least annually.

- **Qualifications** for all roles need to be defined and systematically reviewed.

- **Equivalence and diversity** for all roles, including gender, ethnicity, and disability, which is essential if the enterprise is to be both relevant and creative.

- **Induction programmes** arranged for all roles at all levels, which are not optional.

- **Empowerment programmes** provided to all those that need to develop confidence and the life skills needed to carry out each role.

- **Market dynamics programmes** offered to suit all levels so that all can grasp the essentials of the market in which the enterprise is involved.

- **Building a well-informed electorate** by offering member development programmes that explore the requirements for effective leaders throughout the enterprise. *Learning together,* involving both member and management leaders in programmes of self-development at all levels.

# 14. MYTHS AND MINDTRAPS

### Straight thinking

Few tasks are more crucial to the future development of SHEs than identifying and challenging the many popular fictions that are holding them back.

Myths are narratives that play a fundamental role in society, which are unthinkingly accepted as being true despite the lack of any credible evidence to support them. Throughout history, myths have been used by those in power as a means of maintaining control over the populace. In our time, the false impression about SHEs are mainly perpetuated by those with self-interests to protect, and those who control the popular press, and other media, because SHEs don't fit with their narrow view of the world.

Mindtraps are common errors often made when people don't think through the available evidence before forming a point of view about critical issues. It's too easy to jump to erroneous conclusions or to assume that something is correct simply because it has been accepted as the received wisdom. These mistaken beliefs result in inertia because such ideas are convenient, simplistically appealing, and broadly held by the public - who frequently seem to cling to them even when they are plainly shown to be wrong. This kind of flawed thinking process is equivalent to accepting that 2+2 = 5, having reached a conclusion without reviewing the evidence presented in the calculation, inevitably leading to a wrong assumption. Such careless thinking frequently results in the acceptance of falsehoods as truth. Such false assumptions have to be replaced with evidence-based conclusions, arrived at by clear and logical thought processes. The following are some widespread fictions that need to be challenged.

## OWNERSHIP CHANGES EVERYTHING?

Some believe that self-help enterprises can provide the means of fulfilling their ambition for the public to own and control the means of production, distribution, and exchange. Although community ownership may be one consequence of the intervention of a self-help enterprise within a market, ownership is not an end in itself. It's wrong to believe that running an enterprise simply for the sake of extending collective ownership, is in anyway worthwhile, at least not for its members.

Changing the basis of ownership does not on its own change anything. The disappointing performance of many State-owned undertakings, whether this was achieved by means of nationalisation or communism, all provide ample evidence that merely changing ownership rarely brings the benefits hoped for. Similarly, SHEs nominally-owned by members, but that is in practice run by self-serving cliques, seldom deliver any significant benefits to their grassroots members.

People often expect much from a change of ownership but are more often than not let down by the new people running them. People are routinely disappointed by changes in ownership. For example, when former colonial subjects expected radical change when many organizations became locally-owned, but too often the new owners behaved no better (and sometimes more corrupt) then at a time when expatriates controlled them. Likewise, the mass of people often become disillusioned when governments appoint bureaucrats, politicians, trade union leaders or their nominees to run industries or services on their behalf. The fact is that changing ownership without fundamentally changing the nature of the organization and its most important systems, is unlikely to bring much by way of benefits to the people who are nominally their new owners.

## MUTUAL OWNERSHIP EQUATES TO COLLECTIVISM?

Collectivism should not be confused with self-help and mutual action. Some of the earliest initiatives labelled by some historians as 'cooperatives', such as those pioneered by Robert Owen, a benevolent factory-owner, in the UK and North America, were based on the idea of collectivism. These communities were intended to be self-sufficient and were run using collectively-owned land and other resources. In the main, seeking to place their collective venture outside the influence of the market. Although these were bold experiments in their time, they had little in common with the self-help enterprises that followed later.

Many countries under communist rule, collectivised their agriculture, these collectives usually resulted in extremely negative levels of productivity and in the extreme created food shortages, even famine. Only where there was an external threat and/or a strong religious commitment, were such communities sustainable; for example, following world-war II, the Israeli kibbutz. Over the years, other religious communities, often fleeing persecution used collective communities to survive. Collectivism has not proved to be durable in the long-term; however, as a lifestyle choice, it may well satisfy the inner-needs of some groups. On the other hand, beneficial and mutual ownership, the system of ownership used in SHEs, works well provided that members understand the basis of their ownership; see *Annex II* for definitions, which further explain the differences between these two forms of ownership.

171

## SHEs PROVIDE A PATHWAY TO UTOPIA?

There are those who believe that SHEs can offer an all-encompassing solution to the world's problems. SHEs can, and do, help people to change their lives positively, and participation in SHEs can help individuals to develop cooperative patterns of behaviour. Their experiences can encourage people to take greater control over their lives, even so, it seems unrealistic to assert that such enterprises offer a panacea for all our economic and social ills. Paradoxically, when ideologues claim that SHEs will bring about the realisation of their utopian dreams, their unrealistic expectations have probably done more to inhibit the advancement of SHEs than all of those that have intentionally sought to denigrate them.

Fortunately, new generations, having much greater access to information and knowledge, are much less inclined to accept old-style ideologies. Instead, they are learning to critically evaluate the kind of sweeping promises linked to such beliefs. Healthy scepticism can lead people to choose to make use of forms of enterprise that better reflect their personal agenda in life.

### SHEs ARE 'SOCIAL ENTERPRISES'?

SHEs may be correctly described as 'not-for-profit' enterprises, but this often leads some to fall into the trap of thinking that SHEs are charities. In a similar way, by referring to SHEs as 'social enterprises' (more recently re-branded as the 'social solidarity economy'), can only further compound public misconceptions about them. Concepts, such as 'Social enterprise', are wide-ranging and may be useful to academics, but are not helpful when used to describe any kind of self-help enterprise.

It's essential to realise that many of the enterprises grouped together and labelled as 'social enterprises', are not democratically controlled, with many being run by self-appointed trustees or patrons. Many are enterprises that promote dependency, dispensing benefits to others or promoting specific social or environmental aims. They are often rooted in concepts that directly contradict the self-help mindset. Many of these enterprises are in fact profit-generating enterprises, where some or all their profits are used to support their cause.

This is not to say that such enterprises don't have a role to play in the wider economy or to deny that there some things that SHEs can usefully do together with them. Even so, mixing together enterprises that so often create dependency with genuine self-help enterprises does nothing to build a consensus about the importance of the self-help mindset. It's even more confusing when SHEs are concurrently described as both social enterprises and businesses.

Creating a homogenous market by grouping all outcomes-driven enterprises together may be helpful to those institutions and consultants selling courses and other services, but this is not in the best interests of SHEs. Self-help enterprises exist to serve their members; this means delivering the outcomes that their members want, which is fundamentally different from being a cause-driven enterprise. See *Figure A-1. Forms of enterprise.*

### SHEs MAKE A PROFIT?

Even though SHEs can help increase the profitability of their members', where these are entrepreneurs or businesses. It's not the job of SHEs to generate profits for themselves as corporate entities. SHEs are not designed to be profit-centres in themselves, the benefits that SHEs generate for their members belong to members; and, any surplus created in the process also belongs to the members. It's the members who must decide how any surplus is to be used or distributed. Again, it's worth remembering that the benefits generated by SHEs, are not by any means limited to those that are measured in financial terms. Again, it's useful to be reminded that often when people talk about 'profit' what they really mean is 'margin', which is the difference between all costs and the price realised for any product or service.

Governments prefer to perpetuate the myth that SHEs make profits because they can tax profits. In many countries, the surplus arising from genuine 'mutual trading 'isn't taxed, but any sums distributed may be taxed as income in the hands of the member. Of course, if SHEs are supplying non-members they will be making a profit from them (in the case of a consumer-owned enterprise), or if they are buying from non-members (in the case of a producer-owned enterprise), or if the hire non-members (in the case of a worker-owned enterprise).

Apart from the taxation issue, the fundamental reason why SHEs don't make profits is that they have objectives that are designed to improve the lives of their members. Members use mutually-owned assets to achieve their objectives, and at the end of any accounting period, if they have any surplus, this belongs to their members.

### *A legal opinion about profit*

Lord Wilberforce (a British Lord of Appeal in Ordinary in the House of Lords from 1964 to 1982) said: 'A person cannot make a profit out of themselves'. A solicitor who draws up his own will cannot invoice himself and make a profit for himself from the transaction. Likewise, a group of persons, in this example farmers: who agree to market their produce through a joint effort can propose that they are not 'at arms-length' from their own group. For example, the farmers set the fees and can adjust them up or down at will to produce any result they wish so long as it covers the costs of running the enterprise.

### SHEs CAN BE RUN BY REPRESENTATIVES OF STAKEHOLDERS?

Some SHEs are often described as being 'multi-stakeholder' enterprises, of course, whether this is.an apt description depends on what is meant by this term because it can mean different things to different people. The term is often taken to mean that different stakeholder groups are represented on the board of the enterprise. However, if board members believe that it's their role is to support the interests of a specific stakeholder group, then this conflicts with the important precept that the board has a *collective responsibility* to pursue the purpose of the enterprise and to run the enterprise in the best interest of *all* members.

Most of the examples held up as being successful multi-stakeholder enterprises are in truth no longer bona-fide SHEs. Many of them were either worker co-ops that now accept customers as members or consumer co-ops that grant separate representation to workers in the enterprise. The claims of such enterprises sometimes mislead observers of these enterprises. Closer examination of the operation s of these enterprises often reveals that many are not in reality member-controlled, often ultimate control is being exercised by an external financing body or a board of trustees.

At the same time, community services co-ops, that, for example, run village shops, pubs, transport, and other services, are sometimes referred to as being "multi-stakeholder enterprises". This because some of the people that supply goods and services to the enterprise or are employed by the enterprise are also members. In practice, the most valid basis for membership is a person's commitment to the purpose of the enterprise

Commercial businesses and SHEs alike, claiming that it's their mission to equally satisfy all their stakeholders, (including customers, members/owners, employees and investors) is tantamount to saying that they value everyone that the enterprise interacts with as though they were the same. Such claims leave the management of the enterprise with no clear guidance on what to do when faced with the 'trade-offs' that they need to make between the conflicting claims of the people that make up the different stakeholder groups. For example, in a consumer coop, does preserving the jobs of workers take precedence over getting a fair deal for members? Even more problematic, is the situation where investors are separately represented on the board. Over several centuries, groups have experimented with enterprises that had investors represented on the governing body, only to discover that invariably, sooner or later, the investors take control.

It's also imperative to grasp that because SHEs are mutually-owned, current members, principally the board members, also need to represent an important stakeholder group that cannot represent themselves, these are future generations. Directors have to understand that as well as being charged with the duty of running their enterprise today; they are also trustees acting on behalf of future generations of members.

The idea of the board is made up of representatives from different stakeholder groups is one that can have a most negative impact on the governance of any form of enterprise, including SHEs; see *Chapter 22*.

**OVERSIGHT UNDERMINES THE SUPREMACY OF THE BOARD?**
It's sometimes argued that the activities of an oversight body somehow threaten the supremacy of the board. Such ideas can be a diversion if the board fears that their current powers would be

changed. The board's current freedom to direct the affairs of the enterprise is set within limits established by the rules and any relevant legislation. In practice, the powers of an oversight body are little different from those of the financial auditor, who checks to find how far the financial statements, as well as non-financial disclosures, present a true and fair view of the affairs of the enterprise.

The oversight body has the task of finding out how far the purpose and function of the organization are being pursued and specific objectives are being achieved. Just like the financial auditor, the oversight body should have both the full powers and resources to carry out their tasks and reports directly to the membership. The membership directly elects or otherwise appoint the members of the oversight body. The oversight board members need to have the necessary skills to undertake their tasks; and just as with financial auditors, (especially in large-scale enterprises) they may be professionals, or most likely a combination of member-representatives and professionals.

The issue of trust is often cited in the arguments used by those not in favour of having an independent oversight body. Again, there is no real difference between checking accounting records and checking that an enterprise is carrying out its purpose. In both cases, it's only prudent for the owners of the enterprise to arrange to undertake confirmation. Blind trust is always dangerous, but trust backed up by verification ensures that people are worthy of the trust that they ought to enjoy.

### IS BIGGER BETTER?

When people see the economic power that mega-companies international wield, they often jump to the conclusion that the only way to secure change within a market is to have similar mega-scale enterprises, but this is not always the case. In each specific market, there will be a scale of operation below which it will be difficult to make an impact within that market, even so, SHEs can often organize their members in creative ways to make an impact in a market. Often, SHEs can develop market intervention strategies that cannot easily be copied by commercial businesses, especially if their members exercise solidarity in the face of exploitation by those dominating a market. When SHEs do become large-scale organizations if in the process they lose the commitment of their members, this will considerably weaken their effectiveness within the market.

An obsession with scale by leaders of SHEs has often led to financial overreach, and to an increase in the cost of finance that inevitably affects their capacity to offer a better deal to members. If SHEs accept finance from other than benign sources when they are chasing growth for its own sake, this almost inevitably ends in the members losing control of their enterprise. The correct response of member-directors to expansion proposals, including merger proposals, should always be to establish what is best of the grassroots membership. When SHEs grow too quickly, they usually face multiple problems, including losing sight of their true purpose. The best approach for many SHEs is to aim to have a cellular structure, where independent SHEs own and operate a federal enterprise, this is likely to achieve more than a monolithic type of organization; see *Chapter 12*.

The right scale of operations for SHEs is one that is most effective in terms of achieving the enterprise's goals, and the scale needed to exercise sufficient power in the relevant market.

## CO-PRODUCTION IS A FORM OF ORGANIZATION?

The term 'co-production' refers to a 'management system' where there is a systematic contribution from service users into the provision of services. It's argued that this concept is critical to the effective delivery of knowledge-intensive services. A similar co-productive approach to the generation of knowledge has been applied in the field of biotechnologies. From the various examples of the application of co-production, it can be seen that in knowledge-based industries, this system facilitates the individualisation of service delivery. Service delivery is based upon effective information exchange and shared decision-making, that responds to complex and unique service users' needs. Co-production challenges the idea of a 'passive customer' by creating expectations of both the service provider and the customer having equivalent active roles in the delivery of the service.

Co-production has also been applied to the provision of public services and is sometimes used to describe the relationship between government, private, voluntary and non-profit organizations in the delivery of public services. Co-production is said to have three different elements: co-governance, co-management, and co-production. Co-governance refers to organizations that help in the planning and design of public services, while co-management refers to the production of the service by not-for-profit enterprises in conjunction with the State. Co-production, however, is restricted to user involvement in the production of public services directly, with or without State intervention.

In the UK, there is growing interest in applying co-production to public services, such as social care and health, where the emphasis is primarily concerned with service to an individual rather than with an organizational concept, which is critical in knowledge-intensive services. Engagement and participation are clearly required in the co-productive relationship, which works within a long-term perspective and assumes that both citizens and government have a contribution to make to the provision of the service.

There is often confusion about the term 'co-production' and its application within SHEs, with some believing that it's a type of organization (such as a cooperative or a credit union). Genuine SHEs ought to embody the concepts involved in the co-production approach, whereas, in mutant enterprises, such ideas have often been discarded. In worker and producer co-ops, the ideas behind co-production often form an important part of their market intervention strategy. Good examples are to be found in many horticultural cooperatives where the producers and retailers routinely apply such methods. All types of consumer and community SHEs, if operating the self-help enterprise model, invariably incorporate co-production, co-governance, and co-management systems being integral to the systems forming the self-help model of enterprise.

## SHEs NEED CHARISMATIC LEADERS?

People are frequently taken in by leaders who seem to fit the popular profile assumed to personify a 'real' leader. This usually includes a set the characteristics that such leaders are supposedly expected to possess. The traits required to fit this ill-conceived profile usually include brashness, an overpowering personality, and something vaguely referred to as 'charisma'. On the contrary, history tells us that our greatest leaders have often been unassuming, thoughtful, and placing the needs of the people that they lead above their personal aggrandisement. Examples that exemplify these traits include South Africa's Nelson Mandela, India's Mahatma Gandhi, UK's Clem Attlee Botswana's Seretse Khama, and the UN/Ghana's Kofi Annan.

All too often, people seem to choose leaders who promise much, but then go on to use an organization to amass power and resources for themselves. Evidenced by examples throughout history, including the rise and fall of many royal families throughout Europe, the great dynasties of China, many religious hierarchies, and in those States where communism has since collapsed. Even worse, are those States, still claiming to be communist, that have become personal or party dictatorships. Similarly, in many public companies where they are dominated by their top-level managers and they are primarily being run for their personal benefit. SHEs have not been immune from this kind of takeover.

The ability to exercise leadership is based on the power and influence that the leader can exert over others within the organization. The kind of leader who depends on their power to reward, coerce and make use of their status to keep a hold on power will inevitably damage their organizations and disappoint those they claim to lead. Appointed managers rely on the power that they are given (or is linked to their position). On the other hand, democratically-elected leaders depend much more upon their personal power, derived from their individual traits, and the special knowledge and skills that they bring to their organization. Both appointed and elected leaders, ought to realize that their ability to lead will be severely curtailed if they are unable to personify the kind of behaviour that engenders commitment from those they seek to lead. Leaders perceived as self-serving can still command support because they exercise a high degree of patronage, these 'transactional leaders' rely upon their capacity to give benefits to those who appoint or pick them in return for their support.

SHEs need a different kind of leader, people who are 'authentic' leaders (as described in Chapter 13). Leaders who can recognise

181

what their people need, and who seek to help them first to articulate and then achieve what they desire. These leaders treat people as individuals and provide them with intellectual stimulation by creating the conditions that support creativity. Such leaders inspire people by offering a challenging view of the future and act as role models by living out the qualities and standards they advocate. They are generally more approachable than transactional leaders, involve a wider range of people in decision-making processes, and actively work towards empowering those they lead. Leaders need to be good communicators, know how to listen, and more than anything else - truly *respect* the people they lead.

# 15. AN ALTERNATIVE FUTURE

## The next industrial revolution

Many forward-thinkers are telling us that the world is on the brink of what has been called the 'fourth industrial revolution'. The first industrial revolution, starting in the latter part of the 18th Century, was triggered by the invention of machines powered by water and steam. Since then there have been a series of further revolutions, which have radically changed the lives of people throughout the world. The second revolution started about a century later with the rapid expansion of mass production, the division of labour, machines powered by electricity and machines that made other machines. Then in the late 1960s, electronics, IT, and automated production were the drivers behind the third revolution.

When people talk about a fourth revolution, they are alluding to the anticipated growth of low-carbon technologies, and what has been described as 'the internet of things', or cyber-physical systems. This is the fusion of several technologies and their interaction across the physical, digital and biological domains. Simultaneously, there are further breakthroughs in areas including gene sequencing, nanotechnology, more sources of renewable energy and quantum computing. Together, this group of fast developing technologies should herald a new era filled with opportunities but alongside this are many social risks.

Previous revolutions generated economic growth and jobs, contributing broadly to world development. However, it's unwise to assume that every time there is an industrial revolution it will do the same thing. The next one could be very different because it will automate a far greater number of work tasks and promises to involve the widespread use of artificial intelligence systems and self-driving vehicles. All this will likely result in large numbers of jobs being eliminated or being readily replaced by full automation. Such a merger of people and technology could drive an unprecedented economic cycle full of opportunities, but who will benefit from such a revolution? Such changes appear to be inevitable, but the main question arising is: 'will such a revolution drive the global economy, or simply eliminate millions of jobs creating an expanding underclass of unemployed and the under-employed?' It could turn out to be a revolution that brings extreme hardship for those left without livelihoods, which in turn could lead to significant social unrest.

As with every major shift in economic and social conditions, its consequences will depend upon how people respond to the challenges they face. Perhaps the main difference between the impending changes and earlier revolutions is that the nature of the technological changes forecast may well provide the opportunities for greater devolution of work, the localisation of energy production and other key services; alongside, providing opportunities for more creative and skilled workers. There could also be a need for the more shared use of resources and increased connectivity within communities, which provide many opportunities for SHEs to play a more significant role than was ever possible in earlier industrial revolutions.

## Sovereignty, integrity and realism

In most countries, there are lots of markets crying-out for interventions to be made by SHEs, and in many cases, the kind of interventions required are already taking place somewhere in the world. National leaders need to realise that if their countries are to keep their sovereignty and integrity, then they need to act to stem the unchecked growth of corporatocracy. Recognising the importance of improving their nation's competitiveness in the global marketplace, means realising that where strong and effective self-help enterprises operate, their interventions within the market offer the best way of developing the capacity and resilience of their workforce and facilitating the collaboration of smaller-scale producers and firms, thus permitting them to better compete in global markets.

SHEs ought also to provide the most effective way for people to self-supply many of the most vital services they need. Service providers operated for the mutual benefit of the people that need to use them should be much more likely to be delivered effectively and efficiently than the alternatives of reliance upon commercial businesses or the State.

The scale of opportunities for SHEs is immense but remain out of reach until ordinary people are instilled with the belief that such ventures are both feasible and dependable. Unfortunately, reality cannot be ignored, and the fact is that all these positive outcomes are nothing more than a fanciful hope, unless and until far more effective ways of running SHEs are widely adopted.

People need to be provided with a vision of what is possible, but they also need to be convinced that the enterprises that they are asked to put their faith in, will be truly run for the benefit of all members and be enterprises where fairness, honesty and equivalence are all standard practice.

### Preparing for turbulent times

During periods of economic downturn, recession or depression, there are no fewer resources in the world, nor is there any less underlying desire for goods or services than in times of boom and economic expansion. What does change is the level of confidence of investors have in the economy when it comes to making investment decisions. Any economy that depends solely upon the level of investor confidence to drive it will inevitably suffer from periods of boom and bust so that the presence of a substantial self-help enterprise sector can provide a buffer in times of low confidence.

More people are beginning to see that they have got to demand higher standards of integrity from the organizations with which they choose to become involved. Enterprises driven by need, and by more ethical motives, can replace a dependency upon investors looking only for gains in the market for finance, profit maximization and monies obtained from speculation.

## Shaping new attitudes

Too often, people are ready to listen to those eternal pessimists that would have us believe that it's beyond the wit of humankind to design and run enterprises that serve their members and their communities.

Today, many people feel hopeless because they feel helpless, so they become angry, often being angry with the wrong people. It's vital that people take more control over their lives if they are ever going to feel that they can improve the quality of their lives. Getting people involved with self-help enterprises that can help them to improve their lives has to be a priority. What would it take to get SHEs to fulfil their promise to bring about positive change to the lives of people who are seeking a better life for themselves, their families and their communities? As most people who have sound experience of working in and with SHEs will realise, the answer lies in making SHEs much more effective in delivering what their members want. Yet something else needs to happen if enterprises are to change peoples' lives for the better routinely, this is that those people have got to relearn how to make self-help and mutual action work for them.

**Unlearning the habits and myths that imprison the imagination**
Sometimes, instead of embracing the changes that inevitably have to be made, there is a tendency to continue doing something simply because they have always done it. If they are ready to face up to the fact that they need to learn how the actual market works, and how to make their enterprises operate as genuine SHEs, then they could help to make the market work to the benefit of the mass of people. The privileged few cannot be allowed to manipulate markets, extracting wealth from those most disadvantaged in the market.

Communities can handle the pressures arising from increasing demands for scarce resources, but this will mean creating organizations that are committed to resource optimisation. As a counter-balance to those driven by the concept of 'growth at any cost'. SHEs can help to persuade people to consume less and help them to live better and more fulfilling lives. A good example is those industries supplying water, energy and any non-renewable resource. In these industries, people need to be rewarded for achieving more while consuming less. There needs to a lower level of tolerance of the 'ultra-selfish', who excessively consume and waste scarce resources.

**Public perceptions**
In many cases, the main barriers to the advancement of SHEs have been created by those who have allowed their enterprises to be no longer true to their founding practices. This has resulted in a widely held perception that SHEs are no different from commercial business; arriving at this position from one that in the 20th century was profoundly positive. Although, often hated by those who

controlled businesses that were no longer able to exploit their customers or their workforce.

In countries where the State appropriated SHEs, either directly or by claiming that they were part of a State-backed ideology, the legacy has been to devalue SHEs in the minds of the public. Whatever the reason for the negative public perception of SHEs, this can only be reversed when all SHEs are authentic; this means SHEs need either be rehabilitated or prohibited from claiming to be SHEs when they no longer authentic.

**Removing the barriers to self-help and mutual action**

The overall growth of SHEs is held back by the absence of self-help and mutual action from the curriculum in schools and universities and by governments not providing a positive public policy framework. A 'policy framework' means the system of courses of action, regulatory measures, laws and funding priorities, that serve to support their development and sustainability. The necessary policy framework needs to be positive towards SHEs but at the same time must prohibit government involvement in their direction and the day-to-day running of SHEs. The State needs to supply an environment in which genuine SHEs can be formed, developed, and encouraged to prosper.

In many countries, their public policy framework is a long way from offering the kind of environment needed. Often, the reason why the necessary positive policy framework is not in place is that the public policy agenda is being set by large mutated enterprises, where their representatives, claiming to speak for all SHEs, are lobbying for policies that promote and protect the interests of elites. Many are managers who are primarily interested in creating big neo-commercial businesses that can disburse the super-sized salaries and benefits they aspire to receive.

Political leaders need to be persuaded to support legislation that will cause 'phoney' SHEs not only to return to being democratically controlled by their members but, at the same time, put in place the essential systems of governance and oversight required to ensure that they remain authentic; for a more detailed public policy agenda for change see *Chapter 25*.

### *Self-help enterprises – creating a groundswell*

Every new generation faces new challenges. Some of today's challenges are similar to those faced by previous generations while others are new problems of our time, but many may be met using self-help solutions. In the poorer countries of the world, the most basic needs of the people should be met first, and here SHEs will doubtless focus on what their members need most. Many of the new problems facing people today arise due to advances in science and technology along with significant social changes that many have yet to assimilate.

Everybody involved with SHEs needs to learn to question themselves and to test their beliefs against knowledge gained from their experiences of life and the evidence obtained in the real world, acknowledging that it is always possible to find better ways of running SHEs.

**Many opportunities**

There are many opportunities to start up or join in with an established self-help enterprise. Below are some of the possibilities to consider for those not yet already involved with SHEs. Many of the examples mentioned in the following list are already well established in various countries of the world but if things aren't happening where you then try to make them happen:

- Building homes designed to meet the 'real' needs of people, homes that are more affordable than those offered by the big companies that often dominate the housing market.

- Exercising power over multinational food companies to ensure that people can buy healthy, locally produced food that has been minimally processed. Food that is priced fairly, which means at a price that is both fair to primary producers and fair to the consumer; in some countries, a new generation of 'food co-ops' are operating. The main motivation for the setting up of the earliest consumer co-ops was the desire of people to secure access to unadulterated food. In the 21st century, the science is telling us that the threats to our health, in terms of obesity and the risk of cancer, arising from mass-produced convenience foods are probably at least as high as those prevailing in previous centuries.

- Offering an alternative to the monopolistic drug companies that often focus only on those drugs that can generate the largest profit. Instead, the world needs enterprises that focus on meeting patients' needs, and the most pressing clinical needs of people.

- Operating financial services that work for the benefit of the people that need these services without exploiting them. Instead of these institutions being run only for the benefit of large-scale investors, and the top executives running the finance industry. People need fair rates as savers and fair and responsible lending to those that need credit. Similarly, 'fair' products are needed in respect of - pension provision, insurance, and other important financial services.

- Managing social spaces run primarily for the benefit of the users of such spaces, including - sporting and leisure facilities, natural resources spaces, such as forests, lakes, etc., and community spaces of all kinds.

- Supplying energy, water, and communications services that place the needs of member-consumers at the centre of the enterprise; services that would otherwise be in the hands of monopolies or near-monopolies.

- Jointly managing our waste so that this is recycled into energy and other products of value to our communities.

- Providing transport services - including road, rail, and air transport, wherever the market cannot or will not meet the real needs of passengers/users; particularly in rural areas or where monopoly, or near monopoly, is the alternative. Perhaps it can be imagined that joint action could solve the parking problems in cities where the streets are littered with cars that are slowly killing us with their emissions. Surely, it's possible to organize a method of transport to get around quickly, safely, and without threatening the lives of our children and other vulnerable people.

- Ending the domination of communications networks, TV channels, newspapers, and computer networks, by global companies; where self- help enterprises could supply some solutions to this problem for all democracies.

- Delivering affordable childcare*, eldercare, and other care needs when to rely upon the commercial market results in inferior quality care, not truly based upon the primacy of the requirements of those in need of care. * Self-help enterprises that offer the kind of support that parents need rather than children brought-up relying on ad hoc arrangements (to ensure that they are in a caring, play/learning, environment) when their parents are earning a living.

- Running a workplace that is more attuned to the lifestyle needs of the workforce and the real needs of their customers.

- Delivering health-related services as the alternative to the commercialisation of health services, or supplementing State provision. A good example could be running 'wellbeing societies' that keep people healthy instead of waiting until people get sick and when they need costly forms of treatment.

- Co-ordinating the activities of various types of SHEs so as to implement locally planned projects for urban renewal and for the revival of rural economies.

- Providing legal services in the best interest of the users of these services.

- Running community-led city farms, local food initiatives, and new forms of urban horticulture.

-  Helping students to meet temporary housing needs, also, helping them find employment, including out of term-time jobs, and learning opportunities, including work experience placements.

- Leading change in the higher education system, by providing universities that are dedicated to meeting the long-term needs of the students; including their need for continuing 'life-long learning' to support them in their workplaces. In addition, supporting members to secure their livelihoods and lead lives as empowered citizens. Also, helping people to develop an understanding of the self-help enterprise model, and empowering themselves to develop a 'self-help mindset'.

**Remember:** these are only examples; self-help enterprises can do just about anything – it's up to the individuals who are the members or prospective members of SHEs.

**PART TWO:**

**SYSTEMS FOR
SELF-HELP ENTERPRISES**

# 16. THE POWER OF SYSTEMS

## The role of systems

Human systems act in a comparable way to the kerb-stones, road signs and traffic lights, which are necessary for us to use our roads effectively and safely. Keeping our vehicles on the right road and on the correct side of the road is most important, the alternative is to have vehicles careering about aimlessly. Likewise, our organizations need to keep within the boundaries and parameters agreed and set in advance. The alternative to using appropriate and rational systems is to allow them to operate without clear direction or boundaries, with those running them making-up how they run them as they go along.

As the world changes, many organizations including SHEs, are becoming more complex. In many cases, they are using systems that don't take account of the changes taking place around them. Frequently, there is a mismatch between the practices used in the enterprise and those essential to achieving its purpose. SHEs often adopt practices simply because these are the norm in commercial businesses, disregarding the fact that many such practices are clearly not appropriate for use in SHEs.

### *A reminder - What is a system?*

A human system means a set of interacting and interdependent practices, procedures and habits that work together with the aim of achieving specified outcomes. A complete system is a system that includes all the practices necessary to achieve the overall objective of the system.

**Practices, policies, procedures and processes**

It's essential to precisely know what actions and what behaviour is needed from people, and to communicate this to them. Practices need to be expressed in formal policies that support their implementation. Policies need to be supported by procedures and processes, which in today's world frequently means using computerised methods and portable personal communication devices.

**Complete systems**

Systems have to be complete if they are to be effective. Partially implementing a system usually results in the system failing to achieve its objectives; systems have to be implemented in their entirety.

SHEs will not succeed if they omit vital practices from critical systems. In many SHEs, their leaders often fail to invest adequately in developing their people. Sometimes, there is a vacuum where essential practices have been dropped from a system, with the result that some of the vital foundations of SHEs have been eroded or are no longer present. A stark example of this kind of failure is where the practice of 'only using finance from benign sources' has been disregarded, and instead, finance has been obtained using international capital markets, with ruinous consequences.

Systems are also incomplete when key practices are not translated into clear-cut policies or are not supported by relevant procedures and processes. Where the necessary new habits required to support policy are not formed and embedded, then any new system is patently incomplete. For example, without there being a process for purging redundant practices, there is a danger that these outdated practices can live-on unless and until they are flushed-out.

## Dynamic systems

A dynamic system is one that is characterised by constant change, activity, or progress. SHEs that are wedded to static systems are heading for failure. The capacity to change needs to be built into all systems. When systems are designed, any aspect of the system that is likely to be a barrier to future change needs to be removed before it becomes tomorrow's problem. Typical obstacles to change in SHEs include:

- Perpetuating unsuitable governance. systems
- Failing to provide an adequate system of oversight.
- Using a planning system that isn't directed towards meeting the future needs of members.
- Failing to undertake a systematic review of the market intervention strategy.
- When protecting specific jobs is given a higher priority than achieving the enterprise's purpose.

## Practices

Practices are those actions regularly needed to carry out or perform a specific activity, method or custom, to achieve specific outcomes. Practices are actions as opposed to theories. In SHEs, 'foundation practices' are those practices essential to ensuring that the enterprise is and remains an authentic self-help enterprise. This requires the foundation practices become embedded into the day-to-day operation of the enterprise. Leaders of SHEs have developed sets of practices, and refined them over time, and have designed them so that they sustain their enterprises over the long-term. Usually, leaders of SHEs share such practices freely with others who want to develop and progress similar enterprises. Disappointingly, it's not unusual for leaders of SHEs to insist upon talking about 'principles and values', which often turn out to be nothing more than meaningless platitudes. When instead, what is needed is to follow those proven practices essential to the operation of bona-fide SHEs.

SHEs should not be used as a vehicle for the implementation of any kind of social engineering. Instead, they need to concentrate on the practical impact that they have on the lives of their members. The reality in many SHEs is that a lot of their current practices are there to protect the interests of incumbent senior managers and a clique of self-serving elected-leaders. Such practices need to be rooted out and be replaced by those essential to the success of bona-fide SHEs.

## Developing best practice

Best practice develops out of the practical experience of people dealing with real problems in the real world. Over many years, people in SHEs have shared their experiences both nationally and internationally. Unfortunately, such exchanges of practical experiences do not occur when people are constrained by a dogma, which often sets irrelevant boundaries and stifles creativity. The exchange of information about best practice in SHEs is often hampered when those involved in the process have a personal stake in restricting the exchange of ideas and experience because they seek to create rights to intellectual property, which predictably occur when external consultants or academics control the process.

Some SHEs, (for example, many cooperatives) have adopted a set of practices, commonly referred to as 'principles', which include only *some* of the practices required to sustain an effective self-help enterprise. Such statements of principles do not normally cover *all* the essential practices needed in a self-help enterprise and are therefore incomplete. Typically, such statements are recited but not backed-up by the systems critical to ensuring that these practices are habitually followed.

Advances in technology often supply innovative ways of doing things when old practices need to be updated, for example in the fields of communications, engaging members, accounting systems, and performance management. The reasons for following specific practices need to be understood so that when change is needed the reasons behind the current practices and systems can guide the development of new best practice.

It should be noted that some practices have more than one objective, which can mean that the same practice has a place within several different systems running within SHEs. For example, the practice of providing induction training for members and employees is an essential practice forming a part of many different systems; as is the practice of always fairly treating all members as being equal, is a practice that is essential within all the main systems deployed by SHEs.

**Policies**

Policies supply the boundaries that keep us on the pathway to achieving our purpose. Policies are declarations that give clear guidance as to the actions needed to implement the agreed practices and the standards of behaviour expected from all the people within the enterprise. The membership may directly formulate policies, usually incorporated within the rules, or be agreed by a board of directors (the board) on behalf of the members. Policies may also be expressed in codes of practice. Policies are directions, which only achieve their goals if implemented throughout the organization, and are accompanied by clear, well understood, sanctions applied against those that do not achieve the agreed standards. In all cases, such practices and their associated policies need regular review to ensure that they are adequate under current conditions. Policies should also be in place to ensure the right culture prevails in all parts of the organization. The culture in SHEs should be regarded as an integral part of all systems and not as a separate activity.

## Foundation policies for SHEs

The foundation practices, as set out in *Chapter 9*, need to be consistently applied throughout the enterprise, and be supported by foundation policies. These policies, in turn, need to be supported by proper procedures, standards, habits, and the management system.

'Operational policies' are policies that guide people in the day-to-day transactions of the enterprise. Foundation policies are those policies needed to implement the vital foundations of the enterprise model. Such policies should give overarching guidance to all policy-makers at all levels. These are best set out in concise statements defining the policy and the consequences of non-compliance. SHEs should formulate their own policies, in consultation with their membership, to meet their specific needs. Outside help may be useful when drafting policies but all policies need to be owned by the people that are to make use of them and expressed in terms that are readily understood by them.

## Developing systems

To develop sound systems calls for the application of our energies to design and set systems that are both straightforward and practical. Routine is one of the most powerful tools for removing obstacles to progress, without routine the pull of various distractions can prevent us from achieving our objectives. Critically, the specific aims that each system is intended to achieve need to be completely clear.

At the same time, the practices that make up the system all contribute towards achieving the outcomes needed. Including, for example, the importance of ensuring that the remuneration and reward system recognises people when they achieve the outcomes agreed, and at the same time dispenses penalties for those who do not follow essential practices, policies, and procedures. The practices employed throughout an organization may be a part of more than one system because all the main systems overlap and are interdependent. For example, the practice of mutual and beneficial ownership is part of both the system of organization and the economic system.

Each main system and subsystem need to have a clear set of objectives that drive its design. The precise practices needed to achieve these objectives, along with the processes, routines, and procedures, needed to support them, all need to be identified and then put in to practice. New habits need to become embedded in the minds of the people execute implementing the systems. All systems need to include a process for reviewing and renewing each part of the system. A process that ensures that systems are updated when this inevitably becomes necessary. Finally, steps have to be taken to purge any redundant practices. See *Figure G-16 Designing human systems.*

### Systems and policy audits

Systems and policy audits provide essential checks to ensure that both systems and policies are in fact being implemented. Such audits are needed and take place at regular intervals. All foundation practices and policies have to be regularly reviewed and updated. Without scheduled policy audits, deviations may go unnoticed. Such audits help to prevent backsliding at all levels and help to sustain good habits and the right culture for a self-help enterprise.

Gaps in systems are often revealed when a systematic review of systems is undertaken. Any review of systems ought to reveal where current practices are in conflict. For example, when managers are rewarded for maximising profit, instead of for achieving the outcomes sought by members. Another example is when no proper provision is made for the departure and replacement of members; such provisions need to be incorporated into the planning system. In most cases, nothing more than a common-sense, logical approach is needed to expose where there are gaps in a system.

### Systems for self-help enterprises

The following chapters set out the key practices that underlie the systems essential to the proper operation of SHEs. The precise design of systems fit for any specific enterprise will be influenced by many different factors, including the market in which it operates.

## *Figure G-16 Designing human systems*

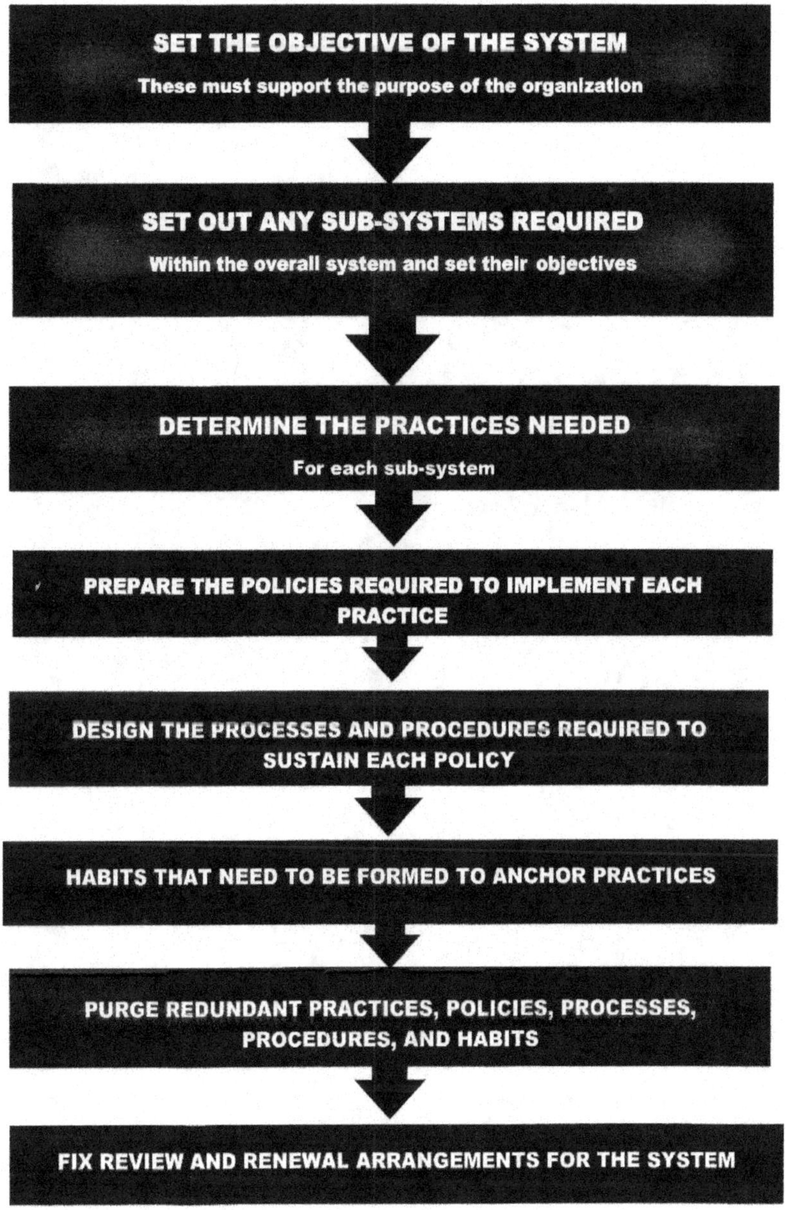

**SET THE OBJECTIVE OF THE SYSTEM**
These must support the purpose of the organization

**SET OUT ANY SUB-SYSTEMS REQUIRED**
Within the overall system and set their objectives

**DETERMINE THE PRACTICES NEEDED**
For each sub-system

**PREPARE THE POLICIES REQUIRED TO IMPLEMENT EACH PRACTICE**

**DESIGN THE PROCESSES AND PROCEDURES REQUIRED TO SUSTAIN EACH POLICY**

**HABITS THAT NEED TO BE FORMED TO ANCHOR PRACTICES**

**PURGE REDUNDANT PRACTICES, POLICIES, PROCESSES, PROCEDURES, AND HABITS**

**FIX REVIEW AND RENEWAL ARRANGEMENTS FOR THE SYSTEM**

# 17. THE SYSTEM OF ORGANIZATION

## What is a fit-for-purpose organization?

This chapter deals with the system of organization necessary to run genuine SHEs. As explained in *Chapter 7*, merely copying the design of any other form of organization will hardly ever result in one that is fit-for-purpose as a self-help enterprise. It needs to be understood that a very specific system which has been specifically designed is required.

In a self-help enterprise, it's essential that all the foundation practices, and the systems required to sustain them, are all embedded into the organization. This design should take full account of how people behave in practice and help to protect the interests of members against the kind of hazards faced by the owners of all manner of organizations. In addition, the system needs to safeguard the continuity of effective democratic member-control.

The overall system of organization includes four essential subsystems, which are:

1.  The foundations of the organization
2.  The governance system
3.  The oversight system
4.  The culture system.

This chapter details the foundation practices that underlie the system of organization while the subsystems of governance and oversight are explained in *Chapter 22.*, and the practices required to sustain an appropriate culture are set out in *Chapter 11*.

## The foundations of self-help enterprises

Previously, in *Chapter 9*, ten foundation practices were identified, these provide the foundations for all types of self-help enterprise and are the bedrock of the model. Sustaining these foundations requires the implementation of a set of practices that together make up a system. The foundations need to be safeguarded within the rules of the enterprise and be reflected in all the policies followed. Ideally, these practices will be reinforced by legislation, which the State provides to facilitate the registration and development of SHEs.

## Foundation practices

The foundation practices of SHEs are restated below; these practices underpin the system of organization. Each of the ten foundation practices listed needs to be supported by a raft of other practices, these are detailed below. Here it will be useful to refer to *Figure E-9 The foundations of SHEs*.

1. **ROOTED IN THE CONCEPT OF SELF-HELP AND MUTUAL ACTION, WHICH REQUIRES:**
   - The self-help mindset to be explained and actively advocated throughout the enterprise.
   - Securing the continuing commitment of members to taking mutual action.
   - Consistently implementing programmes for people development throughout the enterprise.
   - Embedding the critical self-help economic practices throughout the enterprise.

2. **DEDICATED TO ACHIEVING THE PURPOSE OF THE ENTERPRISE, WHICH REQUIRES:**
   - Establishing the core purpose and strategic aims of the enterprise and detailing specific outcomes to be achieved in the more immediate future.
   - Following a clear holistic purpose, as set by its members.
   - Reviewing the strategic aims of the enterprise prior to embarking upon the strategic planning process and the preparation of the annual operating plan.
   - Any surplus distributed is only shared among members in relation to their contribution to its creation.
   - Rewards paid to those investing in the enterprise be only the minimum needed to attract and retain such finance; such rewards are *never* to be made to investors that are in any way related to the surplus remaining (or so-called profits).
   - The adoption of a credible system of oversight.

3. **FOCUSED UPON THEIR MAIN FUNCTION, WHICH REQUIRES:**
   - That the function of the enterprise (market intervention in the best interest of members), remains the focus of the enterprise.
   - Following a sustainable market intervention strategy.
   - They act in the best long-term interest of the membership in its entirety.
   - Undertaking a planning process that focuses on meeting the needs of all members.
   - At all times, making decisions that take full account of the realities of the market.
   - Following a process for regularly updating the market intervention strategy and consistently engaging members.

4. **A VOLUNTARY ASSOCIATION OF EQUAL PERSONS, WHICH REQUIRES:**
   - Voluntary membership without discrimination, membership is a voluntary act and not due to any kind of coercion.

   - Setting out transparent membership qualifications, which are applied consistently and fairly, primarily based on members being committed to the enterprise's purpose.

   - Members are only admitted if they are willing to accept the responsibilities of membership; and provided that the expansion of membership does not threaten the viability of the enterprise.

   - Members are empowered by activities designed to improve their capacity to control their own enterprise, to better engage with the markets in which their enterprise operates, and to safeguard their future wellbeing within a specific market.

5. **DEMOCRATICALLY CONTROLLED BY THEIR MEMBERS, WHICH REQUIRES:**
   - Being controlled by its members using a system of control based upon equivalence, which means, sharing power based on all members having equal rights and responsibilities. Each member only has the power of one vote (or equivalent arrangements where the members are corporate bodies).

   - Maintaining a complete raft of policies that embed authentic democratic control.

   - Setting and following a set of rules and a system of corporate governance that sustain democratic control, which is regularly updated.

   - Supplying all necessary information so as to allow members to scrutinise and control their enterprise.

- Operating a schedule of regular reports, meetings, and elections, such as will allow members to monitor and control their enterprise properly.

- Fully supporting member empowerment by providing education about the democratic processes required.

- Systematically investing in developing people, this includes members, their leaders and representatives; also, managers and other employees.

- Providing both financial audit and purpose and function audit systems; ensuring that oversight reporting is made directly to the membership.

- Providing protection for all those who may have concerns about the conduct of the affairs of the enterprise by means of a whistle-blower charter.

6. **ECONOMICALLY SELF-SUSTAINING, WHICH REQUIRES:**
   - Staying financially self-sustaining, which means being viable, solvent, and having adequate liquidity.

   - Using methods of financing the enterprise that does not have the potential to threaten the sovereignty of the enterprise or undermine its long-term viability.

   - Not being dependent upon external grants, donations or subsidies, for their continuing viability.

   - Following the economic practices that are part of the foundations of the self-help model of enterprise and works according to the self-help economic system.

7. **OWNED BY THEIR MEMBERS ON A BENEFICIAL AND MUTUAL BASIS, WHICH REQUIRES:**
   - Current members make use of the assets of their enterprise and may gain from this. Members are in effect 'trustees', jointly holding the assets on behalf of both current and future members.
   - Members owning their personal investments in the enterprise but having no claim upon the enterprise in respect of any increase in the worth of the assets held by the enterprise; other than by an increase due to the re-valuation of any par-value qualifying investments.
   - Not making any distributions of mutually-owned assets, or their monetary value, to members or any other parties.
   - In case of dissolution any surplus remaining shall not be distributed to members, but instead, this may be donated to another self-help enterprise or to a designated charity.
   - Ensuring that any distribution of surplus made shall only be made to members and in proportion to the member's participation in generating the surplus.

8. **INDEPENDENT AND IN CONTROL OF THEIR OWN DESTINY, WHICH REQUIRES:**
   - SHEs being sovereign entities. Otherwise, they may not be able to act in the best interest of its members. This means being free from the control of the State, free from political interference, and free from the control of investors, patrons, and/or cliques of any kind.
   - Operating a system of governance that is effective in keeping control in the hands of members and supports a high level of direct interaction between members and the supreme governing body (e.g. The board of directors).

- Finance being the servant of the enterprise, not its master

- Limiting the extent of the role individuals or organizations in financing the enterprise: to members and other benign sources of finance and limiting the extent of any one person's or entity's participation to a percentage of the total (for example, not to exceed 20% of the total).

- Not entering any arrangement with any other body or person, including the State or its institutions, unless this is undertaken on terms that will guarantee the autonomy and the maintenance of democratic member-control

- Prohibiting an enterprise from selling-off their total assets, unless it is proven to the satisfaction of the members that the enterprise no longer has any purpose.

9. **BASED UPON EQUITABLE RELATIONSHIPS, WHICH REQUIRES:**
   - Equitable relationships being the basis of all activity undertaken by the enterprise.

   - Voting and all other powers of members being allocated based on all individuals being equal persons.

   - Treating all members as being equal in every respect, and no member or non-member receiving preferential treatment. Members all having not only equal voting rights, but also an equal voice, equal chances, and equal access to the best deals.

   - Equivalence between all members, allowing no discrimination.

   - Being fair and honest in all dealings, with all members and other stakeholders.

## 10. COMMITTED TO LONG-TERMISM, WHICH REQUIRES:

- Prudent accounting practices and policies.
- Provident decision-making.
- Long-term planning to meet members' current and future needs.
- Building long-term relationships with all stakeholders, which is important in terms of ensuring the future of the enterprise.
- Anticipating and removing any significant barriers to essential change.
- Ensuring that market intelligence is gathered constantly and used in all decision-making and shared with the membership.
- Systematically, investing in developing their people, including members, leaders, senior managers and employees.
- Regularly reviewing their organization and following a renewal process.

## Protection against hijack

Attention has previously been drawn to the danger of persons other than the membership in its entirety taking-over control of the enterprise. It's far from exceptional for the real power in SHEs to rest with their senior managers, a clique, or in the case of consumer-owned SHEs, to be in the hands of their employees. In some country's politicians or government staff, exercise control over the day-to-day running of SHEs, having supplanted the members' representatives. Keeping the enterprise under the control of its members is one of the most important tasks of the board.

Whenever the law or the rules are inadequate, because they don't provide the kind of protection needed, predators will inevitably try to take-over SHEs. The demutualisation of SHEs amounts to the theft of their assets from its members; this can so easily occur wherever the law permits it. Leaders of SHEs need to ensure that the rules of their enterprise provide solid protection against the threat of hijack and fully support authentic member-control. This is best achieved by:

- Making reserves indivisible and non-distributable.

- Making sure that only 'economically active members exercise voting rights in the enterprise.

- Limiting any individual member's investment to a stated percentage of the total vote linked to the total equity of the enterprise (for example, 10%).

- Making sure that voting on any change of status needs the assent of a specified majority of members (for example 75% of all members), rather than just those who turn up at a meeting.

### A better organization

One of the main reasons that people start-up SHEs is that they want to have a better organization than those already working in the market. In broad terms this means one that they can always trust to act with integrity, to be fair to all members and remain self-governing. Yet it means much more than this because SHEs should equip members to be more resilient in the face of changes in the market and help members to improve the quality their decisions when facing choices offered by the market.

Members need an ethical organization, which calls for honest trading, fairness, openness, transparency, and freedom from bribery, corruption, nepotism, cronyism, and the improper exercise of patronage. Any deviations from such ethical standards have got to be stamped out at the very first signs of such behaviour.

Corruption can take on many guises, and to eradicate it totally will never be achieved by advocating a vague ethical policy. Defeating corruption requires very specific criteria and codes of practice to be laid down and vigorously enforced. It needs to be accepted that corruption is a real and present threat to every kind of organization, and that relentless vigilance is necessary to prevent it from spreading like cancer. Sometimes, corruption can be the result of systemic weaknesses, such as the lack of clear policies and guidelines, and not always due to conscious wrongdoing; policies. Nevertheless, there can be no room for compromise in these matters.

# 18. THE SYSTEM OF ASSOCIATION

### System of association

This chapter deals with the system of association required in SHEs; this system is founded on the fact that SHEs are associations of equal persons and are often referred to as 'societies' or by other names that make it clear that they are *people-centred* enterprises.

In most countries, companies are incorporated and registered under the prevailing companies' legislation. Currently, in most States, SHEs are registered using separate specific laws. Within the United Kingdom, also in some former British dominions and colonies, the laws allow for some types of SHEs to choose to be registered under the Companies Acts. In a few countries, there are not any specific laws for SHEs, for example in Denmark.

Normally, associations of finance are registered/incorporated using the Companies Law. In companies, both a Memorandum of Association and Articles of Association (or equivalent documents) are needed for a company to be registered using the companies' legislation.

In Company law, the 'Memorandum of Association' is the document that sets up the company, and it's the 'Articles of Association' that sets out how the company is to be run, governed, and owned. The Articles of Association set out the responsibilities and powers of the directors, and how the members exert control over their enterprise. The equivalent single document used for many SHEs is usually referred to as the 'Registered Rules'; or an equivalent founding document, as may be required by the relevant legislation. 'The rules will embody the system of association, so it is vital that the rules are routinely kept up-to-date and not just revised when there is some kind of crisis.

In most countries, the Company law is regularly updated to keep pace with changing conditions, with most governments believing that this is necessary to 'oil the wheels of commerce'. Unfortunately, the legislation needed to support the development of SHEs is rarely given the same priority.

### The rules form a contract

The rules of a self-help enterprise are in fact an agreement between the member and the enterprise. The rules govern not only the relationship between the member and the enterprise but also relationships between members. The rules are a very important document, which needs to be in a format that is easy for members to work with. When a member joins an enterprise, they need to accept its rules as a binding contract between themselves and their enterprise. In some SHEs, members enter into additional agreements with their enterprise; for example, in many marketing co-ops members sign-up to a marketing agreement as well, this governs how, and on what terms, their enterprise will market their products or services.

### Essential rules

Among the essential items to be included in the rules are the qualifications for membership, and in some cases, the rules may allow for provisional or probationary membership. Every contract needs to be enforceable, or it ceases to have any worth. Leaders have to be prepared to use sanctions, but not vindictively, against those who insist on pursuing their own interests at the expense of their joint enterprise.

The level of interdependence between the members in any specific self-help enterprise will set the level of mutual trust needed to make their enterprise work successfully. For example, if a group of workers depend for their livelihood upon the effectiveness of their enterprise, then a significant level of trust and cooperative working between members needs to prevail otherwise the group will fail or disintegrate. In the case of an enterprise that supplies consumer goods to members, the intensity of the level of 'cooperation' needed will be at a lower level; this requires that leaders of these enterprises need to follow a strategy that will constantly engage their members. Such differences in the extent of the level of commitment necessary should be reflected in the rules of the enterprise. Nevertheless, in all cases, the practices necessary to support cooperative behaviour need to be in place if the enterprise is to prosper.

All the main protections for the rights of members, along with their responsibilities, have to be set out in the rules. Any changes to the foundation practices, which should be incorporated into the rules, have to be agreed by the members governing body (normally at the General Meeting), and may only be changed when they are agreed by a qualified majority (for example 75% or more of the members voting).

## The aims of the system of association

The objectives of the system of association are to define and sustain the organization necessary to achieve the purpose of the enterprise. Also, sustaining member democratic control, upholding the practice of mutual and beneficial ownership, as well as all the other foundation practices, which are essential to the system.

The overall system of association involves the application of subsystems; these include systems for:

- Membership and member development.
- Ownership.
- Democratic control, including leadership development.
- Cooperation.

Details of the practices needed for the systems of membership and member development are included later in this chapter. The systems relating to ownership are considered in *Chapter 19*. The systems necessary for effective democratic control and the system for leadership development are elaborated in *Chapter 21*, and the cooperation system is addressed in *Chapter 24*. To reiterate, all of these systems and subsystems are critical to the operation of authentic SHEs. When combined, these interdependent systems form the self-help enterprise model. This means that the successful implementation of the system of association relies upon the systems of organization, economics, management and governance all being applied simultaneously.

### The membership system - essential practices
A raft of practices is needed if SHEs are to keep the right kind of relationship with their members, all of which need to be expressed in the format of clear-cut policies. The following practices need to be part of the membership system:
- **The basis of membership has to be entirely clear**; members need to share a commitment to the purpose of their enterprise.
- **Ensuring that members are recruited without coercion**, and free from discrimination based upon, religion, partisan politics, gender, race, or sexual orientation.

- **The qualifications for membership are transparent**, and members are only admitted if they are willing to accept the responsibilities of membership (this may include contributing to the financing of the enterprise), and that the expansion of membership does not undermine the viability of the enterprise.

- **Ensuring that members are properly informed about the affairs of their enterprise** and are trained in how to take part in the affairs of the enterprise and the use of the information provided.

- **Voting and all other powers of members are allocated based on *all* members being equal persons**. Ensuring that all members are treated equally in every respect, with no member or non-member receiving preferential treatment. All members have equal voting rights, an equal voice, equal chances and equal access to the best deals.

- **Regular dialogue with members** using systems, both formal and informal, that ensure a proper process of two-way communication that works throughout the enterprise.

- **Empowering members**, by providing them with the information, knowledge and skills needed to increase their power within the market, including fully involving members in the strategic planning process.

- **The benefits arising from the activities of the enterprise are shared equally by all members**, or in direct relationship to the individual member's contribution towards creating such benefits. If any surplus is distributed to members, this shall be shared equitably in direct relation to the member's role in its creation. For example: in a consumer enterprise, this will be in relation to their spending with the enterprise,

221

in a worker enterprise this will be in relation to the value of the contribution of their labour.

- **Ensuring that the actions or activities of the enterprise create don't create dependency** or discourages the practice of self-help and mutual action.

- **Following sound practices that sustain cooperative behaviour** between the enterprise and its members, together with building long-term positive relationships with all stakeholders.

- **The members' register is kept up-to-date**. At the minimum, this needs to be on a quarterly basis but should be a real-time activity' The register needs to record which persons are 'active' members who are eligible to take advantage of the benefits available from the enterprise. An 'active member' is one who regularly uses the services of the enterprise; for example, in the case of a shopper, they purchase goods from their consumer-owned shop, in the case of a farmer, they market their crops through their marketing co-op, in the case of thrifty-person, they save and borrow with a credit union or a building society.

**The value of membership**

Members need to be at the heart of every self-help enterprise. The basis of membership, as well as the qualifications for membership, both need to be entirely clear. A major issue for many SHEs is that the basis of membership is not always entirely clear, a situation that can be the source of many problems. it's most important that a complete set of practices, policies and systems be in place to ensure the maintenance of an active and positive approach to the recruitment of members and engaging them with the enterprise.

Compared with the situation a few decades ago, the term 'member' has become devalued because many commercial businesses use the term when referring to customers who join their various loyalty schemes. More importantly, many SHEs having abandoned the self-help mindset but continue to refer to those who are now little more than 'customers', as members. The reality is that the meaning that those running SHEs place upon the term 'member,' is critical to the development of their enterprises. The members of SHEs are in fact the beneficial owners of their enterprises, with the right to exercise democratic control over them.

By belonging to a self-help enterprise, individuals can pick-up signals about their environment from the other members. These signals can concern the market or the threats to their enterprise and/or their community. Their collective knowledge can be extremely valuable, as is their collective vigilance, which can be essential to the long-term survival and prosperity of any community.

### A common bond
In some cases, to qualify for membership, it may be necessary to satisfy a requirement to be part of a specific 'common bond'. The basis of a common bond is that a member has a linkage with all other members; this can be most important within credit cooperatives, for example in credit unions.

The basis of a common bond can include, for example, living in a specified town or city, working for the same employer, being a member of a specified organization, or a member of a designated profession. Changes in the way that people associate have occurred during recent decades, and now that so many people have access to transport and electronic communications, geographic 'common bonds' are often far less relevant than they were in the past.

## The basis of membership

Members need to be aware of the basis of the relationship between themselves and their enterprise. It's wrong to believe that membership is always based on members belonging to a specific stakeholder group. For example, all being consumers, all workers, or all producers. Although in many cases, members will all belong to the same stakeholder group, and this can provide the basis for a 'common bond', which is different from members sharing a common purpose.

In worker cooperatives, a rigorous process for selecting members is essential. Even when a candidate for membership makes it through multiple interviews, she or he needs to be invited to spend the time working with their team, after which, leaders can assess their would-be member's attitude not only to do the job that is to be filled but that they are a 'fit' with other members of a team.

## Fairness and equivalence

If SHEs are to succeed, members need to know that the benefits gained from their mutual action outweigh the hassle that is often associated with working together. The effectiveness of SHEs depends on building mutual trust and gaining this kind of trust calls for a set of rules that govern the behaviour of individual members. Members need to know that there will be sanctions against members who do not stick to the agreed rules of behaviour. Simply emphasising benefits or rights in SHEs is not enough, there has got to be an honest acceptance of the need for members to share the risks and take on their responsibilities. Members need to be convinced that they will fairly share in all benefits and will have a meaningful say in the running of the venture. The sharing of any surplus generated by the enterprise, if distributed, should be in relation to the volume of activity transacted or the effort that each member puts into its creation.

If members are to be motivated to work together, then they have to be convinced that their enterprise will treat them all as equals. This means that they can always expect to be treated equally in both human and economic terms. In practice, it means having equal voting power (one member - one vote), equal opportunities to take part in running the enterprise, sharing benefits on the same basis as all members, having equal access to information and being able to rely upon the fact that their enterprise will always be run in their joint best interest.

## Voluntary membership without discrimination

Mutual action can only be a voluntary activity and not as a result of any kind of compulsion. Members should be able to join, and to leave freely, but without leaving behind any burdens upon the remaining members. Membership should not be free in the sense that it is without cost. Membership should have tangible value and a specified cost. Such costs may include a membership fee or a qualifying investment, alongside their obligation to act as a responsible member.

Membership may sometimes need to be restricted but not in a discriminatory manner; limits can be set where the ability of the enterprise to service new members is constrained by the availability of resources. For example, in a club that can only accommodate a limited number of members or a worker co-operative that has only enough work to sustain a limited number of jobs. 'Open membership' simply means that no applicants for membership will be subject to any kind of discrimination; otherwise, the enterprise can easily become one that exploits those excluded.

## Self-help and the vulnerable

SHEs can cater to the needs of the more vulnerable in society and when they supply such services leaders need to devise methods of maximising member participation that involves all members. Examples of where this kind of enterprise is appropriate, include eldercare and services for those with conditions that limit their competence. In such cases, the overall purpose of the enterprise will be to offer services in the best interest of a beneficiary group. In this type of SHE, the membership will typically include not only those who are part of the beneficiary group but also, for example, their caregivers and the professionals who support them. In such SHEs, members need to share the desire to supply high-grade care or other services to the beneficiary group. Those in need of care or support, plus caregivers, are united by a holistic purpose and in optimising the use of all available resources in pursuit of it.

## Corporate members

Many SHEs need to allow corporate entities to be members. Indeed, there are some SHEs with members who are other SHEs, and where all the members are corporate bodies. Some SHEs have a mixture of individual and corporate members, but this is not often a satisfactory arrangement. For example, when the task of the enterprise is to supply services to other SHEs, the combination of individuals and enterprises is often very difficult to reconcile. Some SHEs are set-up to serve the separate businesses that are their members, in these 'business cooperatives', the members may include corporate entities, individuals, and small groups of entrepreneurs. Such SHEs offer their members one or more services, for example, joint marketing, the wholesale supply of goods, and other business inputs, bank and credit card clearing services, hotel, or other booking arrangements, etc. The main role of this type of enterprise is to increase the profitability of their members' businesses.

Many agricultural cooperatives that began as cooperatives of individual farmers, or family-farms, have changed into business cooperatives; this happens when individual members become large incorporated farming businesses.

### The problem of 'free-riders.'

'Free-riders' are people who enjoy the benefits of the mutual action taken by a self-help enterprise without making any contribution or commitment towards it. Free-riders cannot be tolerated. Otherwise, the support of the members who make a commitment to the enterprise will simply evaporate. Likewise, free, or nominal membership costs, placing no value upon membership, can only undermine the self-help mindset. As with many things in life, what appears to be free, and needing no commitment, or incurring no cost, soon become worthless. Members should constantly be encouraged to show a commitment to their enterprise, and this includes contributing towards the money needed to finance it, and taking part in its economic activities; for example, by buying goods from a community-owned shop, or in the case of a crop marketing co-op, selling their crops through their co-op.

Where there are sales-driven cultures in SHEs, typically in diverse types of consumer-owned enterprises, leaders and managers make the mistake of either neglecting to recruit new members or making admission to membership so easy that it lacks meaning. However, offering an easy route into *provisional* membership, which can help in recruiting new members, can be useful. The full benefits of membership should not be available to those unwilling to make the necessary commitment, including committing to make the necessary investment in the enterprise.

Although, sometimes this commitment may be met by monetising the value of their voluntary labour (often called 'sweat-equity').

People involved in SHEs should recognise what it is that causes cooperation work in practice, and what destroys it. In addition, how to get people to work jointly in their own best interest, and how this, in turn, can be in the mutual interest of the membership in its entirety.

Mutual action entails balancing the needs of the individual with those of the group; it allows the individual to keep their sovereignty while gaining from the rewards of joint action. Some very clear lessons arising from the practice of cooperation gained over many years and in many different situations and locations is the basis of an accumulated experience available to those who need to draw upon it. Regrettably, many of the people running enterprises that are nominally cooperatives or mutuals, appear to have lost sight of this important body of knowledge. The fact is that if SHEs are to thrive, they also need the sound foundation provided by the practices that foster and sustain cooperative behaviour, as set out in *Chapter 24*.

**Exit arrangements**
When setting up SHEs, the founding members sometimes do not give enough thought to problems that can arise if proper exit arrangements are not made for members who may wish to leave the enterprise or who cease to be economically active within it. This issue needs to be covered within the rules of the enterprise, and systems need to be in place if future problems are to be avoided. Best practice has been proven for most types of SHEs, but leaders need to think ahead and to imagine the various scenarios that can arise when members wish to disengage from their enterprise. This being particularly important in all forms of worker and producer

enterprises, in housing co-ops of all kinds, and in many financial services enterprises.

On the one hand, there is the problem of people who are members moving away from the area where the enterprise offers services, or where they are ceasing it be involved in a specific activity; such as when a farmer ceases to grow a specific crop. Other problematic situations arise when members no longer make use of the services of the enterprise, such as when a producer is no longer involved in the specific markets where the enterprise is active. A good example of this is in dairy cooperatives when farmers stop producing milk. These members are often called 'dry-shareholders', which means that they are no longer producing milk. This term has become extended to cover other types of enterprise, where it means that a member is no longer economically active in the markets where the enterprise works, but often still holds so-called 'shares' or other investments in the enterprise. This situation can result in decisions being made by the dry-shareholders that are not in the best interest of producers, but instead, are being made in the interests of people who are there purely as investors.

Proper exit arrangements are critical in situations where members need to hand-over to a new generation of members, and where new members need to replace leaving members. Arrangements need to be in place to ensure that both the leaving members and new members replacing them are both treated equitably. It can become a problem when people come to the end of their working life and need to retire, and if arrangements have not been made to provide them with an alternative income, for example, a pension, then they will simply have to continue to work because they have no alternative. In various forms of consumer enterprises, problems can arise when members are not actively trading with their enterprise, because they may have a quite different agenda from those who are active. In all types of self-help enterprise, it's important for leaders to foresee future problems, and to make sure that exit arrangements are always in place for when these are needed.

### The farmers of Lucky Hill

While working in Jamaica, in the 1970s, I was asked to visit the Lucky Hill cooperative farm. Here a group of farmers were running a cooperative established in 1941 when the pioneering members were young men. Sadly, at the time of my visit, the surviving members were struggling to run the farm because they were getting old and finding it difficult to work on the farm. At the time of establishing the farm, no arrangements had been made for the recruitment of new members or for providing for retirement pensions for those no longer able to continue farming or wanting to leave the co-op. There was little alternative but to plan for the winding-up of this cooperative farm.

It's not unusual to find that when SHEs are established, no proper arrangements are made for the renewal and replacement of members. This is a familiar problem in many workers and producer's self-help ventures. Part of the process of forming any self-help venture needs to involve making provision for the exit and replacement of members.

Farming continues on the land used by the Lucky Hill farmers and the idea of cooperating remains; now it takes the form of individual farmers working together to supply their crops for use in the local production of Jamaican pickles and sauces.

## The elephant in the room

In all types of self-help, enterprise membership needs to be central to every aspect of its activities, where those running SHEs lose sight of this crucial fact, it will surely fail. For all types of consumer-owned SHEs, selling to non-members is a practice that is the source of many of their ills and the cause of their failure to achieve their full potential. Where SHEs regards 'customers' as being more important than members, then the enterprise has a big problem. For most consumer-owned co-ops, building societies or savings and loan associations and mutual insurers, this is 'the elephant in the room'. In other words, a very significant issue that everyone is acutely aware of, but generally nobody wants to talk about.

Consumer-owned enterprises should only be trading with members and 'soon-to-be' members. In worker co-ops, all those employed (working in the enterprise) ought to be a member or a time-limited probationary member. In producer-owned SHEs, offering services provided by the enterprise should only be open to producer members. In all cases, the practice of allowing easy access to the privileges of membership by non-members can completely undermine the integrity of the enterprise as a genuine self-help enterprise. Nonetheless, it is very difficult for SHEs that have devalued membership to return to a position that places membership at the centre of its operations. A carefully crafted plan to reinstate the value of membership is necessary if SHEs are to retrieve their position.

### *Limiting access to membership*

The much-vaunted Eroski supermarket group, (a part of the Mondragón worker cooperatives originating in the Basque region of Spain) in 2015 had only 15,000 members out of a total of 74,000 employees. In these circumstances, it's difficult to accept that it now operates as a genuine self-help enterprise.

## Capacity building

Capacity building is central to the success of all SHEs, for if people are to work together effectively, then they need the basic skills to fulfil their duties. This may involve helping members with literacy and numeracy, and in this century, the required level of computer literacy. Other training needs may include learning how to work within a democratically-controlled enterprise. Sometimes referred to as 'member education', such activities are not to be confused with the education undertaken by the State or those offered by the education industry.

Much of the learning most needed by members is non-formal creative learning and is so much more than offering a few formal courses. It needs to be designed to develop their members' competence to take part in, as well as benefit from, the practice of self-help and mutual action.

If members are to take part fully in their enterprise, they need to be equipped with the elementary skills needed. This includes knowing the rules, how to interpret a set of accounts and to gain enough confidence to take part in the democratic process. It's not at all unusual to find that an emphasis is placed on providing members with knowledge (such as history and theoretical concepts), when the most important need is often for the 'hard' skills, such as interpreting market data and understanding financial and management information.

Capacity building is about drawing upon the creative power of the members and developing their ability to contribute their experience and ideas in the service of their joint enterprise. Unless members learn how to 'co-operate', and to develop the skills necessary to play a full part in their joint enterprise, an elite or clique will soon dominate the enterprise; this 'select few' will inevitably end-up running the enterprise for their own benefit.

## Member engagement

The real value of membership to the enterprise lies in the opportunity to exchange information, both between the membership and the enterprise and between members. This is not by any means limited to using formal democratic processes. Informal exchanges can often be most valuable, and these can take place in informal situations and at all levels of the organization's structure. Even so, all the formal processes for information exchange need to be supported to ensure the integrity of the system of democratic control.

Those involved in running SHEs often complain that their members do not support their own enterprise, and there often appear to be a lack of engagement with their own enterprise. The fact is that most grassroots members are not at all engaged by the theoretical advantages of ownership but are engaged by the outcomes that are achieved as the result of their mutual action that can help change their lives for the better. The challenge of successfully engaging with members is usually only met where SHEs implement market intervention strategies in defined markets. Members of SHEs that are pleased by the results achieved on their behalf are most likely to be ready to engage with them. At the same time, many of the financing problems facing SHEs are best resolved when members are sufficiently engaged that they supply the finance for their own enterprise.

In the case of SHEs that are producer or worker controlled, such members are sellers of goods and services into specific markets, and the members rely upon their SHEs to secure all or a part of their livelihoods. In these enterprises, members are typically more closely engaged in their enterprise when compared to members of consumer-owned enterprises. The fact is that members will fully engage in the activities of their enterprise when they have both a financial stake and are directly impacted by their market intervention strategies. In such circumstances, members will be keen to influence the planning process and to help to sustain their enterprise in meeting the threats to their future that arise within the market.

Member engagement is not a set of activities that can be delegated to a separate department of the enterprise or to be outsourced. Instead, the engagement of members is a task that needs to be fully integrated into the mainstream activities of the enterprise. Although, SHEs with a very large membership will often need specific sections of the enterprise to deal with the administration of membership, communicating with members about their involvement within the democratic process, and for the accounting relating to members' investments in the enterprise.

In the 21st century, this encouragement will involve making full use of cyber-networks and social media, but this needs to supplement regular face-to-face contact. Members need to be fully involved in the enterprise's planning, control and monitoring processes. Engaging members involves supplying relevant information (not 'sales literature' that look like it comes from a commercial business), training and education, all designed to help empower them; including information about how to fulfil their duties as active members.

**Member awareness**
The voice of members who are fully aware of the ways used to exploit people in a market will help prevent their own managers

from using such bad practices in their own enterprise. SHEs need to invest in the future of their members by helping improve their knowledge and the skills, which they need to improve their prospects within the market. It will always be necessary to balance short-term satisfactions against their longer-term well-being. For example, by setting aside savings to cover the risks that they may face during their active lives and to have money in their old age. The wider issue of stewardship, particularly as it relates to the security of the environment, and the dissipation of non-renewable resources are now forming part of an agenda set by SHEs acting in the long-term interest of members.

**Organizing people**
When it comes to organizing ourselves, we often default to traditional hierarchies, using a system rooted in practices that have been used for centuries. This system relies on top-down authority, controlling resources, distributing tasks, and defining relationships, as the way of enabling the organization to work. Hierarchies are typically bureaucratic, where employees often lack positive motivation, and as a way of organizing human activity is far from ideal. If instead, a way of working is deployed that makes the most of the talents and energy of the people who are part of the enterprise, this unleashes their capability for innovation, encouraging the best use of the available human resources.

This approach means concentrating on how to best work through people, rather than by controlling them, which means giving more power to employees and members. Such approaches can result in faster innovation, lower costs, greater agility, improved responsiveness and more influence in the market. At the same time, working out how to deploy the diversity and knowledge available from within the membership. These methods call for a different mindset, but by exchanging an outmoded command and control mentality to one that unleashes the creative power of the people involved, so much more can be achieved.

# 19. THE ECONOMIC SYSTEM

## Economics

Economics is the branch of knowledge concerned with the production, consumption, and transfer of wealth. The application of economics can also help us understand how to manage our personal finances and to run a viable enterprise and help us to get a balanced budget in the national economy. It's helpful to differentiate between micro-economics, which is concerned with the basic elements in the economy (for example, the supply and demand of specific goods and services) and macroeconomics, which deals with issues affecting an entire economy, e.g. unemployment, inflation, economic growth, and monetary and fiscal policy. This chapter deals with the economic system necessary in SHEs.

The set of economic practices underlying the self-help economic system that guides those running SHEs is significantly different from that required in other forms of enterprise and more specifically, those used in commercial enterprises. Nevertheless, all forms of enterprises cannot afford to ignore the discipline supplied by the market and many of the universal economic realities that guide them. These realities include the requirement to remain viable, solvent, and maintain an adequate level of liquidity.

## The objectives of the self-help economic system

The self-help economic system is designed to ensure the achievement of the purpose of the enterprise and to stick to the foundation practices.

## The economic practices of self-help enterprises

Effective SHEs keep to a set of interdependent economic practices; these are set out below, the main reasons for pursuing these practices are also outlined.

### 1. FOCUSING THE ENTERPRISE ON ITS PURPOSE

Achieving the enterprise's purpose has to be at the heart of every decision. SHEs optimise the use of their available resources.

### 2. MARKET INTERVENTION IN THE BEST INTEREST OF ITS MEMBERS

Requires that SHEs develop and implement a viable and sustainable market intervention strategy. (This diverges from commercial businesses that often seek to exploit a market.)

### 3. BEING SELF-SUSTAINING WITHIN THE MARKET

Means sustaining viability, solvency, liquidity and not having a dependency upon the State, a charity, or any other form of patronage. Recognising that SHEs, as with all forms of enterprise, they compete in the market for all resources that they need.

Accepting that there is rarely any alternative but to pay the market rate for finance, labour, land, or any other resources it needs. Therefore, it follows that SHEs need to be able to use such resources, at least as productively as any other enterprise. Otherwise, they will simply not be able to pay the market price for these essential resources. The aim is to optimise the use of resources – doing more with less.

### 4. MAINTAINING BENEFICIAL AND MUTUAL OWNERSHIP

This means SHEs own and control the assets used by the enterprise, whilst individual members own their investments in the enterprise. SHEs cannot offer outright ownership. Instead, they provide members with a method of ownership that secures the long-term future of the enterprise

Typically, enforcement of this practice is achieved by inserting two clauses in the enterprise's rules, which are often cemented by their inclusion within national laws. The first ensures that the assets be applied solely in furtherance of its aims and may not be divided among the members or any other individuals or corporate bodies. The second supports altruistic dissolution, whereby if the enterprise is wound-up, any remaining assets exceeding liabilities are not distributed to the members but instead transferred to another enterprise with similar aims; or, in the absence of this choice, given to a relevant charity.

Members' investments in SHEs, where these are classed as equity, will typically be issued on the basis that they are of par-value – a further explanation of this concept is included later in this chapter.

### 5. ENSURING THE INDEPENDENCE OF THE ENTERPRISE

This means financing the enterprise equitably and using only benign sources. Ideally, financed by its members, but only utilising finance from non-members when this will not compromise member-control.

Money is a means to an end, not an end in its self. The owners of finance are entitled to receive a fair reward for making use of their finance, but they do not directly share in any surplus, because this belongs to the members. Instead, finance needs to be rewarded based on the market rate for its use.

Constraints need to be in place are that prevent anyone concerned with the running the enterprise from securing finance from any source that is not benign. All directors and senior managers should realise that many of those who offer to provide finance will seek to take control of the enterprise, especially if there is any prospect of defaulting on loans. Finance that brings with it any risk that it may compromise the sovereignty of the enterprise is not acceptable; see *Chapter 23*.

## 6. MAINTAINING EQUITABLE RELATIONSHIPS BETWEEN ALL MEMBERS

Being committed to supporting equivalence between all members needs to demonstrate the prices set for goods or services offered or supplied by SHEs are decided by the market within which SHEs has to operate. In all dealings with members, the practice of equivalence applies; all members have to be treated as equals. This replaces the practice of profit-maximization used in commercial businesses. In such businesses, different prices or terms are often offered to different people. In other words, prices are set based on the idea that they charge 'whatever they can get away with'. This kind of 'opportunistic pricing' may include, offering secret deals to some customers, and paying different rates of pay to workers for people doing the same job.

Treating all members with fairness is a crucial factor in maintaining their trust and commitment, which can be soon be lost when members discover that they are being treated unfairly. All members need to be treated as equals in a self-help enterprise; they should all have equal access to the best deals available. This is not to say that there won't be different deals available to members based upon the cost levels associated with individual transactions. For example, any member buying the same goods by the full truckload would get the same price as any other member buying the same volume. Despite this, any member buying goods in smaller quantities should expect to pay a price that reflects the higher costs involved.

SHEs, don't make profits and they only distribute surpluses to members in direct relationship to the individual members' contribution to the creation of any such surplus. The owners of finance do not share in the distribution of any surplus, instead finance is rewarded by means of a fixed rate of interest or by other means not linked to profits; for example, pegged to national bank rates or to rates of inflation.

### 7.  RECOGNISING THE IMPORTANCE OF PLACE

This means that SHEs only operate in locations that further the enterprise's purpose, and where such operations are directly beneficial to its membership. Decisions about the location of their activities are not to be based on the benefits that accrue to the owners of finance nor the opportunity to maximise profit*. SHEs are enterprises committed to a location and to a specific group of people, this often means providing a more secure base for employment and service provision, which commercial businesses would regard as only marginal locations, such as in many rural areas.

*Note: Whenever there is reliance upon internationally mobile finance, and when a commercial business is driven by profit-maximization, speculation, and short-term share-price values; this combination of factors often results in unemployment and the withdrawal of services from areas with lower profit opportunities. Such finance is itinerant, and because many investor-controlled businesses show little or no attachment to any specific location, they often migrate to areas where the cost of labour is significantly lower. When other areas offer the prospect of a higher return, firms withdraw their investment in businesses operating in less-profitable locations.

### 8.  NOT ENGAGING IN ANY SPECULATION FOR PROFIT

This means that speculation (gambling) has no place in the economic process of SHEs. Such activities cannot help most of the members.

SHEs have a duty to serve their membership in its entirety. If one member is to gain, it's inevitable that another member loses. Speculation routinely produces few winners and many losers, so it can never be accepted as the basis for mutual trading.

It forms no part of the role of directors or senior managers to speculate/gamble with the savings of members or their collectively owned assets. The people who create and produce goods or deliver services rarely gain from speculation, because this results in wealth redistribution that only benefits those with considerable wealth. The inevitable impact of compound interest (money begets money) this almost guarantees that the rich will always get richer.

It's sometimes necessary to pursue approaches that minimize risk through a variety of risk management insurance strategies, but these need to stop well short of speculation. Big bonuses, paid to reward speculators are even more of a problem for society because they encourage people to take excessive risks, usually using other peoples' money, which distorts the real market. When managers base their decisions upon securing short-term gains, this ignores the fact that a stewardship approach is needed in SHEs.

### 9. TRADING WITH HONESTY AND INTEGRITY

This means ethical standards need to guide all economic decisions. Integrity, honest-dealing, and the absence of exploitation, misselling, and any kind of cheating, are all essential characteristics of SHEs. Apart from the moral imperative of trading ethically, it makes sense that if an enterprise tries to short-change its members or any other people that it trades with, this will invariably destroy their trust in the enterprise. Such behaviour is the entire opposite of what's needed, which should be to build positive long-term relationships with all its stakeholders.

If people cannot trust their own enterprise, then who are they to trust? The level of integrity expected from SHEs calls for the avoidance of all forms of exploitation, which means not exploiting their own members or any other stakeholders in the enterprise. Conversely, it is about helping members to develop their individual power to fend for themselves, by increasing the power of members to withstand the vagaries of the market and other threats to their living standards and lifestyles. It is about empowering members so that they can respond positively to changing conditions and building their resilience. SHEs need to demonstrate that they differ from those commercial businesses that routinely make profits by exploiting the weakness of their customers, workers, and suppliers.

## 10. ACHIEVING ECONOMIES OF SCALE WHILE RETAINING DEMOCRATIC CONTROL

This means utilising the economies of scale that result when an enterprise obtains cost advantages (savings) through expansion. These arise in purchasing (bulk buying of goods or materials), management (increased specialisation of managers), finance (obtaining lower-cost finance when borrowing and/or gaining access to a greater range of financial instruments), marketing (spreading the cost of advertising over a greater range of sales or output), and technology (spreading costs such as research and development). Diseconomies of scale may arise, chiefly in organizational terms. SHEs need to secure economies of scale whilst supporting member engagement and democratic member-control. Where benefits of scale can be achieved, then the default position ought to be to explore the opportunities for cooperation with other SHEs, always with the intention of offering increased benefits to the membership.

## All ten practices are needed

All ten of the practices are needed to support self-help and mutual action, to avoid the creation of dependency, short-termism and speculation. While at the same time encouraging self-help and mutual action and concentrating on improving the lives and livelihoods of members.

## Stewardship and provident decisions

All economic decisions need to be both provident and equitable; and, all economic practices need to be future-focused. Practices that do not support the long-term achievement of the purpose need to be avoided. For example, rewards and incentive systems that encourage short-term results rather than the long-term interests of the enterprise are never acceptable. Likewise, forms of financing that may bring about growth, but bring significant risks that threaten the very future of the enterprise - are not to be accepted.

The pursuit of policies to sustain the enterprise over time, in the face of fluctuating market conditions, are an essential part of running a successful self-help enterprise. Leaders cannot afford to be wedded to any specific format, but instead, need to be continually evolving. This requires the incumbent leadership to plan for their own replacement in the future. Most of their decisions need to be strategic, not merely short-term. This approach has considerable implications for both the development of leaders and for the methods of raising finance.

## Resource optimisation

Achieving resource optimisation is central to SHEs, this means making full and productive use of all tangible assets and includes productively utilising the space in buildings, securing the best achievable levels of stock-turnover, minimising the cost of giving credit, and controlling all costs within the enterprise. It also means making the best use of peoples' skills, productively and creatively, and working smarter; and, improving productivity by developing the workforce and expanding their know-how, using all finance deployed productively (including achieving an economic level of margin on all finance employed).

Resources are always finite, so there is a need to get full value for money from all resources deployed throughout the enterprise. This concept also embraces the idea of stewardship, which means that SHEs need to take the long view about the impact on their members' future related to non-renewable resources and the impact of their enterprise on the environment.

All forms of enterprises need to run with enough margin between costs and income that allows them to remain viable. Clearly, not-for-profit enterprises do not have the task of securing profit maximization. Managers of SHEs, need to rally their team, build a consensus for the common purpose, and create a culture that supports its achievement.

Some SHEs offer goods or services to their members on a 'cost-plus' basis; members pay the actual cost of buying the goods or services and a share of the administrative costs incurred. Other SHEs set the price that they charge for goods and services in line with those within the market. Any sum of money that is left after covering all operating costs, (including covering any risks involved in conducting the enterprise in generating investment funds to progress the enterprise) is regarded as a 'surplus'.

Decision-makers will make different choices when their aim is resource optimisation. To take an example; if the persons owning the only shop in the village find that they are losing money on the venture, what will they do? In the mindset of profit maximization, they could decide to sell the shop to a house-builder who wants to develop the site, and they may then use the proceeds from the sale to invest in another shop in another town if this would improve their income. In a self-help enterprise, using the mindset of resource optimisation, if the members decide that they want to keep the vital service offered by a village shop they could decide to add other income-earning services (such as a parcel collection service, footwear repairs, dry-cleaning, etc.) and make use of volunteer labour by the members to reduce running costs.

## Distributing surpluses

Surpluses may be distributed to members if they are this will be in relation to the member's participation in generating the surplus; and not in relation to the members' investment in the enterprise. For example, in a consumer co-op, surplus needs to be distributed in relation to each member's spending with the enterprise; and in a worker cooperative in relation to the value of their labour input.

This method of distribution differs from an investor-controlled company, where distributions of profits are shared in proportion to the number of shares held. Sometimes SHEs set aside part of any surplus to support the communities within which the enterprise works or for other purposes agreed by the membership.

It can be difficult to measure the performance of SHEs because many of the benefits are passed directly back to the members. Clearly, the measurement of profit, as used in commercial businesses, is not appropriate in SHEs. The more benefits that are passed directly back to members, by way of better prices or other benefits, then the smaller the resultant surplus will be. Often directors and managers resort to using 'profit' as the measure of performance simply because they have failed to develop the correct ways of measuring results and performance.in SHEs Using the wrong methods of measurement invariably leads to managers working towards the 'wrong' goals.

The results in SHEs need to be expressed as specific outcomes by setting the level of productivity for the resources that are used in achieving these outcomes. Many managers of established SHEs have not been sufficiently educated about the self-help enterprise model. This means that they need to change the way they establish their aims and objectives, and how results are measured. This can be a major challenge for leaders, calling for a change in many of the basic assumptions made by many of the people currently running their enterprise.

Managers in SHEs should be doing more-with-less because resources are always limited, this means getting the best from the people involved in the enterprise by developing more creative ways of working – in other words, working smarter. The productivity of labour in SHEs needs to be at least equal to, or ahead of the industry norms. Gains in productivity can be achieved by skillfully developing the workforce and expanding its competence, whilst at the same time, sharing the gains from productivity fairly.

**The par-value concept**
'Par-value' means that the worth of an item (usually an investment) stays unchanged - the price paid when buying an item stays the same as when was made or purchased when it's sold or cashed-in. In popular parlance, it's said to mean 'a dollar in and a dollar out', However, a dogmatic interpretation of this concept can cause problems for SHEs'. For example, when a member leaves from a worker or a producer co-op and they are to be replaced by a new member unless the true worth of the member's investment in their enterprise is fairly calculated both for the leaving member and new

members. Misinterpreting the par-value concept can also lead to calls for the demutualisation of SHEs.is members are persuaded to find a way of cashing in their investments.

People involved in and advising SHEs, need to consider that 'par-value' means 'equal value'. Fair and equal value is only given when an investment is cashed-in if the proceeds will buy the same amount of resources when it's sold as it did when it was bought; which means taking account of inflation when determining its current worth.

To fully appreciate this approach, requires a more precise understanding of the meaning of the term 'money' and 'wealth'. Wealth means the value of the money that a person owns, plus the value of their assets. People often talk about 'wealth creation' when in fact wealth is rarely created, in most cases wealth is simply transferred between individuals and communities, often by means of deceitful practices.

Those exercising power over others often force transfers of wealth from those people they control, or by manipulating them by a variety of means. People who own physical assets, such as land, property, shares in companies, and other investments can exercise such power. Likewise, those owning brands, patents, copyrights, and other forms of intellectual property, can exercise great power over those without any significant wealth.

### Economic education
All decision-makers in SHEs need guidance as to the economic practices that are acceptable and those which are not. Economic education should be provided throughout SHEs, first targeting all directors, senior managers and other key workers. Education is needed to supply adequate guidance to all those involved in SHEs who make economic decisions at all levels. The provision of a

sound understanding of self-help economic practices and the overall economic system is an indispensable part of the education that needs to be provided for members, member-leaders, managers and staff throughout the enterprise.

### Integration with the management system

The economic system needs to be integral to the overall management system, as well as the system of planning and control, and directly linked to the rewards system. The practices fundamental to the self-help economic system need to be central to how the enterprise is run on a day-to-day basis. Specifically, the KRAs for management need to include the achievement of the outcomes from these economic practices, and KRIs need to be set out that measure performance in these areas.

# 20. THE MANAGEMENT SYSTEM

## The overall management system

This chapter considers the system of management necessary to run a successful self-help enterprise. The objective of the management system is to ensure that the enterprise achieves its purpose and optimises all resources deployed. Whilst the *process* of management in all forms of enterprise is broadly the same, within SHEs the management system should be fundamentally different. Within the management system, many subsystems are needed.

Here the emphasis is on those systems that implement and support the foundations of the self-help model of enterprise. Of course, many other subsystems are indispensable to the enterprise. For example, there are the legal and regulatory obligations of the enterprise, including health and safety standards, employment legislation, food drugs regulations, fire and building regulations, etc. Many of the subsystems needed will vary according to the enterprise's specific markets and industry standards.

## The process of management

Management is about economically using resources to achieve predetermined outcomes. The process of management involves the tasks of planning, organizing, directing, and control (which includes reviewing, adjusting, and re-focusing the enterprise); this process follows a recurring cycle. The management process, in all forms of enterprise, should prioritise ensuring that the enterprise remains fully sustainable, viable, solvent and liquid. Otherwise, all other actions become futile because an enterprise that is financially unsound will soon cease to exist.

It needs to be appreciated that, in addition, management involves setting and maintaining standards of behaviour. These are the standards that are essential if the systems needed are to work in practice, and if a fitting culture is to be sustained.

The management process needs to be conducted within the framework of its distinct form of organization. Each form of enterprise will typically be run using a set of practices, policies and procedures that together comprise the management system.

In SHEs, the management process can begin once the purpose of the enterprise is clearly defined, and the more immediate goals are set. Planning should start at the strategic level, and then at the operational level. Normally, this involves preparing a strategic plan and an annual operating plan. Thereafter, the systems to implement these plans and to control their progress will be activated. This process will be repeated at least annually.

**The fundamentals**

The fundamentals of the self-help enterprise model give direction to the day-to-day running of the enterprise and should drive the design of the management system. Many of the practices essential to the system are very different from those suitable for use in a commercial business. This means that if managers are recruited from other forms of enterprise (including mutant SHEs), they inevitably need reorientation training if they are to work within bona-fide self-help enterprises successfully. Such retraining is even more vital for anyone undertaking a management role at all levels.

**Building the management system**

The directors and senior managers of the enterprise need to define the subsystems needed and set clear objectives for them; formulating a series of practices and the policies needed. It's essential that the overall system and every subsystem is compatible with achieving the purpose and is compliant with the ten foundation practices of SHEs.

The essential subsystems are interdependent and need to work together to achieve the purpose of the enterprise. These include:

1.  Implementing the market intervention strategy
2.  The organization and optimal use of resources
3.  Planning and control
4.  Financial and management accounting
5.  Performance management
6.  Remuneration and rewards
7.  People development
8.  Succession planning
9.  Risk management
10. Regeneration

See *Figure H-20 The management system - an example*

**The practices required**

The practices required to implement the management system include:

### 1. IMPLEMENTING THE MARKET INTERVENTION STRATEGY

The market intervention system will include all the practices necessary to implement the strategy. As explained in *Chapter 10*, these practices will be at the heart of the strategy.

The aim of the resource optimisation system is to ensure that all resources, including people, land, buildings, finance, and intellectual property deployed to achieve the enterprise's purpose. SHEs cannot be content with producing a surplus or maximising profit, or simply ensuring the economic survival of their enterprise. Instead, they need to fulfil their purpose and maintain their viability, whilst at the same time, making the most productive use of all assets. This needs to be closely integrated with the system of performance management, and the remuneration and reward system.

All forms of enterprise, SHEs included, compete in the market for the resources they need to run the enterprise. SHEs need to pay market prices for all the resources that they use within the enterprise, except for the resource of labour if they can call upon their members to work as volunteers. Depending upon their activities, SHEs will need people to run the enterprise, buildings to house their operations, stocks of goods or raw materials, and finance to bridge the gap between their own finance (equity), and the money they need to run the enterprise. All assets deployed need to be utilised so that the costs associated with their use can be fully covered by the income arising from the activities of the enterprise.

Resource optimisation demands the routine measurement of the productivity of all resources and the comparison of this data against relevant criteria. Comparative data can be measured against past performance, by internal comparisons (such as between different departments and outlets) and, most importantly, by 'benchmarking', which means using data that has been exchanged between similar enterprises. However, this should not be limited to data supplied by other SHEs. External benchmarking needs to take place with other forms of enterprises, because SHEs need to match or better all players in the market, competing for both the resources it needs to run the enterprise, and to keep its essential commitment to secure a better deal for its members. In addition, benchmarking can supply the spur to adopt new standards of best practice, and to find innovative ways of improving the productivity of resources.

## 3. PLANNING AND CONTROL

Defining objectives and measuring progress towards their realisation should be a priority for all forms of enterprise. The system for planning and control aims to help set the direction the enterprise shall travel and what outcomes are to be achieved along the way. The control system has to measure what progress is being made towards the strategic aims and meeting the more immediate goals set out in the plan. It needs to show any deviations from the plan and highlight where corrective measures are needed to revert to the plan; or, where conditions have significantly changed, to flag up the need to re-plan.

### 3. 1. Strategic and operational planning

SHEs should concentrate on deciding and delivering those outcomes that will meet the needs of the membership. The planning and control system needs to be 'member-centred', and the methods deployed should be both inclusive and democratic. The planning process in SHEs is not a top-down activity but a two-way process. Regeneration should be central to the strategic planning process, a plan that simply promises more of the same is unlikely to be adequate to sustain the enterprise.

In commercial businesses, the organization is 'the goose that lays the golden egg', which means that it's the future of the business that is paramount; because it's means of money-making for the investors that own it. Consequently, the focus of the planning process in 'businesses' is the organization. Whereas in SHEs, it's the *members' needs* that has to be at the heart of the planning process, and the reason why members have to be fully involved in the process which needs to converge their current and future needs. Central to the planning process is gaining a real understanding of the future that faces members. This means assessing how members are likely to be affected by impending changes in the market and by changes in economic and social conditions. The planning process needs to involve members with the aim of determining the:

1. The threats, opportunities and the obstacles ahead for members.
2. The means of overcoming the threats and obstacles identified.

The outcome should be a plan that sets out what interventions will be made within the market on behalf of the members, and the actions and resources needed. The entire process should give precedence to discovering the future needs of members, not just the needs of the people running the enterprise. The process of planning begins by looking outwards to the overall environment affecting the market and its impact on members, taking account of past interventions and their impact, alongside their current priorities and their longer-term prospects.

The board should then agree on all plans on behalf of the members. The precise arrangements for involving members in the planning process will be inevitably shaped by the scale of the enterprise. Regardless of scale and geographical considerations, with the tools now available, including electronic and internet-based communications, there can be no valid excuse for failing to involve members fully. This means the entire membership can have their say; not just a handful of representatives or activists who often have their own agendas. The process should be a valuable means of finding ways of working more effectively, of learning faster and predicting change.

Both the strategic and operating plans should result in the setting of clear objectives, along with detailed criteria for measuring results. In the absence of clear goals and performance management, the enterprise will simply drift along. In these circumstances, the enterprise will fail to deliver what the members need. Instead, its managers usually resort to setting their own goals, and these may be designed to ensure the preservation or the improvement of their own lifestyles. Invariably, leading the enterprise to shift away from its original aim of serving the best interest of members. When this occurs, the result is typically a mutant enterprise that serves top incumbent managers and a clique of members who are clinging to their elected positions and working to preserve the perks-of-office.

The annual operating plan is primarily conveyed by means of a budget for each part of the enterprise. A budget is a plan expressed in numbers and other fact-based data. Budgets offer the main means of control by the board because management performance can be judged against the plan. Proper control can only be exercised when directors have enough information to ask the right questions and can judge if the answers are at least reasonable, even when not satisfactory.

### 3.2. The process of preparing a budget
The budgeting process enables the management to:

- Think about the purpose of the enterprise and to discover those outcomes that are most vital to members.

- Work out how those outcomes can be best accomplished and to set and quantify the actions needed in physical and financial terms.

- Establish the financial implications of the actions planned.

- Identify the key performance areas and the KRAs in respect of progress toward those outcomes.

- Determine the applicable key result indicators.

### 3.3. The reporting and control system

The reporting and control system compare performance against the budget, and should:

- Measure results against plans.

- Provoke action if results vary from those planned.

- Be critical when setting out realistic plans and securing commitment to the planned outcomes. The figures for the budget should be initially prepared at the lowest level in the decision-making chain. This approach engages those in the front line helping to build their commitment, and substantially increases the chances of successfully achieving the planned outcomes.

- Use 'zero-based budgeting'; this means starting the planning process not by looking back to the past but by looking to the future. Not making any assumptions that the enterprise just repeats what was done last year, the better way is to plan to do what needs to be done to meet the future needs of members. Many people pay homage to the concept of zero-based budgeting, but then revert to using their old method of taking the earlier year's results and then adding or subtracting a bit to take account of forecasted rates of inflation.

## 4. FINANCIAL AND MANAGEMENT ACCOUNTING

Accounting is the process of communicating financial information about an enterprise to its owners, users, and other stakeholders. This information is set out in financial statements and management accounts that show, in money terms, the economic resources under the control of the management, and how and where, these are deployed. The accounting system within an enterprise has three essential jobs; the preparation of periodic financial statements, the preparation of management information that directly aids in decision-making, as well as supporting the auditing process.

Whether the enterprise is simple or complex, the main aim of the accounting system is to keep the enterprise running smoothly. It's difficult to make informed decisions without exact accounting information that allows us to see where the enterprise stands, where it has been, and the trends that can help us to know where it's heading. The accounting system should be a tool that gives information that is readily understood and is presented in a format that highlights the key result areas and the key result indicators.

The accounting system in SHEs needs to do much more than account for the financial aspects of the enterprise. It has to supply details of the benefits that are being provided to members. It should also measure the efficiency of the enterprise, including the use of all resources deployed. Directors and members need to be very suspicious of any accounting methods that are vague or unclear since this usually means that management is either seeking to hide something from the board or don't really know how to manage the enterprise.

### 4.1. Accounting standards

Accounting standards are rules governing how accounts are to be prepared. These standards set levels of disclosure lay down basic accounting principles, define the meanings of terms and specify how numbers should be calculated. The sources of accounting standards include those set out by international accounting bodies, national standards bodies; and the requirements of legislation, including those of appointed regulators of specific industries or types of organization.

It's not unusual for many aspects of accounting standards to vary with the size of the enterprise. For example, most States have separate standards for smaller companies and some other entities. At the time of writing this book, the international statements of recommended practice (SORP) do not properly cover the specific needs of many SHEs. This is because they are specially designed to account for the financial aspects of enterprises, disregarding the accounting needed to measure progress towards the achievement of the purpose of the enterprise. Charities have their own specifically designed SORP; in SHEs, in most cases, they don't yet have a specifically designed set of standards that fully meets their needs; although internationally, credit unions are moving towards having a special SORP.

### 4.2. Financial accounting

All enterprises need to prepare financial accounts as per the accounting standards needed for the specific type of organization. Financial accounts are normally published at least annually, in a set of financial statements which allows those reading them to arrive at an informed opinion as to the financial health of the enterprise. A standard set of accounts, at a minimum, includes:

- a 'balance sheet', which shows the value of everything the enterprise owns, owes, and is owed on the last day of the fiscal year. A balance sheet is a financial statement showing an enterprise's worth at a given point in time by outlining the assets, liabilities, & equity of the enterprise.

- an 'income and expenditure account', (sometimes referred to as 'trading account') which shows the income, running costs and the surplus or loss made over the fiscal year

- notes about the accounts

- a director's report

- an auditor's report

These items will not always be legally necessary in the case of smaller enterprises. Most financial statements are similar for all forms of enterprise, in all cases, it's necessary to adhere to the accounting requirements for specific forms of SHEs, as may be set out in the laws of each country.

The published/statutory accounts should give information to the owners of the enterprise (which in the case of SHEs is the members) about the financial status of the enterprise. The information given by the accounts is needed by directors and managers of the enterprise, as well as by other interested parties. This includes taxation authorities, bankers, trade creditors and the providers of any loans to the enterprise, such as mortgage companies and other external lenders or investors. In addition, the accounts may be called for by any grant giving bodies that may have supported the enterprise, prospective members, current and prospective employees, any trade union acting for employees, and any relevant regulatory authorities, such as the government department responsible for the registration and supervision of the distinct types of SHEs.

The financial accounts should tell the reader whether the enterprise is running with a surplus or a loss, is viable or not, is self-sustaining, is liquid or not, and the enterprise is solvent or insolvent. In addition, these accounts will reveal to what extent the enterprise is over-dependent upon external finance. It's imperative to appreciate that the financial statements by themselves will only inform readers about the financial health of the enterprise, and in the case of SHEs, provide very little information about the effectiveness of the enterprise in terms of it fulfilling its purpose. It's essential to be aware that the statutory accounts (those required by law) will not normally include any budgetary information or anything else that tells members about how effective their enterprise is at delivering the outcomes that members want.

### 4.3. Management accounting

Management accounting is concerned with the provision and use of accounting information that will help directors, managers and members within the enterprise to undertake their control and management tasks and provide them with the information to make informed decisions. A major element of the management accounting system, in all forms of enterprise, is the planning, budgeting and reporting system.

In investor-owned companies, investors gain directly from the financial performance of their company. Therefore, its owners will find most of the facts that they need to know from the regular financial statements. In SHEs, the owner/members receive their primary benefit from the results of the market interventions that their enterprise undertakes on their behalf so most of the important things that they need to know can only be supplied by the management accounts, alongside other information supplied by the directors and senior managers. Therefore, the management accounts of SHEs should record what member benefits are being created, and tangible evidence of the progress towards achieving the enterprise's purpose.

### 4.4. Auditing

The process of auditing supports the verification of accounts and the finding of errors within a given period. Auditing will enhance the level of confidence of the full range of users of the financial statements. Financial audits are usually performed by qualified accountants, who are the external auditors and experts in financial reporting. External auditors are needed to express a view about the validity of the financial statements and may issue a certificate subject to qualification when they are not fully satisfied. The financial audit is one of many assurance services supplied by accounting firms. Many organizations separately employ or hire internal auditors, who do not attest to financial reports but instead concentrate on providing internal controls. In the case of SHEs, auditors are bound to report to members any significant items that do not meet the relevant legislation. Directors and members need to study their auditors' report, and then decide if the report raises issues that call for any further investigation and reporting.

The directors arrange for the choice and appointment of external auditors, which have to be confirmed by the members, in a way that will ensure their independence and competence. The directors should see to it that all necessary procedures and systems of internal audit are in operation to protect the assets of the enterprise. The role of auditors and auditing in the system of governance is considered in *Chapter 22.*

### 4.5. Accounting practices

Leaders and members need to know that all accounting has to be undertaken according to the following standards:

- On a continuing basis, as this affects the valuation of buildings, machinery, redundancy costs etc.

- With consistency, to prevent manipulation of the numbers by selective changes in the approach to accounting, which may involve placing a monetary value upon research and development, stock valuations, or debtor provision, for example.

- On a prudent basis, so income and surpluses are not counted before they have come in, which would be imprudent. It's prudent to consider losses which have arisen or are likely to arise, after the year-end and these have to be accounted for, based on the knowledge that is available to the board up until the date of signing-off the accounts.

- On an accrual's basis, including all transactions that relate to the actual accounting period. This may be different from the sums of cash paid and received during the same period.

- By separate valuation of assets and liabilities, it's necessary to prevent the practice of offsetting, for example, where both good and bad investments are put together in one group to disguise the fact that some are non-performing.

## 5. PERFORMANCE MANAGEMENT

The aims of the performance management system are to ensure that the enterprise pursues its purpose, highlights deviations from this path, and on a day-to-day basis, make sure that planned outcomes are in fact realised, and that the optimisation of all resources deployed is achieved. Performance management spotlights the performance of the enterprise in each department and section. In addition, measuring the contribution of managers and other workers throughout the enterprise, where this can be used to chart the effectiveness or otherwise of the systems and processes in use by the enterprise.

### 5.1. Empowering people to get results

In most large SHEs, leading a team towards achieving the enterprise's objectives will mean leading people who are themselves the leaders of smaller teams. The main job of the chief manager becomes that of giving a context within which creative management can take place at all levels within the enterprise. The most successful managers are those able to keep a balance between the individual flair and creativity of their people and the systems essential for achieving the objectives of the enterprises. The chief manager needs to have the capacity to construct the kind of environment necessary to get the management team to work positively towards the enterprise's purpose as a precursor; the board needs to generate the kind of climate that will allow the chief manager to work creatively.

The future of all kinds of organizations depends on their ability to attract, keep and deploy creative people; these are people need to feel empowered to do their jobs. The enterprise depends heavily on its managers' ability to get other people involved and committed. Instead of coming to work to receive instructions and be controlled by successive layers of supervision, the managers, and the workforce, in general, need to share a vision of the enterprise's future and they need to perceive that this as part of the culture of the organization.

Regrettably, many enterprises have become masked in hypocrisy, with the members' leaders mouthing platitudes about democracy, equality, and human values; while their managers are pursuing their own agendas designed to maximise personal benefits from the enterprise. All concerned need to be constantly on guard against allowing this kind of culture to drive out the positive culture required.

The creative management and empowerment of individuals can only take place within the framework of clear objectives and the strategies to achieve them. There needs to be a set of systems holding the organization together and keeping it on track. Some people mistakenly believe that empowerment means letting people do things in their own way, in effect, the management abdicating their responsibilities for directing and controlling the enterprise. It does mean granting a great deal of freedom to act and delegating decision-making to the person who should deal with a problem or take advantage of an opportunity. Empowerment is only possible in the context of shared vision with understood aims and common values converted into practice. Individuals need to be backed by the systems, resources, and psychological support that only a skilled team manager can provide.

### 5.2. Key result areas and key result indicators

It's essential that managers are judged against relevant performance criteria, and that the KRIs deployed are directly related to the KRAs needed to deliver the enterprise's purpose. Concurrently, salaries and other rewards ought to be geared towards achieving these objectives. Directors should understand what kind of information is needed, and the key management ratios are appertaining to the trades, industries, or services in which their enterprise is involved.

Leaders of SHEs need to start by prioritising the goals of their enterprise and by measuring to what extent they are achieving its required results. Otherwise, people simply revert to the practices of commercial businesses, where the only result that counts is the amount of profit gained. Even in commercial businesses, where profit is rightly their purpose, there does need to be limits on how this is achieved. Too many businesses pursue profit to the limits, set by the boundaries provided by criminal laws.

When the directors of an enterprise run away from the task of setting clear objectives they sentence their enterprise to behave like the proverbial 'headless chicken'. Directors can often be diverted from this vital task by those who do not want the enterprise to be too clearly directed because this limits their opportunity to pursue their own, individual agendas. There are those who want to set quasi-objectives to be measured against vague criteria relating to a social audit. Such separate exercises can have their uses, but they are no substitute for a fully integrated management system that sets objectives, develops strategies for their achievement, and defines operational objectives.

## 6. REMUNERATION AND REWARDS

The success of SHEs depends upon the alignment of the interests of all those involved in running the enterprise. There cannot be any compromise about something that is so fundamental, so those who are committed to any conflicting agenda should have no part to play in the enterprise. The remuneration and reward system (The R&R system) is a vital tool to be used in securing the alignment of the interests of all the people involved in the enterprise.

### 6.1. The objectives of the R&R system

The objectives of the R&R system are to support the achievement of the purpose and to optimise the use of all resources. The system needs to motivate all the people involved in the enterprise, including members, directors, managers, and employees. This requires that the system only rewards people that truly help the enterprise to achieve its purpose and is essentially fair to everyone involved.

Where managers do not deliver the required results, the root of the problem often lies with the absence of clear-cut objectives and associated measures of performance. It's not unusual for the Chief manager and the management team to be allowed to set their own performance criteria, usually borrowed from commercial businesses, and not tailored specifically to meet the needs of SHEs. Without KRIs that are directly related to achieving the enterprise's, purpose causes severe problems for SHEs, because if the rewards system is geared towards achieving profit maximisation, there will be no chance that the enterprise will ever achieve its purpose. It's essential that the R&R system is geared towards achieving the aims and. outcomes set for the enterprise. Therefore, defining objectives and measuring attainment has to be a priority for all SHEs, for without this framework nothing else makes much sense. It's not unusual to find SHEs using R&R systems that reward people for doing exactly the opposite of what is needed.

The planned results need to be set-out by finding the specific outcomes to be achieved and the levels of productivity of the resources. Managers and other employees behave no differently from other human beings, if they have a bonus scheme that is tied to sales growth, or any another result that is not directly linked to delivering benefits to their members, then that is where their energies are likely to be targeted. In short, it needs to be clear that all financial incentives are fully aligned with their members' interests.

### 6.2. Achieving fairness in the system

Fairness is a vital feature of any successful R&R system. When managers base their decisions upon short-term gains, this ignores the fact that a stewardship view is what is needed in most cases. While excessive rewards may motivate a few top earners, the full cost of such high rewards needs to take account of the costly effect of demotivating the rest of the workforce, and other stakeholders both inside and outside of the enterprise. Where the members believe that payments to top managers are overgenerous, this can undermine the director's commitment to their enterprise because it's often perceived to be unfair to member-directors, members and other employees.

There are many people who believe that those who are only motivated by money cannot be trusted. As an example, this point of view has recently been given credence by the unprincipled behaviour of many highly-paid bankers. Nevertheless, the idea that money entirely motivates top managers is demeaning if it were true this would mean that people should never trust them because mercenaries will always go where the rewards are highest, and job satisfaction plays no role in their decisions to work for a specific organization. Experience shows that across the spectrum of diverse types of SHEs, there are many managers being paid below their market value, but they have chosen to work in SHEs because they feel that they are achieving a higher level of job satisfaction. There are also some managers in SHEs who would not realistically command the level of salaries that they imagine they are worth in other enterprises.

It needs to be remembered that the people who lead and manage SHEs also have a duty to their families and other dependants. This can result in them being pressured to move on to positions that yield higher incomes if they are perceived to be being paid at rates below the market-worth for their ability, time, and commitment. Fair rewards and recognition are needed if SHEs are to keep good people. SHEs cannot afford to employ people who are simply looking for their main-chance, people solely motivated by an ambition to become part of a wealthy élite.

### 6.3. Constructive practices

A set of practices that, together, can give a constructive framework for such a system is likely to include that:

- All payments are directly linked to the contribution made, as confirmed by the achievement of specific outcomes.

- Payments are set considering the current market rate for the experience and skills needed.

- The basis for deciding levels of payment is open and transparent, avoiding any possibility of favouritism.

- A generic set of procedures is followed in implementing the R&R system which is open to scrutiny.

- Upper limits are set for managers' rewards packages, based upon a multiple of the average payment made to the general workforce, or on the gap between the highest and lowest hourly rate of pay.

## 7. PEOPLE DEVELOPMENT

Probably the single most damaging mistake made by leaders of SHEs has been their unwillingness to invest sufficiently in developing the people involved in running their enterprises. Often, when SHEs have spent money on education and training, so much has been wasted on activities that have done little to develop their power to deliver life-changing benefits to their members. Frequently, whatever education has been provided too often has been only theoretical. In most cases, what the people involved in running SHEs need to grasp the essential practical tools needed to carry out their specific roles. Only rarely has enough attention been given to securing an enduring understanding of the markets in which their enterprise is involved, or in providing practical guidance about the application of the self-help enterprise model.

It's counter-productive to conduct education and training for members and staff unless the directors and the senior management team have themselves achieved a correct understanding of the self-help enterprise model. All new members and employees need to be given at least a basic induction programme upon joining the enterprise. Directors and senior managers need to undertake a full induction before being let-loose within a self-help enterprise. The aims of the people development system should be to ensure that all those involved in the enterprise are equipped to make the greatest contribution towards achieving the aims of the enterprise. This applies equally to members, their representatives and employees, at all levels. Ensuring that people can fulfil future vacancies and roles is most important so needs to be closely linked to the succession planning system.

### 7.1. Sound practices

The following practices can be expected to be part of the system:

- All employees/members undertake induction and refresher programmes so that they fully understand the self-help enterprise model; there can be no exemptions for directors or senior managers.

- All training and education given or funded by SHEs recognise that people require the specific professional skills to fulfil their responsibilities as well as understanding that their main objectives of the enterprise.

- The directors and managers of the enterprise receive regular briefings about the standard of behaviour expected from them, particularly in respect to the equitable treatment of members and all other stakeholders. Regularly emphasising the kind of trickery and marketing ploys used by many commercial businesses that are not acceptable within SHEs.

- Ethical dealings and honest communication need to be regarded as the norm for all people involved in the enterprise, and the policies designed to make this happen need to be supported by adequate supervision, and by the remuneration and rewards system. With re-training being given to improving behaviour continually and in the case of default, sanctions applied when their behaviour does not improve.

## 8. SUCCESSION PLANNING

Succession planning is a process for finding and developing people with the capability to fill key posts, including all leadership roles in the enterprise, it encompasses both member-leaders and senior managers. The system seeks to sustain the enterprise by making sure that enough people with the required competencies and qualities are available to fill all key post as they arise. It will help identify where external recruitment is likely to be needed so that steps can be taken to prepare people for upcoming vacancies and for any new positions planned. The aim is to develop a pool of talent, rather than to create 'crown-princes/princesses' in waiting.

This system needs to be closely aligned with the strategic planning process.

The following practices are likely to be part of the system:

- Detailing all key posts throughout the enterprise, including professional and democratic roles, and also mapping the vacancies along a timeline.

- Enlarging the size of the pool of talent available for each post by offering specific development programmes to cover future vacancies, in line with the people development system.

- Pinpointing those individuals within the enterprise who have the capability to undertake the projected vacancies. Preparing personal development plans, including the provision of mentoring, for all those showing the skills and aptitudes needed.

- Preparing members of the wider community to undertake key roles within the enterprise, by providing briefings and general education programmes that explain the role of their enterprise in the community and the basics of the self-help enterprise model

## 9. RISK MANAGEMENT

Life is inherently unpredictable and the occurrence of extreme events, such as major natural disasters, are not always with our power to predict. So, when planning, it's necessary to prepare to face the unexpected. Risk management is the process of finding, analysing, and responding to risk factors throughout the enterprise. Such risks range from general risks to assets (such as fire, flood, accidents or criminal activity) to those risks that arise from the activities of the enterprise. For example, the risk of a food poisoning event occurring in any enterprise that is producing, processing, or handling food; or outbreaks of disease or infestations in animals or agricultural products.

Most enterprises will be subject to very specific hazards, often including those that that could destroy the enterprise if not well managed. In the case of some risks, insurance cover can mitigate the risk. Even where risk is covered by insurance, the cost of this can be prohibitive, unless sound policies are in place to remove the impact of such risks. Sound risk management will reduce not only the likelihood of an event occurring but the size of its impact. The risk management system needs to be designed to do more than just show the risk; it has to quantify the risk and help to predict the impact of that risk. Decisions sometimes need to be made as to whether any specific risk is unacceptable if so a decision needs are taken to abort the activity that gives rise to the risk.

Risk management needs to be undertaken as a continuous, disciplined process of problem identification and resolution. Surprises will be diminished when the emphasis is on proactive rather than reactive management.

In commercial businesses, if their customers or suppliers fail due to an unpredicted event, it may or may not affect them, while in SHEs, any risk to its members often becomes a risk that also impacts their enterprise because members and their SHEs are often inseparable. One of the most valued benefits provided by many SHEs to their members is helping their members to mitigate their risks. When designing the risk management system for SHEs, full account needs to be taken of the risks facing their members and how those risks can be best managed.

## 10. REGENERATION

Regeneration means renewal through the internal processes of a body or system. SHEs need to deploy a system of regeneration, otherwise when changes take place within their markets, and in the economic and social environment, they may be too slow to respond. This may result in their failure to continue to be relevant to the needs of their members and, so they become side-lined. For example, SHEs need to constantly re-evaluate their market intervention strategy and the systems needed to implement it. In addition, there has to be a systematic review of all systems and the practice that underlie them. Regeneration should be linked directly to the strategic planning process, as well as being built-in to the design of all systems throughout the enterprise.

The aim of the regeneration system is to ensure that the organization changes whenever necessary to maintain the enterprise's relevance to both current and prospective members. The practices needed to achieve this aim will usually include:

- Policy audits are regularly conducted to ensure compliance, and to show where changes are needed.

- The design of all systems includes provision for their systematic review.

- The strategic planning process starts with the assumption that regeneration will become necessary and needs to be considered as the plan is developed. A key task of the oversight body is to scrutinise the strategic plan to confirm that it makes adequate provision for regeneration.

# *Figure H-20 The management system – an example*

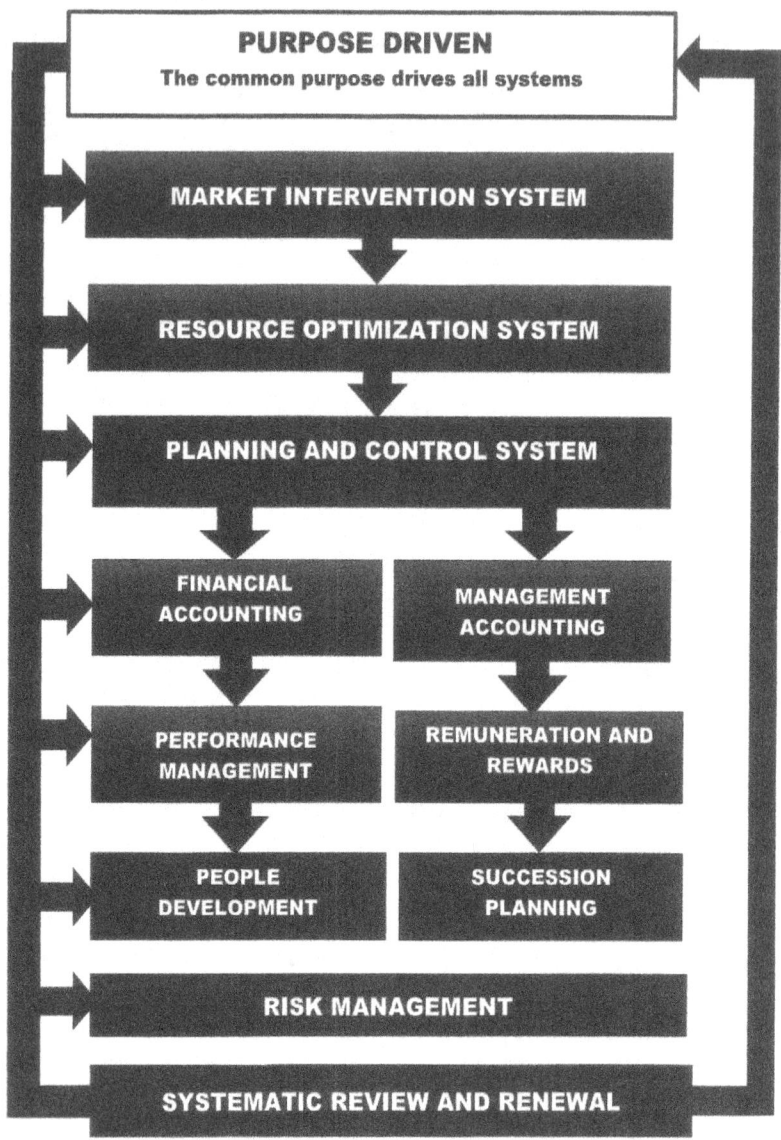

# 21. DEMOCRATIC CONTROL

## The objective

This chapter deals with the system of democratic control within SHEs; this is an important subsystem of the system of association. SHEs have to be democratically-controlled because, where they cease to be subject to democratic control they inevitably stop working in the best interest of their members. The objective of the democratic control system is to ensure that effective control is maintained, and the enterprise is run in the best interest of the membership in its entirety.

## Democracy

Democracy supplies an alternative to conflict, by offering a mutual approach in place of adversarial ways of behaving. Democracy is by no means a perfect system, but when compared to the alternatives it's the best system available. When democracy is not working effectively, this usually occurs because all the practices necessary to make it work are not in place.

It needs to be kept in mind that in many organizations there are people who have a personal stake in preventing democracy from working properly. In SHEs, democratic control is a means to an end, and not an end in its self. It's a crucial element in SHEs because effective democratic control is a prerequisite to ensuring that the enterprise serves its members and achieves its purpose.

## Democratic decision-making

Sometimes, many of the people managing SHEs are disparaging about the impact of democratic control on the enterprise. The detractors of democracy often ignore the reality, which is that democratic decision-making can often improve both the quality and accuracy of decisions. Sound decisions are made when competing arguments are considered before arriving at a consensus, or if this fails, by resorting to a majority decision.

The process of decision-making is usually enhanced when a mix of talents are brought together, and a diversity of experiences enters the equation. This includes those differences that arise from personal identities, such as gender, cultural heritage or race. Diversity can help provide useful differences in the problem-solving approaches used, adding value to the process.

Increasingly, scientists, professionals, and other people facing big problems collaborate in interdisciplinary teams, and when people are diverse, they regularly outperform groups of the smartest conformist individuals. More creative decision-making will help to lessen the impact of uncertainty, complexity, and change. This is regardless of whether our enterprises are small or large.

The opinions of specialists and experts are obviously important, and even more so when it comes to scientific and technical matters, but when it comes to broad issues, which are usually among the more important matters, the opinions of ordinary people, who can take an overview of the situation, are often much more relevant in arriving at the 'best' decision. Often, specialist professionals will favour a decision that defends the interest of their profession, rather than one that is in the best interest of a wider community. Specialists characteristically deride democracy when it does not suit their own interests, and sometimes when they do not get others to accept their advice, they should be responding by presenting their case in terms that ordinary people can understand.

Democratically, empowered citizens should make all the big decisions that affect the citizens of the State. In the same way, the members make all the most important decisions affecting the members of SHEs. The example provided by the jury system, which plays a vital role in the administration of justice, supplies a reminder of why 'experts' alone, are not to be left to make decisions about really important matters.

### The importance of member-control
During the 18th and 19th centuries, the mass of people in many countries began to grasp that they could not rely upon anyone but themselves to make the changes needed to secure far-reaching improvements in their lives. Those setting up early SHEs recognised that democratic control was essential because unless SHEs are under genuine member-control, they cannot be relied on to deliver the benefits that members need from their enterprise.

When a group of people set up an enterprise with the aim of serving their mutual interests, the only guarantee they have that the enterprise will constantly be committed to this purpose is that it remains under member-control. SHEs face many threats to the maintenance of democratic member-control from both within and outside the enterprise. Internally, from groups of members pursuing a personal agenda or from senior managers. Externally, member-control is under threat from those having a financial stake in the enterprise or those who are conniving to secure such a stake, as well as from people with a partisan political agenda, and in some countries from the State itself.

SHEs need protection from all the many threats to their sovereignty. Protection needs to be inbuilt within their rules and within the specific laws catering for SHEs. In a lot of countries, the laws relating to SHEs are far from adequate, this means that the law cannot be relied upon to protect members from the threats they face. In practice, the comprehensive application of the self-help enterprise model supplies the best protection of the rights of grassroots members. In many SHEs member-control has been lost and needs to be re-established. The first step in this process is for members to gain a clear understanding of the self-help enterprise model. In many countries, changes in legislation will be needed before SHEs can be genuinely member-controlled.

## Forms of democratic control

Members of SHEs often have very different ideas about what is meant by 'democratic control' and its application within their enterprise. A collective understanding of the meaning of 'democracy' in any specific self-help enterprises needs to be established. There are sometimes diverging views as to how, and to what extent members should take part in managing, directing, and controlling their enterprise.

There are three main systems of democratic control. The first is 'direct democracy', which is usually only suitable in small-scale organizations, and uses when this is desired and where it's practical for all individual members to be involved in making decisions about the day-to-day operations. Individuals, in even the smallest of organizations, do not always achieve the level of involvement needed, and may sometimes expect more than even direct democracy can deliver. It's worth remembering that, in practice, when everybody is responsible, then often nobody will take responsibility.

The second is 'populist' democratic control, in this system individuals are voted directly to senior management roles. This is widely practised in the USA, where direct elections are often used to select people for positions such as chief of police, the mayor of the town or city, and the superintendent of schools. In some UK cities, the practice of having directly-elected mayors and police commissioners could well bring the populist system into wider use. This approach has some very serious drawbacks when used in SHEs, not least because it can result in senior manager roles becoming politicised; or, in enterprises being run by people voted into office based on their celebrity status rather than on their ability to do the job.

The third system is 'representative democracy'; this is the method most widely used within SHEs. In this system, members elect representatives to carry out a variety of roles within their enterprise. Such elected representatives will normally appoint professional managers and administrators to carry out the day-to-day running of the enterprise. Representative democracy calls for the separation of powers between people undertaking different elected roles within the enterprise. This system, if it is to work properly, requires the deployment of a range of inbuilt checks and balances.

Whatever the system of democracy, at the very least it should supply mechanisms for controlling the excesses of those in positions of power. In addition, there need to be procedures in place for the replacement of under-performing leaders, and for retaining the commitment of people. This also means member involvement in all major decisions about the future of their enterprise. Democracy is not a static system; it needs to adapt to meet changing circumstances; yet, it should always remain rooted in the practice of equivalence, because SHEs are 'associations of *equal* persons.

## Democratic rights and responsibilities

When referring to democracy in the context of a self-help

enterprise, is not just about democratic rights; such rights are to be balanced alongside the responsibilities of membership. In a democratic system member are entitled to:

- Exercise ultimate control, which rests with a governing body chosen from and by the membership; typically, this will be a general meeting open to all members

- Elect their representatives and member-leaders, to rescind their delegated powers and recall their elected officials, as set out within the rules governing the enterprise

- Scrupulously fair and transparent arrangements for all elections

- Arrange for the monitoring and auditing of all aspects of the enterprise

- Be consulted on all major plans and policy issues

- Have access to all relevant information. However, some information may be excluded from the public domain if it could be damaging to the overall interests of the membership. Even so, this information should never be hidden from those that the members appointed to exercise oversight on their behalf.

- Be given help in improving their collective capacity to take part in the democratic process.

- Have equal opportunities, without discrimination, to stand for any office for which they are qualified.

- Ask questions about the running of their enterprise, and to have them honestly answered.

- Register complaints, and to petition the directors on any matter concerning their enterprise.

- Change or amend the rules, with the agreement of an enhanced majority of the members.

In a democratic system, members have duties to perform, including:

- Voting in elections and holding representatives to account
- Participating in the affairs of their enterprise, especially in the strategic planning process
- Abiding by the rules of the enterprise
- Act always with integrity and fairness.

## The impact of scale and coverage

Many SHEs that started in a small way have grown into large and complex organizations, often outstripping the abilities of their elected leaders and current managers; and also, their ability to finance their expanding operations. The pressure to deliver economic benefits to members inevitably results in them pursuing economies of scale. These might be achieved through mergers between smaller enterprises, or via amalgamation with a larger enterprise, but in the process, many of the fundamental characteristics of a self-help enterprise are often lost.

Organizations that were once small, local, and based upon a system of direct democracy can run into problems when they grow. So often they discover the need to change their system of democracy to one based on representatives acting on behalf of members. To achieve this conversion successfully calls for both committed leaders and the full involvement of the membership. The best scale for SHEs is one that balances the economies of scale within the framework needed to support an effective system of democratic- control; see *Chapter 12*.

## Roles and duties

If representative democracy is to work properly in a large-scale enterprise, then the following roles are typically needed:

- **Member representatives** – should act as a conduit for two-way communication between members and the leadership, and may involve them providing scrutiny of leaders on behalf of members

- **Member-directors** – are tasked with achieving the purpose of the enterprise by developing, overseeing, and implementing strategies, plans, policies, and procedures, and scrutinising the actions of senior managers.

- **Oversight board members** – undertake their duties on behalf of the members, and are responsible for ensuring that the leaders and managers are fixed upon achieving the agreed purpose of the enterprise, and are always working in the best interest of the membership in its entirety

- **Executive directors** (full-time professionals) - may share some of the duties with member-directors, and in law, they may be considered de facto directors of the enterprise and have the same responsibilities. This as well as having the day-to-day responsibility for conducting the activities of the enterprise. Executive directors may or may not be members.

It should be clear that the main task of member-directors of SHEs is to secure the achievement of whatever the members want from their enterprise. What they don't want is an organization that will 'rip-them-off', or if given the opportunity, to make a quick-profit which usually ends up in the pockets of those running the enterprise.

In a larger scale SHEs, an alternative to multilayers of committees, which often have no decision-making powers, needs to be developed. The election of locally based 'envoys' could be an alternative, with them having the role of facilitating the two-way communication between the grassroots members and the board of the enterprise. The roles of all jobs within the democratic process should be set out in a job description including the qualifications (not merely academic or professional) needed for each specific role.

## The professionalisation of democratic roles

In recent times, there has been a transition from a tradition of having unpaid or 'expenses-only' representatives and directors, to having members paid to undertake all types of roles within their enterprise. Many of these roles have become sinecures, occupied by individuals that keep their positions by dint of the practice of patronage and cronyism.

Whenever paid democratic roles are considered in SHEs, clear rules and systems, have to be in place to ensure that all posts are open to all members based on merit. The election of members to undertake such roles should be made by an informed electorate. All those seeking paid office need to show evidence that they have, at the very least, a proper understanding of the self-help enterprise model, the dynamics of the markets in which their enterprise is to intervene, and a proper understanding of the systems needed to plan, finance, manage and control them. Although, the rules of some SHEs set out standards for would-be candidates, in many cases the rules need to be strengthened to debar opportunists.

Sometimes, there is a requirement to undertake training courses prior to being eligible to stand as a candidate, but in all cases, the relevance and the quality of all training need to be designed to empower members to carry out their roles. In many cases, stricter standards for would-be candidates for office are needed, but this should not be used to filter out people that do not fit a preconceived view of the kind or class of person favoured. Greater emphasis may need to be placed upon the acquisition of the 'hard-skills' needed, such as a clear understanding of the dynamics of the market, the comprehension of management information, and the use of statistical data.

SHEs cannot ignore the fact that many of the people putting themselves forward for leadership roles in SHEs do not have the competence to undertake the role. Members who have had limited experience, need to be supplied with the skills and attitudes required to do the job properly. Job descriptions are essential for all posts, and their performance measured and reported to the electorate. At the same time, members' leaders need to show a real passion for securing a fair and honest deal for their members, and, most critically, be persons of the highest integrity; *see Chapter 13*.

### Constituencies and voting systems

Members' representatives are sometimes given the role of serving a specific constituency of the membership. Traditionally, this has been based on a geographic area or region, but in many SHEs representation is based upon the roles and activities, or the special interests of groups of members. Whatever their constituencies, the basis of representation should be reviewed on a regular basis, to ensure that they accurately reflect the various segments of the membership.

Voting systems in SHEs are typically based upon a first-past-the-post system, where the candidate who has the most votes is declared the winner of the election. Although, there is now some interest in other systems, such as a transferable vote system; under this system, no one is chosen until one candidate secures more than

50% of the ballots cast. Candidates with the fewest votes are dropped from the list, and their votes are distributed to the remaining candidates, based upon the voters' second choice. The choice of proportional representation, by which candidates are chosen based on the proportion of votes cast for a political party, is usually regarded as unsuitable for use in SHEs because it can create factionalism, which tends to destroy the essential cohesion and consensus needed for SHEs to succeed.

In practice, many elections are conducted by supplying the members with a list of candidates. Members are then entitled to cast as many votes as there are vacancies, but no more than one vote for any individual. The persons voted in are those on the list with the highest number of votes. This system does not always give a satisfactory way of reflecting the members' choices, because members typically vote tactically, for one or two favourites to avoid boosting the vote of their lower-rated choices.

**The value of time**
In bygone days, people were often glad to become involved in a self-help enterprise, not just to gain access to a service or other member-benefits, but often it gave people the opportunity to become part of a wider social group. Attending meetings and taking part in various committees, often provided a welcome relief from the isolation of rural life or the tedium that many faced in the days before the wide range of entertainment and leisure pursuits now available. Today, people value their time more than ever before, and the pressures on time will surely increase in the future. People will seek to increase their economic well-being, but it can be expected that there will be an even greater emphasis on enhancing their quality of life, and this will entail not spending time doing things they would rather not do.

There is a growing impatience with meetings for the sake of meetings, and with organizations that waste their time with needless bureaucratic processes. Democracy may be a wonderful and necessary thing, but the novelty can soon wear-off if it doesn't result in better services, better value-for-money and improved responsiveness to members' specific needs. What most people now want is less hassle and less wasted time. People are now most likely to judge the relevance of SHEs to their lives against criteria that include whether it's worthwhile investing their time, effort, and savings, in them.

## Changing what needs to change

All forms of enterprise need to adjust in response to the changes taking place within their markets; otherwise, they become irrelevant. In the case of SHEs, if they do not evolve, they soon cease to enjoy the support of their members. The ability to change needs to be inbuilt within the enterprise so that both the democratic system and the market intervention strategy are changed whenever they need to respond to the changes taking place both within the market in which they work and within the fabric of society.

In many SHEs, essential changes to the democratic system are not being made because the present arrangements suit the people that are the current post-holders. This is particularly the case where elected members are paid and are in receipt of other perks of their position. It's vital to ensure that all democratic practices are regularly reviewed, to assess their current usefulness and relevance. There are a variety of current practices that will impair the quality of the democratic control process these include:

- An over-emphasis of the views of the articulate members, and those with the 'time' to participate.

- Members often confuse the roles of representation, policy-making and management action – and fail to provide proper oversight of those running their enterprise.

- Elected members being unable to play a proper part in the policy-making and direction of their enterprise unless they have the ability, professional support, the time, and the necessary information to make effective decisions. Meetings can be dominated by people who simply 'turn-up and spout'. Instead, members need to be schooled so that they come to meetings properly prepared to express their views.

- Members, once selected, tend to want to hold onto power regardless of the level of their effectiveness, and the procedures are not always in place to remove them when they are ineffective. Limits may be placed on the number of consecutive terms any member can serve.

- If steps are not taken to develop the available talent, and to implement a system of compensation for the time devoted to the affairs of the enterprise, then the only people holding office will be those with an adequate pension or other unearned income, with the result that the enterprise becomes short of new blood and creative thinking.

- Arrangements are seldom made to subject all involved to adequate scrutiny.

- The main threat to the effectiveness of the process of democratic control arises when people are selected who are driven by their prejudices, including those based on religion, partisan politics and other single-issue causes.

**Practices that support sound democratic control**

The system provides the means for getting the best out of all the people involved in the democratic process. Practices that help sustain and enhance democratic control include:

- All members being routinely made aware of their rights and responsibilities, which is best promoted in the format of a 'members' charter.

- The rules of the enterprise provide adequate protection against threats to the sovereignty of the enterprise and sustain the equivalence of all members.

- The overall direction and policy-making of the enterprise are in the hands of persons appointed by, and responsible to, the membership, and that the majority are fully-qualified members of the enterprise.

- The membership makes all significant decisions about the purpose, outcomes, and the rules of the enterprise.

- An oversight board elected by and reporting directly to the membership, ensures that the enterprise consistently pursues its purpose, and stays under democratic control; to this end ensuring that enough qualified candidates come forward and that all elections are actively contested

- Setting limits on all fees for members' representatives, and for all other benefits. The board should set these, subject to the final scrutiny by the membership at an AGM.

- The performance of all post-holders is subjected to regular scrutiny, and the completion of an annual report, which should be made available to the membership. Members need to learn to judge and select their leaders based on the results that they achieve, and the practices and standards that they follow.

- Fixed limits on the number of terms that any elected member may serve in any given post need to be fixed.

**The overall system for democratic control**
The system of democratic control requires a set of subsystems these include:

- **A member information system** - giving all necessary information to allow members to watch over and control their enterprise. Including, a schedule of regular reports, meetings and elections; making full use of media and electronic communications, developing a well-informed electorate. Providing equal access to the membership, standardised election addresses, the prohibition of external funding or partisan political or religious endorsements.

- **Decision-Making, consultation, and feedback system** – supporting the conduct of members' meetings; including, standing orders for the conduct of all forms of meetings, embracing those using all forms of electronic communications, and supporting a regular dialogue with members.

- **A system that ensures free and fair elections**, by supporting the proper conduct of elections, and where necessary, giving external validation of the propriety of the arrangements.

- **A member training and development system**, for both incumbent and prospective directors, oversight board members, and all other members' representatives. Supplying induction programmes for members to ensure that all have the competence to fulfil their respective roles.

- **A remuneration and rewards system, which covers all elected posts** - giving a transparent method of rewarding those members that carry out the duties of directors and other roles on behalf of members. Such rewards to be entirely fair in relation to the demands made upon such members and only paid if they meet the criteria laid down for the role.

- **A system that ensures arrangements are in place for the oversight of the board and senior managers**. When necessary, providing for the removal of persons not acting in the members' best interests or who are proved to be self-serving or ineffective.

- **A support system for all elected office-holders** – offering access to an independent secretariat and professional advice to support all member-directors.

- **A member engagement system** – including a set of practices to ensure the full involvement of members in decision-making and in the strategic planning process; including, regularly reviewing the rules of the enterprise, its purpose and specific planned outcomes; and, monitoring progress towards their achievement.

- **A system for measuring and controlling the costs** involved in the operation of the system of democratic control and ensuring that this is true value-for-money. The democratic costs need to be quantified, and practices need to be changed whenever shown that they do not work.

# 22. GOVERNANCE AND OVERSIGHT

## Corporate governance

Governance, often called 'corporate governance', is all about the exercise of authority and control within an organization as a corporate entity. The governance system encompasses the overall direction, management and control of the enterprise, and the relationships between all the people involved. The way that power and control are exercised is crucial to both their current performance and long-term future.

This chapter explores the system required to sustain sound governance within SHEs, including the arrangements to provide effective oversight; this is referred to separately because for SHEs it's such a vital part of the system.

The governance system is a matter of concern not only to the members, directors, and managers in the enterprise but is of concern for all parties having dealings with the enterprise. For example, employees, creditors, bankers and other stakeholder groups, and especially those supplying finance or extending credit to the enterprise. A sound system of governance supplies the basis for securing the level of confidence that is essential if people are to place their money at risk within the enterprise.

## Inadequate laws

The framework of an enterprise's governance system will be stipulated within the rules; these have to comply with any requirements specified in the relevant legislation. If such legislation is in any way inadequate, this could mean that the most effective system of governance may not be available. SHEs that are held back by inadequate legislation urgently need to combine with other SHEs to lobby for the introduction of better laws.

**Designing the governance system**
The system of governance is designed to ensure that:
- The enterprise stays under fully effective member control.
- High standards of management accountability are maintained.
- Openness and transparency prevail between managers and the board, and the board and the membership.
- Members can be confident that the enterprise will always act in their best interests.

The role that the enterprise plays in the daily lives of its members should influence the design of the system of governance. SHEs that supply their members with vital services, such as housing and employment, or that are fundamental to their livelihoods, need a system of that intimately involves members in active everyday participation. SHEs that supply consumer services that may be important but not central to the members' livelihood, usually adopt a system using delegated powers placed in the hands of elected directors. For example, in SHEs that offer goods or services that are readily available from alternative sources

Small, locally-based SHEs normally use a system of more direct democratic control for their enterprise. Where an enterprise has hundreds or perhaps thousands of members, and it works across a wide geographic area, then it will need a different system of governance.

**Organs of governance**
Governance systems are based on their organs of governance, each

of the organs that constitute the system needs to be allocated a set of clearly defined tasks. This along with matching powers and the limits of these powers specified. All of which need to be documented and communicated to all concerned. An effective governance system relies on having the correct organs of governance.

The human body supplies a relevant analogy. We enjoy good health when all our organs are working well together. Likewise, the organs forming the governance system each has to carry out its allocated role, and no organ can carry out the task of another. The health of the organization will suffer if any organ doesn't work properly, or if an essential organ is omitted Problems relating to the exercise of power and control in SHEs usually arise because of the way powers are distributed between the various organs.

The organs of governance within SHEs, in all but the smallest enterprises, will normally include the general meeting of members, the board of directors, and the chief manager. These three basic organs will also usually have supporting organs, which together make-up the governance structure the supreme organ of governance in all SHEs is the general meeting of members.

Decisions on how best to distribute powers between different organs should achieve a balance of power between the different organs. Ideally, all relationships between the various players should be based upon mutual trust, but to achieve such relationships calls for transparency of dealings between all the parties, which is achieved with the aid of control and monitoring systems.

### The board needs to achieve unity of purpose
All the organs of governance need to work in unity towards achieving the organization's purpose. In many SHEs, there will be

space to represent the views of different sections of the membership or other stakeholders. Within the system, there may be some organs, while part of the system, (such as consultative committees), that have an advisory role but no decision-making powers.

The system may well allow for the participation of other stakeholders within the process, but when the board meets to make decisions, everyone sitting around the table needs to be entirely committed to achieving the common purpose of the enterprise. The reality is that SHEs need to respond quickly to changes taking place in the market and other conditions. When tough decisions need to be made by leaders, members need to be confident that their board will take decisions that are in the best interest of the members. therefore, the board cannot comprise people who believe that they are there to represent the interests of different factions of the membership or of the concerns of different stakeholder groups.

## Some causes of defective governance

Governance is about the exercise of power in the organization. It's not about tinkering around with structures or the roles of the individuals involved. The twin handicaps of unclear intentions and an unsuitable system of governance are the root causes of many of the problems facing SHEs. A poorly designed governance system can cause an enterprise to be inflexible, slow to react, and lack decisive direction.

SHEs are often damaged by the misconception that SHEs have separate economic and social purposes. In SHEs their purpose is always socio-economic; see *Chapter 6*. Where leaders allow themselves to be persuaded that they need separate organs to deal with economic and social activities this always leads to confusion. For example, some SHEs have a 'principles and values' committees; this usually means that one group of people discuss esoteric theories, leaving another group to get on with running what they perceive to be not much different from a commercial business. SHEs need to have complete unity of purpose, and the governance system needs to reflect this reality.

Another source of weakness in governance is created by the ambitions of some leaders to create conglomerates, instead of concentrating on the specific markets that need to be changed to benefit their members. The result of mistaken over-expansion is that members usually cannot control their enterprise, and. where over-complex and cumbersome structures are introduced, true member-control is impossible.

To be fully effective, SHEs need be both lean and nimble, which means using flat structures with the minimum levels of hierarchy, rooting-out unnecessarily bureaucratic practices and procedures. This means being dedicated to the elimination of waste and extravagance, when and wherever it occurs.

## Members in control
Members need to take on their responsibilities within their SHEs, rather than just hoping that their elected representatives will deliver what is required, or alternatively simply rely on their managers, who may or may not be fully committed to the enterprise's purpose. Outsiders may never be fully able to appreciate the real needs of the membership, and they can end up pursuing a different agenda from that of the membership.

Members need be able to make their views known to those exercising powers on their behalf, including both directors and managers. Two-way communication is an essential component of the system of governance, for example, the planning and control system ought to start and end with the membership.

## Abuse of power

Where the management of an enterprise is only nominally in the hands of its elected members, and the real power is in the hands of one or more professional manager; this is plainly *not* member-control. The unequal balance of power between part-time member-directors and full-time professional managers comes about when managers control critical information and resources within the enterprise. Where this occurs, the organization is wide-open to the abuse of power, which results in the transfer of both the control and the benefits arising from the enterprise away from the members. The inevitable result is that the enterprise mutates into an organization that no longer serves its members.

## The duties and responsibilities of directors

The directors need to ensure that the books and accounting records are adequate to meet statutory requirements, up-to-date and designed to help safeguard the assets of the enterprise. Directors have to ensure the prompt preparation of accounting and management information that supports the proper control of their enterprise. Directors need to be aware that if they allow the enterprise to continue trading when it's insolvent, then they could become personally liable for any financial consequences. Such an outcome may occur due to overtrading which leads to cash flow problems, and most often because of a lack of working capital.

Directors of SHEs not only have the job of directing their enterprise today, but they are also trustees acting on behalf of future members. The method of ownership used in SHEs (beneficial, mutual ownership) means that the current directors have a responsibility to look after the interest of future generations of members.

Keeping control over their enterprise is essential. Maintaining control by the board calls for a range of support mechanisms, to carry out their role; both individually and collectively. The process of equipping the board for its job starts with adequate training, including an adequate induction for new board members and developing the capability of directors on an ongoing basis. Even if not specified in the rules, the board collectively has a duty to ensure that all directors get the support they to act independently of the chief manager whenever this becomes necessary. This means that the board has access to independent professional advice and has the services of a company/society secretary, normally appointed directly by the board to discharge their legally required duties.

The chairperson is normally a part-time non-specialist, while the chief manager is a full-time professional, so an imbalance of power is bound to occur between the lay-members, led by the chairperson, and the senior management team, led by the chief manager. The fact that the chief manager usually controls much of the information presented to the board, as well as all the enterprise's resources on a day-to-day basis, means that he/she is in de facto control of the operation of the enterprise. What is important, is that the exercise of the powers of the chief manager should always be carried out within the boundaries set by the of policies laid down by the board.

**Collective responsibility**
The board always carries out its powers and responsibilities collectively. The delegation of some of the board's specific tasks may be allowed, either to a specific individual or to a sub-group of the board, but in all cases, the action is taken with the authority and the backing of the full board. The board should not become only a collection of individuals serving disparate groups of members or

stakeholders. When the board meets, all directors have a duty to act in the best interest of the entire membership; although never ignoring their responsibilities to all other stakeholder groups.

## Decisions that are the prerogative of the board

The rules of the enterprise will specify some matters that are reserved to be decided by members at their general meetings, and the be other matters that are reserved' as decisions for the board. Further to this, there needs to be a detailed schedule of all matters that are reserved as a decision that can only be made by the board. The matters to be specified in this schedule will depend on the nature and the activities of the specific enterprise but are (for example): likely to include

- Decisions reserved for the board within the relevant legislation, including the approval of reports and financial statements
- Recommendations to be made to members concerning any revisions to the rules
- Reporting arrangements both to the board and to the members
- Recommendations on any matters needing the approval of members, including the distribution of any surplus, raising finance from members, and the allocation of voting power
- All matters relating to the recruitment of members, discipline procedures for members and policies affecting - relations with members
- Actions needed as the result of the reports of auditors and any audit committee
- Policy towards and relationships with federal, national, and other levels of the federal organization

- Proposals for any merger or transfer of engagements to any other enterprise
- Review and approving of all long-term strategies and plans
- Establishment and checking of an annual operating budget for both revenue and capital expenditure.
- All property and land transactions, including purchase, lease sale or other acquisition or disposal.
- Approve all major items of capital expenditure (with a specified cash limit).
- All significant policy decisions, on such matters as:
- Changes to management structures
- Methods of raising finance
- Important employment policies, including matters of health and safety
- Opening new and closing facilities and activities
- Remuneration policy for the board and senior managers
- New acquisitions and disposal of parts of the enterprise
- Appointment and dismissal of key senior managers, normally limited to the chief manager, board/company secretary, and other senior posts reporting directly to the chief manager
- Selection and appointment of outside non-executive directors
- Approval and monitoring of operational control systems.
- Matters relating to the membership that could detract from its value and how members are to be recruited.
- All matter deemed to be foundation policies, see *Chapter 16*.

## Board/management relationships

Whether SHEs succeed or fail is often highly dependent upon the quality of the board/management relationships. This, in turn, depends upon the board creating the right climate for the practice of creative management in the enterprise. The relationship needed between the member-directors (non-executive directors) and top-level managers in SHEs, does not mirror those in investor-controlled companies. Senior managers in SHEs are often appointed without the crucial difference being made clear to them, and without them receiving an adequate induction. Such an induction needs to include a thorough briefing covering the self-help enterprise model, and the systems, practices, and policies, that they will need to implement.

The board of directors, working closely with their senior management team is the best arrangement for running SHEs. In successful SHEs, there is a constructive partnership between the directors and the senior managers, where each fully appreciates the distinct role of the other.

## The role of the chairperson

The chairperson undoubtedly has a pivotal role in securing the success of the enterprise. He/she should be able to sustain a sound working relationship with the chief manager; this needs to be achieved without any loss of independence or suggestion that the chairperson is 'in the chief manager's pocket. The chairperson needs to discharge the following duties:

-   Ensuring that the board operates as independently as it should.

-   Maintaining a fair balance between the individuals that make up the board.

- Ensuring that all directors are enabled and encouraged to play an active and positive role in the board.

- Seeing that all directors receive prompt and relevant information so that they can make proper decisions and monitor the performance of the enterprise and the people running it.

The chairperson needs to have the ability to stand back from the day-to-day running of the enterprise, always keeping an eye on its purpose and main aims of the enterprise. Whilst at the same ensuring that the board stays in control of the enterprise on behalf of members.

### Non-member non-executive directors

The unequal power and knowledge of the chief manager can be counter-balanced by the appointment of non-member directors, who are often referred to as 'outside non-executive directors. Such directors can support the elected board members by bringing additional knowledge and skills to the boardroom. However, it can be very damaging to any enterprise if self-serving or incompetent people are appointed, so it's crucial to only appoint outside directors who are fully in tune with the purpose of the enterprise and committed to helping achieve it.

Outside non-executive directors may be able to make two uniquely important contributions in the boardroom; these are to help to review the performance of both the board and the chief manager and to take the lead when any conflicts of interest arise. It's essential to realise that there will be times when the specific interests of senior managers and the wider interests of the enterprise will diverge, and at such times the role of an outside director can be critical

## Sub-committees of the board

The rules of the enterprise may specify that specific subcommittees of the board are to part of the system of governance. The board may decide to set sub-committees to deal with specific issues, but where these are formed care has to be taken not to set-up an 'inner-board', with some board members being excluded from decision-making processes. It needs to be remembered that *all* board members are equally responsible for the conduct of the enterprise.

Even when the board delegates specific tasks to a sub-committee, the sub-committee only makes a report and recommendations to the full board, which then takes any necessary formal decisions. An audit committee has already been mentioned, but other tasks that may lend themselves to sub-committees include the review of senior managers' salaries and conditions, the development of member involvement, and other areas for which a group smaller than the full board may be more effective.

Other sub-committees may include:

### A remuneration and governance committee

- A remuneration committee ensures that pay and other rewards support the strategic aims of the enterprise. It should aid the recruitment, motivation, and retention of senior managers while at the same time following the requirements of any governmental regulation. This committee should have delegated responsibility for proposing rewards for all senior managers, directors and the chairperson, including any pension rights and other benefits and compensation payments. The committee should recommend and check the level and structure of remuneration for senior management. This committee may also review corporate governance issues to ensure that these are updated when necessary, along with the required corporate governance policies and procedures.

### A disclosure committee

- In large-scale SHEs, it may be appropriate to establish a disclosure committee, usually chaired by the chief financial officer, to consider the materiality of information, determine disclosure requirements and identify disclosure issues according to the relevant legislation). At the same time, this committee coordinates the development of an appropriate infrastructure to ensure that information required to be disclosed in the reports is communicated to the management team.

## Senior managers

The quality and commitment of the senior managers, particularly the chief manager, is, of course, critical for any enterprise, and the board is responsible both for recruiting and keeping effective managers. Crucially, the board needs to create an environment where creative management can flourish.

The board needs to supply the boundaries within which management freedom can be exercised; this freedom is inevitably accompanied by the danger that such power may be abused. Therefore, a careful balance needs to be kept between management freedom and adequate controls. It's best if the chief manager and the financial controller/chief accountant are de facto directors and take part fully in the affairs of the board. These managers are subject to appointment and removal by the board, and their position is distinctly different from that of the other directors who are appointed directly by the members. There will be some decisions in which senior managers do not directly take part, for example, in deciding the action needed following the review of their own performance, salaries, and conditions.

The service contracts of senior managers should not normally exceed a three-year term, and in most cases, an annual rolling contract is most suitable. When senior managers don't perform to the required standard need to be replaced, and the sooner any difficult decisions are made in this respect, the better are the prospects for the enterprise. it's unacceptable for managers to receive huge severance payments if this appears to be a reward for the delivery of poor results. Proposed management contracts that provide for big payouts if a manager turns out to be unsuitable ought not to be accepted by the board.

The board has a duty to promote openness and transparency in all matters of significance to members. The details of the personal contracts with senior managers should be known to all board members, and at least the broad range of salaries need to be published in the annual report of the enterprise. This along with the way that any performance-related payments are to be made. Likewise, full details of any severance payments or other significant benefits bestowed on senior managers cannot be kept secret from the members; this same degree of openness needs to apply to all additional payments and any other benefits provided to member-directors.

### The meaning of oversight

Everyone needs oversight. Without it, most people tend to drift away from their purpose, and/or become distracted by all manner of personal and external events. Sometimes, they become diverted by their individual weaknesses, obsessions and the temptation to misappropriate property and funds. Whenever those running an enterprise are not the same people who own it, a vigorous system of oversight is essential. In the absence of such a system, the owners are likely to find that the main benefits from the enterprise go to those running the enterprise, instead of going to the owners. In this context, 'the owners' means the shareholders in the case of a company, trustees in the case of a charity, and members in the case of a self-help enterprise.

Most people running organizations are well aware of the need to provide adequate financial oversight yet frequently fail to provide sufficient checks on how those running their organization are carrying out the enterprise's purpose and function. The oversight system needs to provide a series of checks and balances designed to prevent the organization from drifting away from its projected destiny. In some cases, the people running the enterprise become so fixated on ensuring that their organization survives that they lose sight of the reasons for its existence.

Universally, corporate bodies are at risk from those who misappropriate funds and assets. Systems of the audit, both internal and external, should minimise these risks. In times past, the main concern was that employees might steal the petty cash, but now it's not unusual for managers, often aided and abetted by others, to steal the entire enterprise. Financial audit systems are of course essential, but oversight needs to extend beyond the financial aspects of running the enterprise. SHEs need auditor that will reveal whether the enterprise is working towards achieving its purpose. This is not to be confused with any other auditing that may also be conducted; for example - social audits, democracy audits, environmental impact audits.

In small concerns, an independent financial audit may provide sufficient oversight to make sure that the enterprise is working for the benefit of its owners. In large and complex organizations, a more extensive and robust system of oversight is needed. This calls for a specific body to carry out this task. For example, in major German companies and French financial services enterprises, it's common for oversight boards to carry out a range of duties. Credit unions often provide oversight by including a supervisory committee within their governance structure, although in many cases this is limited to some audit responsibilities.

**Oversight bodies**
An oversight body is the organ of governance tasked with providing oversight on behalf of the members; it needs to give all the necessary powers to carry out its task. It will be appointed by the members and will report directly to the members. It should ensure that the enterprise:

- Remains focus on its agreed common purpose and its proper function. The body needs to report at least annually, directly to the membership.
- Strategic plans are always purpose-driven and developed in full consultation with the membership.
- All senior management posts are filled only by those able to show their commitment to the true purpose of the enterprise, and that their performance is reviewed annually to assess the worth of their contribution.
- Membership is properly valued and constantly promoted.
- All elections for members' representatives and leaders are properly conducted.
- All senior managers receive thorough and effective training on how to work in a bona fide self-help enterprise.
- The remuneration policy is designed and implemented to support the achievement of the purpose.

- All finance is only obtained from benign sources.

- The enterprise is not in any way involved in speculation.

- Regular constitutional reviews are undertaken so as to that the system of governance and rules remain 'fit-for-purpose'.

- Capacity-building activities are offered to develop effective member participation.

- All elections for members' representatives and leaders are properly conducted.

- All directors receive thorough training on how to properly carry out their duties within a self-help enterprise.

- The process of renewing and refocusing the enterprise is undertaken on a regular basis so that the enterprise is continually revitalised.

The investigative powers of the oversight body need to be similar to those of an independent financial auditor. The membership may appoint members or outsiders they trust to carry out these duties on their behalf. Just as they appoint independent financial auditors, the members may appoint professionals having the skills and experience to fulfil this role. The leaders of SHEs need to work together to arrange for the training of people to fully comprehend the role and duties of an oversight body. Members of such bodies need to be supplied with guidelines about how they should complete their tasks.

### The financial oversight system

The objective of the financial oversight system is the prevention of fraud and malpractice. The board has the primary responsibility for safeguarding the assets of the enterprise, with the directors acting as trustees on behalf of the members. The board should be able to exercise this task without hindrance from the chief manager or anyone else. It's no use pretending that those involved in SHEs are above temptation or do not need to be subject to the checks and controls that should be in place in any form of organization.

Every SHE should be subjected to an independent audit. The requirements in this respect are usually set out in the legislation under which the enterprise is registered. The board should not restrict auditing arrangements to these legal requirements if more comprehensive auditing is necessary - to ensure that the board and members are fully satisfied with adequate safeguards and controls. Such audit systems should protect the interests of the members and the other stakeholders who may have a financial interest in the enterprise.

The annual audit should give an external and objective check on the way in which the financial statements have been prepared and presented. Although auditors need to work with and not against management, they should still be professionally objective - always. This means not only having the necessary professional skills, but staying impartial, critical, and detached. The auditors should be able to report directly to the Annual General Meeting of the membership, and every director should receive a copy of a management audit letter/ report, prepared by the external auditors concerning the affairs of the SHEs. Auditors should be changed from time to time to avoid the development of a relationship that is too cosy with the senior management team.

### Audit committees and auditors

It's good practice to set up a separate audit committee to oversee internal controls within the SHE and to follow up matters brought to its attention by the external auditors. Such an audit committee should meet independently of the chief manager and have a separate chairman who reports on behalf of the committee both to the full board and directly to the members' meeting. Where there is a two-tier board structure (i.e. the members appoint a council of delegates which in turn appoints the board), then the audit committee should report directly to the council of delegates. The tasks of the audit committee will include considering remedial actions and procedural changes for improving control, and monitoring progress towards implementing improvements.

The role of the external auditors is important, and to keep them as truly independent, the following practices need to be part of the system:

- Changing the auditors at regular intervals to prevent the development of relationships with management that become too familiar.
- Declaring in the annual report all fees paid to auditors, both for audit and other services.
- Obtaining added professional services from a firm other than the auditors.

## The governance of subsidiaries

SHEs sometimes create subsidiary companies. If such subsidiaries directly intervene in a market in the best interests of their members, then they can be a valid extension of the function of the parent enterprise. However, if subsidiaries are simply a means of raising revenue or accessing finance, then they are no different from any other profit-driven enterprise. When charities run subsidiaries with the objective of raising revenue, these too, are profit-making ventures and will usually be treated by the tax authorities in the same way as any commercial business; the only difference being that a subsidiary company owned by a charity may be permitted to donate, free of tax, a sum equal to their profits to the charity that owns them.

SHEs may, where the law allows, set up subsidiaries of various types, such as wholly or partially-owned companies, or joint venture companies. In all cases, it's essential that these are fully aligned with the controlling parent enterprise's arrangements for governance and oversight. Otherwise, they can become the means of circumventing important controls, for this reason, member-directors from the main board of the holding enterprise should be appointed to the board of any subsidiary enterprise. These board members will have the responsibility for regularly reporting, to the full board on the affairs of the subsidiary. For more about subsidiaries see *Chapter 23*.

**Tools for good governance**

There are some important tools needed to make sure that the system of governance works as it should, these include:

- **Policy manuals:** It's essential for every board to have in place policies that clarify the components and implementation of its legal fiduciary responsibilities. Having a board policy manual, best maintained by a professional (for example the society or company secretary) and shared with all board members, enables the board to be always guided by their up-to-date policies. Among the essential policies are the board's own standing orders. The policy manual may also include details of the governance structure and other information about how the board operates. Other organs that are part of governance structure should have their own statements of its role and responsibilities; these are always subject to formal board approval. Monitoring any board member's possible conflicting interest needs due diligence and oversight. The board needs to demonstrate its commitment to preventing not only actual or material conflict, but act where there is any suggestion that there is a potential conflict of interest. Possible conflicts of interest need to be covered in the policy manual.

- **Recording decisions:** Most organizations maintain a record of the work conducted at meetings in the form of 'minutes' of the meetings of their governing body. Sometimes minutes provide only the briefest summary of the meeting, whilst others give a blow-by-blow account of all that took place at the meeting. It needs to be realised that within SHEs the minutes of board meetings, need to give a record of all decisions taken at the meeting, and where new policies are framed at the meeting, then this results in the policy manual being updated. In addition, the minutes need to summarise why the decision was made; this is most important because this record should build-up the institutional memory of the enterprise, which is crucial in terms improving the quality of decision making, and it aids those who follow in the footsteps of the current board, to appreciate why past decisions were made.

- **Codes of ethics:** In all organizations, those involved need to know and accept the required standards of behaviour, here codes of ethics can be helpful in maintaining standards. However, unless the code is applied to the letter (particularly at the highest levels, including the board and senior managers), it will be subject to much criticism and become counterproductive. The code of ethics ought to help keep members commitment and to give members assurance that fair treatment will be the norm throughout the enterprise. Any code of ethics needs to be developed, in full consultation with all those involved, and it should be regularly reviewed. Compliance with the code should be checked at set intervals by persons with this specific responsibility. Every enterprise needs to develop its own code, which is likely to cover matters such as how it treats both its members and other stakeholders. Practices that can lead to corruption (such as accepting and giving gifts) as to what is expected by way of the disclosure of information need to be clarified in the document.

- **The power of patronage:** Corporate bodies, and the individuals running them, often use patronage to increase their power in the market and, in many cases, they seek to influence political processes too. Those running SHEs need to take great care when dispensing aid because it can become counter-productive and generate dependency, which is opposite to the idea of self-help and mutual action - which underpins SHEs. More importantly, senior managers and cliques of members often use the dispensing of financial support to influence or distort the democratic process within self-help enterprises. For these reasons, all decisions about dispensing patronage ought to be under the direct control of its owners – the members. Controls need to be placed over any kind of support, gift, grant, sponsorship, or donation (which shall only be distributed with the express authority of the members in a general meeting). Other than very small donations made on the authority of the board up to a limit authorised by the members.

- **A whistle-blower's charter:** The system needs to provide the route for those with enough conscience to 'blow the whistle' on any person who is damaging the enterprise by their behaviour. Such negative behaviour can come in many guises. It is a sad fact that most people with guilty secrets are very adept at hiding their failings from those with the power to put a stop to their bad behaviour. Organizations often depend upon whistle-blowers to help keep wrongdoers from seriously damaging them, so it's important that there is a clear, well-publicised route so that any accusation is sure to reach top-level decision-makers. In addition, the policy needs to give adequate protection for those whistle-blowers who have the courage to speak out when they become aware of any kind of behaviour that is a threat to the success of the organization.

### It's all about people

No matter how carefully the structure of an organization is designed, it will only succeed in fulfilling its purpose if the people involved are clear about what this is. People need to have the knowledge and skills necessary to run their enterprise effectively and are supported by a positive culture. These imperatives are only met when the enterprise is run by people who are totally committed to its purpose. This calls for a recruitment process that screens-out people with incompatible attitudes, and an induction programme that, at a minimum, supplies a clear explanation of the self-help enterprise model. SHEs need people who have the required mindset and talents, which are provided with the knowledge, experience, and skills, necessary to carry out their specific roles.

This applies in the same way to member-directors, member-representatives, all senior managers, and all the workforce.

Unnecessary layers of decision-makers need to be eliminated, and there is no need for committees that are there purely for their own sake, these often needlessly filter out direct feedback from members. When there are too many organs within the structure, the result is often the slowing down of the decision-making process, with too many people trying to justify their own role. See *Figure I-22 The governance structure – an example.*

### Guidance about governance

Many of the organizations supporting specific types of SHEs have set out recommendations as to the best practices, along with codes of ethics relating to governance for their sector of SHEs. Leaders of SHEs need to check that they have up-to-date information available, which is essential if they are to make sound decisions. Nonetheless, it needs to be realised that not all recommendations will place sufficient emphasis on the need for rigorous independent oversight. Effective governance depends upon the enterprise having competent directors who follow all the established practices, policies and systems. Both new and experienced directors need to be given a regular briefing and on a regularly review their governance system. Members should constantly be made aware of the fact that if they do not keep control, then by default or design, control will pass into the hands of others. They need to work out what kind of information they need, and the key management ratios are appertaining to the trades, industries, or services in where their enterprise is involved.

# *Figure I-22   The governance structure – an example*

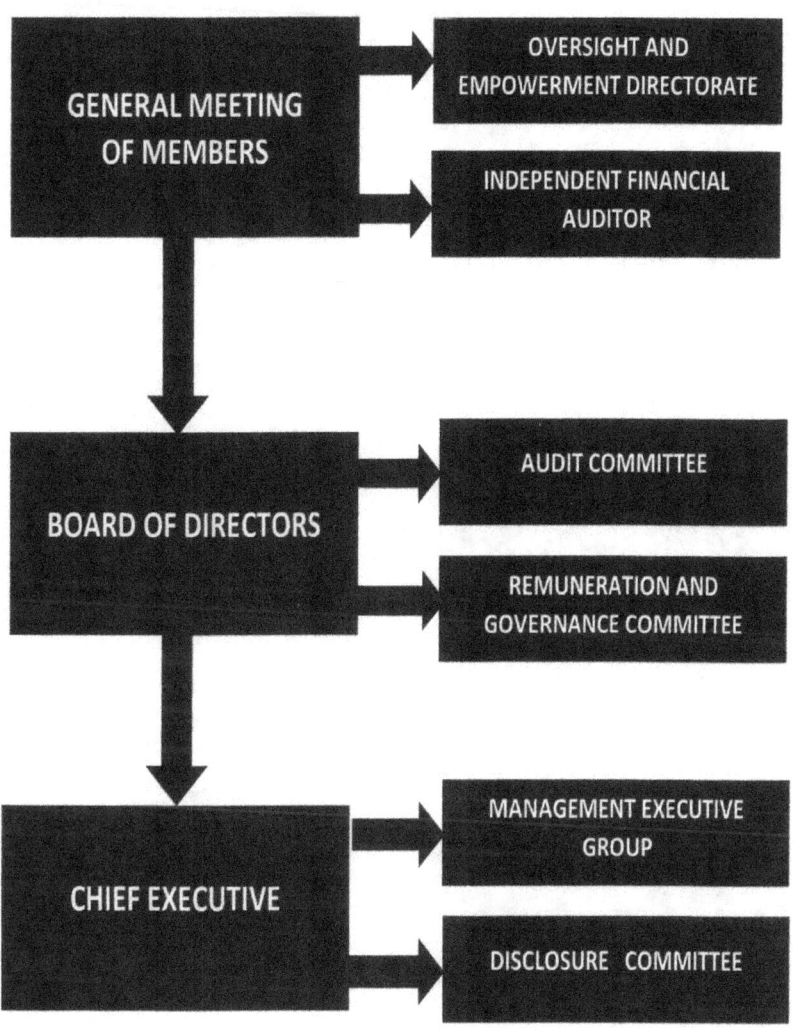

# 23. FINANCING SELF-HELP

### Finance and financing

Finance means the money used in running an enterprise, and when people speak about 'raising finance' to fill the gap between the money an enterprise has, and the money needed to run the enterprise. Finance is a key resource for all forms of enterprise because it unlocks access to all other resources, including land, buildings, labour, knowledge, technology and goods for trading. In SHEs, one of the core tasks of leaders is to optimise the use of the finance employed in pursuit of the enterprise's purpose. This chapter describes the system of financing needed in SHEs, which is an important subsystem of the economic system.

The ways, means, and methods, of financing SHEs, all need to be designed to secure the viability of the enterprise, whilst at the same time keeping its sovereignty, and its democratic control by its members. This means that only benign sources of finance are acceptable within SHEs, which is to say that sources of finance that are likely now or in the future, to in any way threaten the sovereignty of the enterprise should never be employed. Finance must *not* be permitted to become the master of a self-help enterprise. Whenever finance secures the upper-hand, members lose control, and inevitably the enterprise will not be able to achieve its true purpose.

The financing system needed in SHEs is one that ensures finance is available at the lowest cost that's compatible with attracting and retaining it. While at the same time maintaining full sovereignty and member-control. This can only be achieved by implementing the complete set of practices that make up the self-help financing system. This needs to be supported by a very clear policy document that governs the way that finance is raised by the enterprise.

## Diverse ways of financing distinct types of SHEs

The main differences between the distinct types of self-help enterprise often arise from the ways that they finance their operations. In the case of both building societies and credit unions, members' savings creates the underlying source of finance. Insurance mutuals use the premiums paid by members, and the investment earnings to cover the costs of claims and administration.

In clubs and similar ventures, members' subscriptions supply the basic finance needed. In consumer co-ops and community ventures, members' investments will be the source of the basic finance, often by the issue of so-called 'shares. In most SHEs, once well established, their finance for further development will come primarily from retained surpluses.

Many SHEs have no shareholders as such, only members who collectively own their enterprise. For example, many friendly societies and social clubs are collectively owned by their members, but members are not called shareholders. Indeed, even in those SHEs that refer to members as shareholders, members are not shareholders with the same rights as in an investor-owned company.

In SHEs, investors, both members and non-members, only have a claim on the cash value of their original investment in the enterprise, plus any added interest due to them. The real assets, including buildings, equipment, stock, and intellectual property belonging to the self-help enterprise is held mutually on behalf of members by the enterprise. Therefore, these are not divisible, or available to share between members in the case of dissolution of the enterprise. As explained earlier in the book, the method of ownership needed in SHEs is beneficial mutual ownership, which means that neither surpluses or reserves may be distributed in relation to investments held within the enterprise. It's worth noting that in many countries but excluding the UK and its former colonies, the term 'shareholder is not used in the context of SHEs, they generally use more precise, less confusing, words.

### The framework for financing SHEs

It's necessary to stress again that SHEs are associations of equal persons, so their financing needs to be arranged in ways that don't conflict with this fact, or any of the other foundation practices. To reiterate, this means only using finance obtained on terms that will ensure that the enterprise remains committed to its foundation practices. All financing arrangements need to be checked for their ongoing compliance with these practices.

Some elements of these requirements are often included in the relevant legislation for specific types of SHEs. For example, setting out the limits on the proportion of, and the total amount, that can be held by an individual member and restrictions placed upon the distribution of any residual funds in case of winding-up. It is the duty of members and their representatives to defend the financial integrity of their own enterprises, which means that the rules of the enterprise and the foundation policies have to enshrine these practices. Member-leaders need to resist pressures to accept financing arrangements that could undermine the foundations of the self-help enterprise model.

### Objectives and practices

The objectives of the financing system are to ensure the enterprise secures the finance it needs while optimising the use of this resource at the lowest cost compatible with maintaining the sovereignty of the enterprise, its mutual ownership while remaining under the democratic control of its members. To meet these objectives calls for the application of a raft of interdependent practices, which includes:

- Following the economic practices that constitute the self-help economic system

- Not being dependent upon external grants, donations, subsidies, or any other external support for their continuing viability

- Members have no claim upon the enterprise in respect of any increase in the value of the assets held by the enterprise, which the enterprise owns on behalf of its members. Members own only their personal investments in the enterprise

- Not making any distribution of mutually-owned assets to members or any other persons

- In case of dissolution any surplus remaining shall not be distributed to members, but instead, this may be donated to another self-help enterprise or to a designated charity.

- Ensuring that any distribution of surplus shall only be made to members and only in proportion to the member's participation in generating the surplus; and not in any way linked to the amount of finance supplied by any member or any other investor.

- Rewards for the use of finance are to not to be made in any way that is related to the surplus created by the enterprise, instead such rewards are limited to a fixed rate of interest. Alternatively, limited to keeping the purchasing power of the value of the investment (for example, limited to the level of inflation over a lengthy period).

- Limiting the extent of the role that any person or organization has in financing the enterprise. This because the enterprise is an association of equal persons, so no one should be able to exercise power simply because they play a greater role in financing the enterprise.

- All finance available for use within the enterprise should only be deployed if it can be used productively in pursuit of the purpose of the enterprise. This same dictum applies when reinvesting surpluses back into the enterprise.

## Maintaining sovereignty and member-control

When new SHEs are being set up, there may be pressure from the members to get their enterprise started, because the most important thing to members can seem to be that they get hold of the finance needed to get the enterprise underway, regardless of the longer-term consequences. Decision-makers within SHEs need to be aware of the threats to both sovereignty and member-control, and if the members are to keep control of their enterprise, it's essential that only those members making use of its services control the decision-making processes. This means that if any member stops using the services of the enterprise, they should relinquish membership, and forgo the right to take part in the control of the enterprise. When a member is no longer primarily interested in the services of the enterprise, then their motive for involvement usually shifts towards securing a return upon any investment they may have in the enterprise. The presence of large numbers of economically and democratically inactive members results in the enterprise ceasing to serve its membership. SHEs should never accept finance from any source if it threatens effective member-control. Which in SHEs should always rest firmly in the hands of the economically active membership.

## The cost of finance

The actual price (the cost of finance) that needs to be paid for using an investor's finance will depend upon many factors, including the overall level of confidence in the economy, the relative attraction of other forms of investment and, very significantly, the current and projected level of inflation. Timing is critical when investing in new facilities or services. If an enterprise borrows at fixed rates when interest rates are high, it may easily become uncompetitive when rates fall. When the risk of investing in a specific enterprise appears high, then the cost of finance can be expected to be high. The length of time an enterprise needs to lock-in the investment is yet another factor determining its cost. The ease of realising or converting an investment into liquid cash will significantly influence the cost of borrowing. Most of all, investor confidence is the key to getting finance at a reasonable rate.

Only if the enterprise is regarded as responsible in the way that it operates, and is seen to be well managed and entirely viable, can it expect to obtain finance at competitive rates It should never be forgotten, that whatever the cost of finance, an enterprise can only afford to use any finance if the net result is a sufficient margin earned by the activity invested in. Any funds invested in an enterprise need to produce a return that will cover all costs incurred, including the cost of finance.

## Risk factors

SHEs that have been prudently managed over many years often become exposed to an elevated level of risk when they embark upon expansion without having the correct method of equity financing in place. In SHEs where their equity (reserves created by the retention of surpluses and by increases in the value of freehold property through inflation) is used to secure more finance. The cost of servicing such debt can become a heavy burden, which needs to be carried by the enterprise's current operations. The impact of this is often underestimated, while its ability to generate the income needed to service the debt is often overestimated. This situation often results in the management trying to trade-out the problem, by making further investments in the enterprise, often with even more costly finance on even more costly terms.

The reason for adopting such inappropriate investment strategies can usually be traced to the fact that the enterprise's leaders were not focusing on the real purpose of their enterprise. Instead, were pursuing growth for its own sake. This can happen whenever leaders do not grasp the value of the self-help enterprise model, in particular, if they do not follow the economic practices that should guide their decision-making.

### Sources of finance
There are three main sources of finance available to SHEs, these are:

1. Members.

2. Retained surplus arising from the activities of the enterprise.

3. Individuals and institutions that are non-members

Traditionally, SHEs have placed great store upon financing their own operations primarily using funds supplied by their members. Credit unions have always emphasised saving before borrowing, and the first rule of the original Rochdale Equitable Pioneers was 'that capital should be of their own providing and bear a fixed rate of interest'.

If possible, each member should contribute finance in direct proportion to their use of the services that the enterprise provides, and in some cases in proportion to the benefits they receive. When members make use of services on an equal basis, then each member should contribute the same amount of finance. Ideally, members should supply the money to finance their enterprise, but of course, conditions are rarely ideal. This means that to meet members' expectations its first necessary to draw finance from the members when they have the funds available, and only after to consider obtaining finance from other people and institutions that are willing to offer it, such finance is referred to as 'external finance'.

It's imperative that all finance, irrespective of its source, be employed in such a way that it will fully cover the cost of the finance deployed. All prospective investments to be made within the enterprise need to be properly evaluated and watched. Ineffective managers sometimes do not use finance efficiently and then try to convince members that the productive use of finance is not a necessity because the enterprise is a self-help enterprise. Except in rare cases, such as when grants are available, all finance has to be paid for at a cost that is set by the market for the specific kind of finance needed. Even where apparently 'cost-free' money is available, the application of the self-help mindset should make leaders highly suspicious that there will be covert strings attached.

If SHEs are well-managed, they will only accept finance from benign sources, and the enterprise will be run following the self-help economic system, which includes not engaging in speculation, and ensuring that provident decisions are always made. This commitment should mean, that although finance will not be attracted from those looking to get-rich-quick, it needs to be attractive to those looking for a safe haven for their savings.

### *The wrong type of finance: The UK's Co-operative Bank*

In May 2013, members of UK cooperatives were shocked by the news that the bank's chief executive had resigned following the downgrade of the bank's debt, Ostensibly, the cause of these events had its origins in the financial downturn, problematic loans, and the increases in the sums of capital required to be held to meet new regulations in the banking sector. However, the underlying issues run much deeper than this.

The management of the bank seemed to believe that they were running a commercial business, with the aim of profit maximization, a 'business' that just happened to be owned by a cooperative. Management had been given a free hand to borrow millions, making use of international capital markets; which they could not repay. This resulted in the bank being no longer owned by the Co-operative Group. Instead, it's now majority-owned by a group of international investors.

The group sold its final stake in The Co-operative Bank in September 2017. This had been a wholly owned subsidiary until 2014 when the group was forced to sell the most of its holding to investors to raise funds for the bank. The Co-operative Bank includes the internet bank Smile and the former Britannia building society.

All decision-makers, both member-leaders and senior managers, be fully aware of the basics about financing their enterprise. This is a subject that cannot be left to the 'experts' or placed in the 'too difficult to understand box'. Leaders should always apply the cardinal rule, which is that: when it comes to financing their enterprises – *if you don't fully comprehend what is being proposed - then don't agree to it.*

## Finance from members

It's reasonable to expect that when members want their enterprise to undertake an activity, then they ensure that their enterprise can secure enough funds to finance this. Nevertheless, members are not always able to provide all the financial resources needed to take advantage of current opportunities, and where the members are unable or unwilling to support their own enterprise, by both investing their own money into it and by utilising its services, then this may call into question both the need and the prospects for any such a venture.

The presence of large numbers of members or non-members who obtain benefits from the enterprise without making any investment in it will always undermine the prospects for the enduring success of any self-help enterprise.

Enterprises need to supply both members and would-be members with a clear picture of the enterprise's plans and prospects. The leaders of the enterprise have to ensure that they supply the information on which both members and all prospective providers of finance, can make sound judgements about whether to invest. In most countries, the laws relating to the disclosure of information about all forms of investment are increasingly demanding more transparency. In most cases, this means that SHEs are becoming more strictly accountable under the relevant legislation governing such investments.

When SHEs are locally-based, and the relationships between the enterprise and their members are close, the members will be well placed to assess the risks that they are taking with their savings, and it is usually easier for SHEs to attract investments from members. Where SHEs work across a large geographical area, and the enterprise is a complex organization, then much more sophisticated methods of raising finance from members often become necessary. The answer to both financing problems, and to successfully engaging with members, is usually to be found in organizing SHEs that implement market intervention strategies in specific markets. Members that are enthusiastic about the results achieved on their behalf by their SHEs are most likely to be ready to both engage with their SHEs and to contribute financially.

## Two types of members' investments

There are two types of member investments. First, there are those investments required as a condition of membership; these investments carry with them the benefits and responsibilities of membership and most importantly the power of a vote. The second type of investments are those made optionally by members in their enterprise; Such investments may be made entirely voluntarily, but in some cases, these are also required as a condition of membership but don't bestow any additional voting rights.

When members are called upon to make investments in their enterprise to qualify for membership, interest may be paid on these investments, but the member does not share in any surplus based on their financial holdings or share in any capital gains, nor in any distribution of residual assets (in case of the winding-up of the enterprise). Such member's equity may be withdrawable but not normally transferable other than in case of their death. Members' equity investments are often 'qualifying investments', which means the minimum level of investment required is set as a condition of membership. In some cases, a higher level of investment may be required, for example, if a member wishes to stand for election as a director of the enterprise.

There have been many examples of SHEs finding that when member confidence in their enterprise is shattered due to events that cause members to believe that they may lose money that they have invested in the enterprise, they may be a rush of members seeking to cash-in their investments. Even though the board usually has the power to halt withdrawals, in these circumstances, the result will often be that the enterprise is forced into administration or liquidation if there is a lack of liquidity

As with all aspects of their operation, fair and honest practices should be applied to how enterprises are financed, which means treating all members. (past, present and future) equally. When there are increases in the value of the enterprise's assets (particularly those created as the result of inflation) ways, need to be found to allow members to fairly share such windfalls with members and not simply add these to its accumulated reserves. Because these mainly only benefit future members. Collectively owned reserves that are excessive can result in management believing that they have 'cost-free finance' at their disposal and that the need to secure the financial commitment of their members becomes unimportant.

### Different forms of finance sourced from members
**Please note:** Some of the sources of finance mentioned below are only suitable for use in specific forms of SHEs.

- **Par-value withdrawable shares:** These are members'
  investments linked the rights of membership and under
  normal circumstances, withdrawable on demand. However,
  the value of these so-called 'shares' does not exceed its
  original purchase price. Further aspects of withdrawable
  finance are considered later in this chapter, and the 'par-
  value' concept was examined in *Chapter 19*.

- **Community shares:** The term 'community shares' refers to a
  type of withdrawable investment; a kind of share used in
  the UK, issued by cooperative societies, community benefit

societies and some other. Community shares are withdrawable, non-transferable shares in a society with a voluntary or statutory asset lock. The Charity Commission for England and Wales and the Office of the Scottish Charity Regulator are the regulators for these schemes, which means that enterprises running such schemes are in practice treated as if they were charities.

- **Loan finance:** Many SHEs accept investments from their members by way of loans, either for a fixed period or repayable after a stated period of notice of intention to withdraw. These types of loan finance are often used when the limit set on investment in so-called 'share capital' is reached.

- **Fixed-term bonds:** SHEs sometimes issue fixed-term bonds whereby the member places finance at the disposal of the SHE for a fixed period. Such bonds usually bear a fixed rate of interest or a rate of interest set at regular intervals, say, annually. This type of bond is not usually tradable and stays in the name of the member, who can withdraw it only by giving a set period of notice or upon the end of the time agreed when the investment was initially made.

- **Small savings accounts:** Some SHEs can offer savings accounts in which small sums of money may be invested in the enterprise; this is, of course, one of the main services of credit unions. Other types of SHEs, usually find their activities in this connection are limited by the banking laws of the country.

- **Compulsory contribution schemes.** Members are called upon to make added investments in their enterprise, either upon joining the enterprise or at some later specified date. If the financial outlay for these investments is large, members may be allowed to invest over a period (12 months, for example). In most instances, it is advisable that the level of investment required from each member is in line with the member's expected use of the enterprise's services. For example, in many milk processing cooperatives, members usually invest in their enterprise in proportion with the volume of milk they have available to process.

- **Compulsory surplus retention:** This practice involves an added charge on the members, by increasing the price of goods bought or services supplied. Obviously, accounting records need to be of the highest standard to ensure that the funds retained are allocated to the individual member and don't become counted as trading income. Otherwise, value-added tax or other taxes may be calculated incorrectly. Retentions can be considered in aggregate and can constitute an important part of the long-term funding arrangements for the enterprise.

### Withdrawable investments

It's helpful to know that the terms 'shares' and 'shareholders' in SHEs were used in the absence of more precise terminology. When early SHEs were started, their founders (and the legislators of the day) simply adopted the terms already in use within companies. It's also worth noting that in some languages (other than English) specific words are often used to describe members' equity linked to voting rights in SHEs.

A 'share' in a company is an equal part of the company's total value. Ordinary shares in a company receive no fixed reward but instead entitle the shareholder to a proportion of the company's value. Shares in a company are permanently invested in the enterprise; they cannot be withdrawn, only sold. These conditions do not apply to SHEs. Instead, these so-called shares, do not grow or decrease as the value of the enterprise changes and does not offer the basis of entitlement to any participation in the surplus produced by the enterprise

## Retention of unallocated surplus

The most attractive method of financing for SHEs is by the retention of surpluses. Unlike investor companies, SHEs do not generate a surplus to satisfy shareholders, but instead, the creation of surplus is an essential by-product of undertaking the activities of the enterprise. If the policy of the enterprise is to generate internal finance, then it will be necessary to include such provision within the margin applied, and this approach will be reflected in its pricing structure for any services supplied by the enterprise. If alternative service providers are acquiring finance directly, by share issues, then their prices will only reflect the cost of servicing this finance. If SHEs are accumulating finance by what amounts to a surcharge, then SHE may become uncompetitive. Therefore, there is a clear limit on the extent to which retained surplus can be used to finance SHEs.

Undistributed surpluses increase the equity base of the enterprise and reduce the need for raising other forms of investment or borrowing. When surpluses are not distributed but held back by SHEs to use in the enterprise, great care has to be taken to ensure that members are treated equitably. Surplus generated from trade with one specific group of members should not be distributed to a different group of members. Allocations should be made in proportion to the member's use of the SHE. Typically, the greater the investment that members can call their own, then the stronger is their sense of commitment to using the services provided by their own enterprise; and the member's sense of ownership. This can also ssupply an added incentive to be involved in the democratic process and to develop a proactive relationship with their representatives and the management team.

### External finance

If SHEs are to attract and keep outside investment, they should make available a prospectus that will allow investors to make considered investment decisions. Investors need to be convinced that the rewards are enough to cover the level of risk involved. The viability of any enterprise will be a determining factor, and regardless of how socially beneficial a loss-making enterprise may be, this cannot be the basis for securing any kind of investment. The transparency of financial reporting, the quality of long-term planning, the reputation and performance of the management, are crucial to securing investment funds. It's essential that investors' funds be used only to finance wholly viable operations, including both new and current ventures, and not be used to finance trading losses.

Investment should only be part of a carefully crafted plan based on realistic budgets that show a high probability of their achievement. Both members and non-members considering investment in SHEs are increasingly likely to demand quality of information, usually in the format of a properly prepared prospectus.

### Sources of external finance

The following are some of the external sources of finance used by SHEs:

- **Bank finance:** SHEs will usually take advantage of what may be described as normal bank finance, such as negotiated overdraft facilities or fixed-term loans (at fixed or variable interest rates).

- **Seasonal loans:** Crop production is usually highly seasonal, with post-harvest prices for crops and distribution costs being unfavourable. Seasonal finance, using short-term bank borrowing, may be necessary to finance the storage of crops and to even-out their producer-members' cash-flow.

- **Mortgage-linked finance:** Loans secured against specific properties may be obtained (at fixed or variable rates) from financial institutions; mortgages may be a first or second mortgage against a single asset or a basket of assets.

- **Permanent interest-bearing shares** (PIBS): For several years UK Building Societies have used permanent interest-bearing (non-voting) shares (PIBS). This kind of finance could be used much more widely throughout SHEs if the right kinds of mechanisms are in place. 'Perpetual preferred stock' – is already available to investor-controlled companies. In SHEs, this type of investment has a fixed value in an enterprise's accounts but is tradable (able to be bought and sold at current market value). There is not usually any fixed date on which the invested finance is returned to the holder, although the issuing enterprise will always hold redemption privileges. This kind of investment usually ranks only before members' qualifying investments for repayment in the case of winding-up.

- **Loan finance and bonds:** Loans and bonds like those available to members may be made available to non-members, either on the same or different terms. SHEs should not obtain finance by using bonds linked to surplus or asset growth. The problem with surplus-linked

335

instruments is that the management of an enterprise is normally able to decide the amount of surplus that will be given to any outside investor by manipulating the prices of the services supplied by the enterprise. Asset growth-linked investments are even less likely to be used by SHEs but are a means of raising finance when the investment can be related to specific assets held by the enterprise. These can be particularly useful at times of high inflation. Tracking bonds may be used; these attract a rate of return equal to that obtainable on the national stock exchange.

- **Sale and lease-back:** Some SHEs are using sale and leaseback to finance current operations, but this can be expensive especially in term of the set-up fees involved. The 'family silver' is something that can be sold only once, and the same applies to the sale and lease-back of SHEs assets, usually land and buildings. Such arrangements may be worth considering if the deal is provided by a trusted specialist self-help enterprise financing body offers a less-risky deal.

- **Fixed-interest tradable securities:** Larger scale or medium-sized SHEs may group together and arrange to issue securities. This will usually mean that fixed assets are used as collateral/security against a bond issue that may be tradable. This type of financial instrument needs to be issued when interest rates are low. The purchaser can then either sell the bond at a premium (if the interest rate payable by the enterprise is higher than the current market rate) or at a discount if the rate proves to be lower. Such bonds can either be of a fixed duration or on an open-date basis, and they may be linked to the security of specific assets or be

336

ranked as creditors. The enterprise can buy back the bonds at their market rate if it wishes to reduce the level of finance invested.

- **Government finance:** In many countries, the government makes special finance available for SHEs. It should be noted that if an enterprise accepts such finance (particularly a subsidised rate), the government may acquire indirect control if the enterprises if it becomes dependent on this kind of finance. If finance is to be secured from governmental sources, or from other agencies offering 'soft loans'; detailed scrutiny is essential of the loan terms, because such loans can lead to a loss of sovereignty. It is important that any relationship with the government is clear - because the autonomy of the enterprise has to be maintained.

- **Crowd-funding:** This kind of finance is usually provided lending intermediaries that are profit-making enterprises that generate revenue by collecting a one-time fee on funded loans from borrowers and levying a loan-servicing fee to investors, either a fixed amount annually or a percentage of the loan amount. Because many of the services are automated, the intermediary companies can run with lower overheads and offer the service cheaper than traditional financial institutions, so borrowers may be able to borrow money at lower interest rates and so lenders earn higher returns.

- **Peer-to-peer lending:** Most peer-to-peer loans are unsecured personal loans, i.e. they are made to an individual rather than a company, and borrowers do not offer collateral as a protection to the lender against default.

Some companies offer enterprise loans, where the interest rates are set either by lenders who compete for the lowest rate on the reverse auction model or are fixed by the intermediary company based on their analysis of the borrower's credit. Borrowers assessed as having a higher risk of default are assigned higher rates. Lenders mitigate the risk received by choosing which borrowers to lend to, and by diversifying their investments. Lenders making peer-to-peer investments are not normally protected by government guarantees, so the bankruptcy of the peer-to-peer lending company that arranged the loan may put the lenders' investment at risk.

- **Green bonds and social investments:** In many countries, newer forms of financial instruments are being developed, often referred to as 'Green Bonds' or 'Social Investments'. These are bought by 'ethical investors', who are ready to invest in environmentally-friendly and socially-beneficial activities. Usually, these bonds/ investments will be a means of providing fixed income investments for benign investors, which can be an attractive type of finance for SHEs.

**Financing institutions**

Financing institutions specifically designed to meet the needs of SHEs are not widely available. Development banks run as separate institutions. The presence of effective self-help enterprise development banks, or similar institutions, can be the key to achieving the development and stability of a strong self-help enterprise sector. This is most successful when financial support is directly linked to high-quality consultancy and advisory services provided by specialists in self-help enterprise.

338

### *Financing SHEs – re-stating the essentials*

The arrangements for financing SHEs are absolutely critical to their success and their survival as independent member-controlled enterprises.

Since their inception to the present day, the most significant failures of SHEs have more often than not been caused by adopting means of financing that are inappropriate for use in SHEs. All member-directors, outside directors and all senior managers need to be fully briefed, and confirm that they understand the dangers inherent in accepting financing that carries with it the risk of loss of sovereignty, or commits to providing any reward to investors based on sharing in any surplus (or profit) or distribution of the value of assets.

# 24. COOPERATION AS A SYSTEM

## Cooperation

Cooperation is not something to believe in like Santa Claus or a religion; it's something that people do. It's much like rowing a boat, individuals may study the technicalities prior to rowing, but in the end, they have to get in their boat and row. The successful operation of SHEs relies upon the application of the system of cooperation, as do all forms of mutual action.

Cooperation, as a system, includes a set of interdependent practices that work together as a whole; and has the aim of achieving specified outcomes. The system of cooperation needs to be implemented in its entirety, it's the essential system that supports many of the other systems that are needed in all self-help enterprises; and without it, SHEs are unlikely to achieve anything worthwhile. The prime goal of the system of cooperation is to ensure that people work-together harmoniously to achieve their common goals.

Cooperation is based upon reciprocity – that is to say, 'give and take'. It can never be all 'give', or all 'take' by any member; otherwise, the result is exploitation, not cooperation. Members who want to enjoy only the benefits of cooperation without contributing to the common cause will inevitably undermine any form of cooperative endeavour. Cooperation between individuals, and between groups, calls for open and reliable communication and the creation of a culture of mutual trust. People motivated to cooperate regularly find that this mode of behaviour becomes natural and effortless once the habit of cooperating becomes the norm.

The following practices are required to make cooperation work:

## 1. A COMMON PURPOSE

The starting point of any mutual venture is the members' agreement on, and commitment to, their common purpose, this is what should unite them and persuades them to cooperate. Their common purpose inspires their commitment and drives their enterprise. Therefore, it's essential that their purpose is unmistakably defined. Leaders of any cooperating group need to build a consensus among its members as to the specific outcomes that they plan to achieve as a result of their mutual action. Their purpose needs to be defined holistically so that it comprehensively sets out the expectations of the members of the group

## 2. LEADERSHIP

It's essential that members are selecting and support leaders who are committed to working towards the achievement of the agreed purpose. The group needs to find and develop its own leaders, as their role is critical to the success of any mutual venture. Such leaders need to be competent and knowledgeable about the tasks that the group seeks to complete. Practices need to be in place that will support the development of current and future leaders.

## 3. EMPOWERMENT

Ensuring that all members of the group are engaged by the purpose and are systematically empowered to make the greatest contribution. This includes them being involved in the decision-making processes. Learning new skills is never easy, but once mastered they become automatic, it's a worthwhile investment when such skills and attitudes stay with individuals for the rest of their lives.

## 4. EQUIVALENCE

To be motivated to cooperate, people need to be convinced that they will be treated as equal members of the group. This means that they can always expect to be dealt with fairly and enjoy equal rights and responsibilities within the group. Similarly, members of the group need to know that the benefits gained from their cooperation will be distributed fairly and that they will have equal access to information about their joint enterprise. Maintaining equivalence requires that the enterprise is democratically controlled, and all arrangements need not only be fair but also need to be seen to be fair to all members.

## 5. VOLUNTARY ASSOCIATION

Cooperation can only be a voluntary activity and therefore cannot be based upon any kind of duress. Members of the group have to be able to join and leave freely, but without leaving behind any unfair burdens on the remaining members of the group. This is not to imply that membership is without cost, or that people can be accepted as members regardless of the group's capacity to service their needs. Membership will be open to all those who share a unity of purpose. Potential members satisfying the conditions for membership will not be subjected to any form of discrimination, and all members need to be treated as being equal.

## 6. ETHICAL BEHAVIOUR

Members of the group need to practice ethical behaviour, which means being fair and honest in all their dealings. Otherwise, the relationships between members and the other stakeholders with whom they interact will degenerate, resulting in the breakdown of cooperation.

## 7. RULES

Getting people to cooperate involves having a set of rules that are widely understood and followed by all members of the group. These rules supply the basis for practising cooperative behaviour and are in fact a formal contract between both the enterprise and its members, and between the members themselves. This contract needs to be enforceable or else the rules cease to have any worth when they are disregarded. Leaders need to be ready to use sanctions against those who insist on pursuing their own interests at the expense of other group members.

### Obstacles to cooperation

Dishonesty, duplicity and unwarranted selfishness are infectious forms of behaviour that become rife when people are treated unfairly and feel powerless. In contrast, cooperative behaviour can become contagious, where, as members, people feel valued and believe that they are being treated fairly; then they are usually ready to commit to their joint enterprise. The benefits brought by such behavioural changes can help both individuals and their communities, and this result of a ripple-effect can be life-changing for many people.

Individuals are often torn between belonging to a community (including their SHE) and maximising their own personal welfare. For cooperation to work, people need to be adult in their outlook and to be treated as responsible individuals. So, as well as social norms, formal arrangements such as legal contracts, laws, and rules need to be in place to ensure that all members gain fairly from the activities of their enterprise. For instance, the accuracy and fairness of decisions could be ensured by introducing quorum-thresholds, requiring well over a simple majority of voting members to make any significant rule amendments.

## Wearing different hats

Members of SHEs need to be able to agree-to-differ, putting aside any divisive differences, most notably disparate religious beliefs, political leanings, and prejudices - that might lead them to treat people differently. Instead, they should direct their energies towards the important matters that they do agree upon. This means focusing on achieving the purpose that unites them. Members can wear different hats (putting aside any individual loyalty to causes and external beliefs) to work on making their joint enterprise a success. Of course, outside of their self-help enterprise members are free to wear their religious and political hats, but they need to leave these at home whenever they meet to conduct the affairs of their enterprise.

Many of the individuals involved in SHEs may, in addition, have wider interests in securing social change, but partisan politics have no place inside SHEs, and this position applies uniformly to the advocacy of religions. Successful SHEs need to achieve a consensus among many people that may hold a widely differing view about matters political or religious. These are matters about which members must agree to disagree, whenever they have diverging opinions.

## The value of belonging

Belonging can be important to members, but people often only miss the true value of their enterprise when it's gone or mutated. When individuals feel that they belong to something, it often gives them much more freedom and energy. Most people gravitate to situations where they receive positive feedback and avoid ones where it is negative, thereby building networks around organizations associated with positive outcomes.

To achieve a sense of belonging, people need to share similar ideals and common experience that results in their bonding. If just clicking a link on a website to enable members to join an organization, it's unlikely to encourage a lasting commitment; this is much more likely to be the outcome from staying up all night, with a determined group of volunteers, to get the community shop or pub ready for the grand opening.

Sending a donation may get our name on a list of sponsors but working in an overcrowded room full of like-minded people to agree a set of rules for a new self-help venture lets us belong to a group striving to make a difference. Tough situations shared, often engender a durable sense of belonging. A true sense of belonging builds confidence and can give members a lasting sense of security and well-being; because when people truly belong they are never alone.

Most people will only become and remain engaged with their enterprises if it provides real benefits and treats them fairly. Members soon become apathetic when SHEs behaves in the same way as commercial businesses, treating people) as nothing more than a market ripe for exploitation. Why would anyone bother being involved in a self-help enterprise that treats them unfairly?

**Cooperation not conspiracy**
People with an entirely selfish intent may also work together to achieve their own ends, but this can amount to collusion or conspiracy. It's not unusual for businesses to collaborate to improve their profitability, but if instead, they try to manipulate the market against the interests of the consumer or their suppliers, then it is most certainly not cooperation, but a cartel – a combination of independent enterprises designed to inhibit competition or fix prices. Genuine cooperation involves honest-intent and a commitment to offering a fair deal for all stakeholders.

# 25. EMPOWERMENT

## Self-help – the neglected freedom

'Freedom of association' is the right to join or leave groups of a person's own choosing and for the group to take collective action to pursue the interests of members. This includes the freedom to set up our own organizations to do things for ourselves in cooperation with others. Such 'freedoms' were hard won in many countries, yet it seems citizens are often losing their rights by default. Too many people appear to be convinced that they can't do anything for themselves, so instead rely on government or big business to meet all their needs and solve all their problems.

Today, in many countries, there are charities that are obligated to governments or commercial businesses. Often being reliant on State funding and/or corporate donations. The idea that people can deal with problems and change things by their own efforts hardly ever enters the collective psyche. If people are totally dependent for their survival and well-being upon organizations in which they have no real influence, then they are hardly free individuals. It's only by joining together with others that people are likely to achieve their real potential. If people lose the capacity to help themselves, they are giving away important freedom, and it's only a few short steps from dependency to a form of enslavement.

## Empowering citizens

The value of effective SHEs, their contribution towards developing the national economy and the overall well-being of the nation, have been recurring themes in this book. Governments too, in most countries regularly extol the potential role of SHEs in economic and social development. Since the beginning of the 20th century, many governments have had separate departments involved in supporting SHEs in a variety of ways, but sadly not always achieving a great deal in terms of long-lasting positive outcomes.

Several of the United Nations' (UN) agencies are actively engaged in promoting and supporting SHEs; most notably, the International Labour Organization (ILO) the Food and Agricultural Organization (FAO) and the United Nations Development Programme (UNDP). Both the colonial powers and the independent States that replaced them envisaged that SHEs could play a significant role in national development.

Governments can help encourage the start-up of SHEs, their further development and help to safeguard their integrity as genuine SHEs but should not be involved in the running of enterprises. Any over-reliance upon the State by SHEs is always counter-productive because it takes away their essential sovereignty and negates democratic control.

Those wishing to support SHEs, including governments, non-governmental organizations (NGOs) or any other agencies, need to take great care not to destroy the 'self-help mindset', for without it SHEs predictably perish or mutate. Leaders of SHEs need to guard against accepting 'hand-outs' from any source because these can easily become suffocating patronage. Leaders need to be able to distinguish between what helps to foster self-help and what will undermine the very purpose of their enterprise.

### What should governments do to support SHEs?

If governments want to support the development of effective SHEs, then the best contribution they can make is to provide them with a positive public-policy framework. The raft of public policy priorities needed by SHEs will vary from country to country, but in most, the framework required will include a body of legislation that is supportive of their establishment and development. This alongside regulations and policies that will help SHEs to acquire the resources they need to operate, provide protection against many of the threats to they face, and to protect the interests of their grassroots members.

There are many impediments to the development of self-help enterprises; typically, the most damaging is the failure of the State to provide them with a progressive and up-to-date legislative framework. Internationally, sound advice is available as to the detailed requirements for drafting progressive laws to support the advancement of SHEs and putting in place such a body of law can be the prelude to the burgeoning of a new wave of SHEs. Crucially, the law should provide protection of the various names of the different types of self-help enterprise (for example: 'credit union', 'building society', 'cooperative'), and the misuse of these terms by enterprises that are clearly not bona-fide SHEs need to be both prohibited and policed.

Other significant impediments to the development and sustainability of SHEs that are within the ambit of the State include:

- The failure of many officials and professionals to acknowledge the 'self-help option', the problem is often attitudinal, when civil servants, policy-makers and the public in general, have no valid perception as to what SHEs are.

- Unfairness in the planning system and in other areas of regulation, which are generally framed only to meet the needs of commercial businesses.

The principal obstacle for SHEs to overcome is within the realm of public policy, where 'self-help solutions' ought to be considered the 'first option' rather than being the last resort. The following are among the policies most supportive to the advancement of SHEs. The government needs to:

- Provide adequate protection for the interests of grassroots members, and measures to prevent SHEs from being hijacked by managers and cliques of members; including the requirement that proper oversight is built into the rules of all SHEs.

- Introduce laws and regulations that permit and support the development of financing mechanisms, which makes it easier to raise finance without compromising the sovereignty of SHEs or forcing them to take on the mantle of being charities.

- Implement measures to ensure that 'asset-locks' are in place to prevent the demutualisation of SHEs. Also, the misappropriation of mutual assets needs to be a 'criminal offence' carrying substantial penalties.

- Consider the special needs of SHEs in respect of their treatment within any legislation that is primarily designed to address problems in commercial businesses. For example, when the regulation of the banking industry unfairly impacts SHEs.

- Grant start-up tax-breaks designed to encourage new enterprises or those needing help to become established in the face of unfair bias in specific markets.

- Stimulate investment in SHEs, by providing tax breaks for individuals and institutions investing in special funds for this and/or making available management advice coupled with finance.

- Facilitate the setting-up of a self-help enterprise development bank, with the power to make available start-up finance alongside advice for new ventures. Also, providing a market for the trading of financial instruments issued by SHEs, which are not available to speculators.

- With the support and the full involvement of local SHEs, support the establishment of self-help development hubs. They should provide practical support for developing SHEs at the regional and local levels but must be led by those with direct experience of developing SHEs.

- Facilitate the setting-up of a self-help enterprise development Trust, which can provide advice and support to all types of self-help enterprises. This ought to be a registered charity that could benefit from donations made by prosperous self-help enterprises. The Trust may also own and administer the rights to the use of any franchised systems, and own all common trademarks used by SHEs.

- Make good the neglect of SHEs within the education system by seed-funding the setting-up of a central school for self-help enterprise to provide education, training and personal development programmes for the directors and managers of SHEs. Including, providing e-learning programmes plus residential group work for members and employees at all levels. It needs to be stressed that this body can't be a conventional academic institution, although it will be expected to collaborate with universities.

- Support research that needs to be undertaken into the best ways of promoting and supporting new SHEs that need to intervene in situations where markets are clearly not

351

working in the best interest of citizens. In addition, explore the potential role for 'transitional' self-help enterprises.

-   Ensure that SHEs are, in all respects, treated at least as favourably as any other form of enterprise; including within the education system.

In both developing nations and where support needs to be given to fledgeling SHEs in any nation, specific services need to be provided to help educate the people about the potential of SHEs to improve their living conditions. This kind of 'consciousness – raising' is often best undertaken by NGOs, provided that they can demonstrate a genuine commitment to promoting the self-help mindset and helping to set-up bona-fide SHEs.

Government departments or agencies can be helpful to SHEs if they provide model rules and assist with the process of registration; also, when they provide auditing services to small-scale SHEs and until such time as independent private audit providers are ready to provide audits covering the purpose and function of enterprises. Nevertheless, the involvement of governments directly in the management of SHEs is generally counter-productive so has to be resisted.

**Mainstreaming SHEs**

Self-help enterprises should be an integral part of the mainstream economy, being ready to step in whenever the market is not performing as it should. This is probably best achieved by adopting legislation that governs *all forms* of enterprise within a single body of law. An example of this kind of approach to legislating for all forms of enterprises is to be found in New Zealand. Here single Companies Act that includes a special chapter that caters for cooperatives. Using an overarching Companies Act is far from perfect, it does have the important advantage of ensuring that everyone studying any form of enterprise will become aware of the role of SHEs within the economy. Concurrently, those parts of the education system that claim to meet the needs of enterprises should no longer be permitted to ignore the self-help form of enterprise within their courses and other activities.

Governments tend to place the responsibility for the registration, supervision and administration of the relevant legislation within a department that is most impacted by the involvement of SHEs. For example, where the most significant SHEs are in involved in agriculture, the responsibility will be given to the Department for Agriculture, while if the most high-profile SHEs are involved in providing financial services then it will be likely placed in the Department responsible for the finance and banking sector. Irrespective of where the responsibility for the administrative support aspect of SHEs is placed.

## A self-help champion

If the government wants to get self-help and mutual action onto the national agenda, this calls for the appointment of a 'Self-help Champion', preferably placed inside the office of the Prime Minister or the President. The task of the 'Champion' and their team is to make sure that the necessary positive public policy framework becomes a reality and that self-help and mutual action is promoted through all government departments and agencies.

## Education and training gaps

Currently, much of what is offered as being education and training in respect of SHEs is little more than the repetition of theories about them. Much of the training provided often comprises nothing more than a series of statements outlining the theoretical advantages of SHEs and very little by way of advancing the important 'hard skills' that are actually required. What little education that is supplied is often delivered without any attention being given to the development of the essential the skills, attitudes, and systems that are vital to their success. The people involved in running SHEs, need to be provided with the tools needed if they are to run successful enterprises. To attempt to teach anything about SHEs without having a good understanding of the 'self-help' model of enterprise is like trying to teach medicine without having a grounding in human anatomy.

## Making change happen

Many people who are involved in supporting SHEs are also enthusiastic supporters of achieving more extensive changes in society; sometimes, advocating political and social changes, the wider application of democratic control, alongside the fairer distribution of wealth and power throughout society. However, it's essential that those advocating such change appreciate that SHEs need to focus on achieving their common purpose and that other functions call for separate organizations.

### *SHEs – The next big wave*

All over the world, there are lots of thoughtful people who realise that if future generations are to enjoy anything like a satisfactory quality of life, then big changes are needed in the way that the world's resources are organized, managed and allocated. They understand that if people simply keep doing what they now do, then nothing of meaning will ever change. Many are searching for alternative ways of living their lives because they know that the rampant, consumerism, that now pervades our lives is unsustainable. They are looking for ways of bringing a better balance to our lives – something beyond the constant pressure from those who already control substantial resources to gain more, while others get less and less.

More people are rediscovering that lasting solutions for many pressing problems are to be found in the practice of self-help and mutual action. However, if SHEs are to contribute, they need to be led by people who will put ethical standards into practice and help those they lead to combining their own hopes with those of others with similar needs. At the same time, governments committed to empowering their citizens are needed, but they must be proactive in enabling citizens to set-up SHEs that can challenge the dominant players in any market, whenever they aren't serving people as they should. An alliance needs to be forged between all those that can benefit from truly effective self-help enterprises, creating a 'big tent' that brings together all who understand that if power remains in the hands of the ultra-selfish, there can be little hope of future generations enjoying fulfilling lives or of safeguarding the future of planet earth.

Perhaps just by working together more cooperatively in our enterprises, people may learn that by balancing their own interests with those of the wider community they bring about profound change. A realistic solution to conflicts between communities and nations may be found when people learn how to work together. Self-help and mutual action can provide many of the tools needed to build a better future, for ourselves and for future generations.

# FIND OUT MORE

The following list supplies links to websites sharing information about organizations and concepts mentioned in the book:

**Agricultural co-ops - international:**
http://icao.coop/sub1/sub1.php?smenu=sub1&stitle=subtitle1_1

**Arla Foods - Scandinavia:**
https://www.arlafoods.co.uk/overview/farmer-owned

**Building Societies Members Association (UK):**
http://bsma.org.uk/index.php/building-societies/

**Building societies UK**: https://www.bsa.org.uk/about-us

**Co-operative Bank Plc. (UK):**
https://en.wikipedia.org/wiki/The_Co-operative_Bank

**Cooperative banks – international:**
https://en.wikipedia.org/wiki/Cooperative_banking

**Cooperative Bulk Handling – Australia:**
https://www.cbh.com.au/about-cbh

**Corporatocracy:** https://opinionfront.com/corporatocracy

**Credit Agricole, France:**
https://en.wikipedia.org/wiki/Cr%C3%A9dit_Agricole

**Credit unions - international:**
https://www.woccu.org/impact/credit_unions

**Desjardins bank - Canada:** https://www.desjardins.com/ca/about-us/desjardins/who-we-are/index.jsp?navigMW=mm&

**Empire and Co-operation**, by Rita Rhodes:
https://www.birlinn.co.uk/Empire-and-Co-operation-9781906566562.html

**Eroski supermarket group:** https://en.wikipedia.org/wiki/Eroski

**European consumer co-ops:**
https://genos.univie.ac.at/fileadmin/user_upload/genossenscha
ftswesen/Genos/consum.pdf

**Farmers' co-ops in the USA:** http://ncfc.org/about-ncfc/

**Fishery co-ops - international:**
http://www.icfo.coop/members/members01.php

**Fonterra = New Zealand:** https://www.fonterra.com/nz/en/about-
us.html

**Food co-ops - USA:**
https://en.wikipedia.org/wiki/Food_cooperative

**Food co-ops, for example,** http://wholefoods.coop/ownership/

**Friendly societies - UK:** http://www.friendlysocieties.co.uk/

**Health & care co-ops - international:** https://ihco.coop/about/

**Housing co-ops:** http://www.housinginternational.coop/housing-
co-operatives-worldwide/

**Indian Farmers Fertiliser Cooperative:**
http://www.iffco.in/content/index/about-us

**International Labour Organization, co-operative branch:**
http://www.ilo.org/global/topics/cooperatives/lang--
en/index.htm

**John Lewis Partnership - UK:**
http://www.johnlewispartnership.co.uk/about/the-partnership-
spirit.html

**Lucky Hill farmers co-op, Jamaica:**
https://www.tandfonline.com/doi/abs/10.1080/00086495.1949.11
829188?needAccess=true&journalCode=rcbq20

**Migros, Switzerland:** https://en.wikipedia.org/wiki/Migros

**Mondragon co-ops - Spain:** https://www.mondragon-corporation.com/en/about-us/

**Mutual insurers - international:**
https://www.icmif.org/introducing-icmif

**Rabobank -Netherlands:** https://en.wikipedia.org/wiki/Rabobank

**Rural revival in the UK:** https://www.plunkett.co.uk

**Savings and loan associations - USA:**
https://en.wikipedia.org/wiki/Savings_and_loan_association

**Social-and-solidarity-economy (The):**

https://oxfamblogs.org/fp2p/beyond-the-fringe-realizing-the-potential-of-social-and-solidarity-economy/

**Suma Wholefoods, a UK worker co-op:**
http://www.suma.coop/about/

**Worker Co-ops - international:**
https://en.wikipedia.org/wiki/Worker_cooperative

# ANNEX I - TYPES AND ACTIVITIES OF SHEs

## Overview

This annex provides brief descriptions of a selection of the many different types of SHEs. The listing demonstrates the extent of the range of types of SHEs and the diversity of their activities. This list is not intended to be definitive, not least because new types of SHEs and the activities they undertake are being constantly developed.

There are two *classes* of SHEs, those serving sellers, and those serving buyers. SHEs of sellers include –worker co-ops, those selling their labour, skills, and knowledge, - producer co-ops, which market produce and other goods on behalf of their members, and – service co-ops, that supply joint-services, in the main too small and medium-sized enterprises (SMEs). SHEs that seek to, buy, or negotiate, for goods and services on behalf of individual members, is often identified as being 'consumer-owned enterprises', include consumer co-ops, building societies, savings and loan associations, mutual insurers, credit unions, community cooperatives, and other types of SHEs providing goods and services to their members in their capacity as consumers.

## Legislation

Some types of SHEs are recognisable because they make use of specific legislation to register as corporate entities. For example, in the UK, The Co-operative and Community Benefit Societies Act, Credit Unions Acts, Building Societies Acts; although, some cooperatives are still registered under the Companies Acts. The legal form used by any group of people setting up a self-help enterprise will depend upon the legislation that is available in the country concerned. The choice of the type of SHEs deployed will be influenced by the knowledge/experience that the group involved has, or by the advice that may be available to them from any promoting body. Most groups setting up SHEs will select a type of enterprise used successfully by other groups with which they have had contact.

## COMMUNITY SERVICES

### Community health service association

Members can include healthcare professionals, residents, and supporting agencies. Income to cover the cost of health services is collected by regular payments from members.

### Cooperative clinic

Owned and run by health professionals or jointly with the community. Like associations (above)

### Electricity and communications supply co-op

Jointly owned equipment run by the cooperative to supply electricity and/or communications services used by members on a fee-paying basis.

### Flood warning group

Self-help groups supply members with a two-way information service that supports the quick transmission of early warnings about natural disasters to their members.

### Food for work Venture

The group organizes the required labour and the distribution of food to those who have undertaken the work.

### Community development co-op

This type of co-op draws members from all parts of the community, including consumers, workers, and local organizations. The services offered will depend on the needs of the community but can include village shops, local pubs, health services, schools, local transport, and income earning ventures.

### School and learning co-op

Members of the community, often in collaboration with other bodies, offer educational services for their members and their families.

### Transport services co-op

Transport supplied by the cooperative to member-users, often based on a contract with individual vehicle owners.

363

## Village improvement society

The society will have members from all parts of the community and will undertake projects, which improve village life and the living environment.

## Water users' association

The association organizes and supports the local water supply.

## Wildlife protection society

The society organizes the management of wildlife and usually contracts with governmental conservation agencies to protect wildlife in the interest of the community and the nation.

## CONSUMER SERVICES

## Consumer co-op

Cooperatives run retail shops and other services needed by their consumer members. (often working with other cooperatives to jointly supply their own wholesaling services)

## Defence and advocacy association

The association supplies legal advice to its members; it may be an organization jointly owned by local people or legal professionals. The association supplies defence against exploitation or attack from any source.

## Food and nutrition buying club (food co-ops)

Members bulk their purchasing power to obtain lower-cost nutritional food. Sometimes, they adopt a 'box system', this means that they obtain a variety of foods according to seasonal availability.

## Funeral service co-op

The cooperative undertakes the funeral arrangements for the member; sometimes this is a separate organization, or club, into which the member subscribes on a regular basis. In other cases, funerals are only one of the services offered by a consumer cooperative.

## Pharmacy services co-op

Operated by its members as a consumer cooperative, often running as an adjunct to a cooperative clinic or health centre.

### Renewable fuel/energy supplies co-op

Several types of cooperatives, especially agricultural supplies cooperatives and consumer cooperatives provide members with renewable fuel/energy supplies.

### Disadvantaged groups

Where members are from a specified vulnerable group, needing to secure access to services, such as employment opportunities, credit for productive purposes. And. vulnerable groups, for example - children, older persons, disabled, or other similar groups.

## AGRICULTURAL PRODUCERS/ FISHERY SERVICES

### AGRICULTURAL cooperative bank

A bank usually jointly owned by several agricultural cooperatives or credit societies, which will either lend mainly to farmers, through its member organizations or direct to farmers.

### Agricultural credit co-op

Provides seasonal farming credit, and usually involves collective guarantees for loans from banks or credit agencies.

### Agricultural marketing co-op – agency model

Markets produce on behalf of members, but ownership stays with the individual member, rather than the co-op, until the sale of the produce to a buyer.

### Agricultural produce buying co-op

The cooperative takes ownership of produce when bought from members, often linked to processing or packaging to add value to crops.

### Artificial insemination (AI) services co-op

Collective purchasing of artificial insemination and other veterinary services, the cooperative may employ its own staff or contract for services.

### Crop and livestock insurance mutual/co-op

Mutual cover for risks to crops and/or livestock which usually needs laying-off risks by reinsurance.

---

### Farm input supply co-op

The cooperative normally runs depots that carry stocks of farm inputs for sale to members as needed by them.

---

### Farmers' association

An association of agricultural producers is often undertaking advocacy and representation on behalf of producers; it may also become involved in offering economic services to members.

---

### Farmers' market

The association or cooperative runs a market where farmers or their family members sell their own produce direct to the public.

---

### Fishery co-op

The cooperative will normally supply its individual members with fishing equipment and market their catch.

---

### Fish farming association/co-op

Offers fish for stocking fishponds, etc. to members and may market fish on behalf of members.

---

### Forestry co-op

Markets forestry products on behalf of members and may offer a forestry management service to members.

---

### Grain or cereal bank

Members place grain in collectively owned storage which is used to store crops for their own consumption when needed, and or for selling when prices have risen to higher levels than at harvest time.

---

### Land settlement association

Offering joint services, such as input supply, machinery, and produce marketing, to individual farmers, usually renting or owning adjoining plots.

---

### Livestock association

Individually owned livestock jointly managed by the association, this may involve trekking to new pasture, holding grounds and arranging veterinary services.

---

### Livestock marketing co-op

May involve the cooperative in providing members with any of the services as above (by an association) but will usually include marketing on behalf of the individual member, in most cases the farmer will be paid on the dead weight of their animal.

### Machinery ring

A joint enterprise of owners of farm machinery, which may be contractors or individual farmers. Some supplying machinery services to farmers, and booking services, for which they will collect a small fee, from both the machine owner and the farmer using the service, to cover costs.

### Multi-purpose agricultural co-op

A cooperative that supplies a wide range of services to its members, which can like those offered by specialised co-ops.

### Purchasing group

Joint purchasing of agricultural inputs, by bulking orders and negotiating a price with the supplier: the group often holds no stocks of supplies.

### Water/irrigation management association

The association that jointly manages water supplies, often, sharing out the available resource, supporting pumps and other equipment and offering irrigation services.

## FINANCIAL, RISK MANAGEMENT/SOCIAL PROTECTION SERVICES

### Building society (Savings & loan association in the USA)

The society collects savings from members on a regular basis and makes loans to members to buy housing or the materials to build homes.

### Cooperative bank

Supplying banking services to members, also see agricultural cooperatives banks. Note: the various types of cooperative banks are described at the end of *Chapter 10*.

| |
|---|
| **Credit and savings society**<br>A society of persons who make regular savings and can qualify to take loans from the society. There are several distinct types of credit and savings societies, many based on the Raiffeisen system developed in Germany in the 19th century. |
| **Credit Union**<br>A type of credit and savings cooperative, based on self-help practices, needing members to save before they borrow and encouraging them to use loans only for productive and provident purposes. |
| **Friendly society**<br>The society collects regular payments from its members and makes payments to members in times of sickness, unemployment, or other hardships. |
| **Insurance mutual/co-op**<br>Members pay regular insurance premiums to the insurance mutual/cooperative, and in return members receive payments to cover the loss and costs incurred if an insured risk occurs; members may receive bonuses as a form of profit-share, should surpluses be available for distribution. |
| **Reinsurance Mutual**<br>An insurance mutual/cooperative that spreads the risks that its member organization cover by reinsurance, sharing the risk between mutual insurers. Internationally, the International Cooperative and Mutual Insurance Federation (ICMIF) helps arrange reinsurance for its member- organizations. |
| **Sickness and accident club**<br>Like a Friendly Society (see above) |
| **Local currency provider**<br>Operates a members-only closed currency in a defined geographical area with the aim of improving the local economy. |
| |

| **LAND, CONSTRUCTION AND HOUSING SERVICES** |
|---|
| **Community land trusts**<br>Acquiring and managing land for the benefit of the community Enabling communities to solve their own problems through self-help, community action, especially land used for housing or community assets. |
| **Construction brigade/co-op**<br>Construction workers organized into a brigade or co-op to undertake major construction tasks, which may include giving training for young workers and new entrants. |
| **Housing co-op - Ownership model**<br>Members jointly own housing, which it jointly manages, and is often used to secure housing finance by joint guarantees from banks and other credit agencies. |
| **Housing co-op - Tenant management model**<br>Housing stock often owned by the government or local authorities but managed by residents. The cooperative may collect rents, supplies common services, and undertake repairs, and in some cases help by offering employment and childcare facilities etc. for members. |
| **Housing co-op - Self-build model**<br>The cooperative jointly secure buildings, land, finance, and supplies construction materials, and may supply construction advice and employ technical specialists to help members with their building project. After the completion of the housing, it may change its role to that of managing all common parts and provide joint services. |
| **Refugee, returnee or ex-combatants association**<br>The association organizes refugee (or demobilization) camp services and seeks to offer income-earning employment. The same or a separate association supplying services to help re-settle refugees or ex-combatants when they return home. |
|  |

| **EMPLOYMENT AND ENTREPRENEUR ORGANIZATIONS** |
|---|
| Enterprise marketing and service co-op. Shopkeepers or others jointly buy supplies for their enterprises, and/or jointly market their individual products. |
| ### Craftsmen and artisans' co-op<br>Jointly buy supplies needed for their trade, and or jointly market the individual products of artisans or artisans and can offer other services such as managed workspace and accountancy services. |
| ### Eco-tourism /farm tourism co-op<br>Jointly market accommodation and other tourist services and sustain main tourist assets/attractions to sustain tourism in the area. |
| ### Employment mutual<br>The mutual help to find employment for its members and to support them when they are seeking work. The members may be self-employed people who receive help from the mutual marketing of their services to individuals or firms that can make use of their services. |
| ### Market operator co-op<br>A marketplace runs jointly on behalf of vendors and/or individual craftsperson or small-scale producers. |
| ### Migrant labour and remittance service co-op<br>Migrant labourers arrange to remit safely part of their members' earnings to their families; this is often a service offered by a credit union. |
| ### Mutual guarantee society<br>Jointly offer security to secure enterprise loans from banks and other credit agencies. |
| ### Pharmacists' co-op<br>The members of the cooperative are pharmacists who buy drugs and other goods jointly; sometimes they offer cover when the pharmacist is absent. The most successful, manufacture drugs under their own label. |
| ### Taxi and transport operators' co-op<br>Offers central services, such as dispatching, often negotiating contracts with hotels etc. on behalf of taxi owners. |

## Worker co-ops

Enterprises that are owned and run by the people that work in them. Such co-ops can be engaged in any kind of activity that has the potential to be a viable enterprise.

## SOCIAL, CULTURAL AND SPORTING SERVICES

## Social and sporting clubs

Members self-supply recreational, social and entertainment facilities for members.

## Supporters trusts

Providing supporter-members with a stake in the sports, they follow.

## Musical enterprises

Where musicians, who are members, jointly run their own band or orchestra, on a cooperative basis.

## Artists and entertainers' co-op

Offering services to members, who are artists and entertainers, these services may include acting as an agent, joint marketing, management, and other services.

# ANNEX II - WORDS WITH IMPORTANT MEANINGS

**'A business'** - means any form of enterprise conducted with the aim of generating profit. It's necessary to understand the differences between 'being a business' and 'doing business' (conducting trade and commercial activity); and 'conducting an enterprise in a business-like manner'.

**Agent** - means a person who acts for another. The term also has legal significance in matters of contract law. SHEs act as an agent on behalf of their members and the rules of the enterprise formalise the relationship between the enterprise and its members.

**Beneficial, mutual ownership** - means that the current members of an enterprise have the use of its assets and benefit from their use. Current members are, in effect, trustees jointly holding the assets on behalf of both current and future members. Members own their personal investments in the enterprise but have no claim upon any increase in the value of the assets of the enterprise, which are owned on behalf of all its members, current and future.

**Benign finance** - means finance that is secured only from persons or institutions that will not threaten, currently or in the future, the sovereignty of the enterprise or its members' democratic- control over the enterprise.

**Business cooperation** - means a type of SHE in which the members are themselves enterprises (either corporate entities or individual owners). These SHEs supply their members with many types of joint services, such as marketing, wholesale supply of goods and other inputs, bank and credit-card clearing, and hotel or other booking arrangements.

**Collectivism** - means an arrangement whereby all the assets of an enterprise are jointly controlled, and the individual has no ownership or investment rights. A collective is not be confused with a self-help enterprise.

**Commercial business** - (including sole-traders, partnerships, and private and public companies) means a business conducted with the goal of generating profits; an investor-controlled business is a commercial business run for the benefit of the investors who own shares in it.

373

**Common bond** - means the shared basis of the relationship among those wishing to become members of an enterprise. It is widely used in credit unions (SHEs of savers and borrowers). Examples include residence in a specified town or area, employment by a designated firm, or membership of a specified profession, church, or other organization. In many countries, it is a requirement of membership to satisfy a 'common bond', which should be set out within the rules of the enterprise. A common bond is different from having unity of purpose.

**Common purpose** - A holistic purpose, agreed by members, that unites the membership by setting out a shared- vision of what they want their enterprise to achieve on their behalf. Their commitment to their purpose takes precedence over any differences between individual members allowing them to set these aside.

**Cooperative** - a specific type of self-help enterprise, often defined within national laws, may be identified by reference to the Statement of Cooperative Identity, published by the International Co-operative Alliance (ICA).

**Corporate entity** - is formed when an enterprise is registered under a law that provides them with a 'legal personality', meaning that they can sue and be sued as a corporate body, that is separate from the individuals who jointly own it. Individual/sole-traders and partnerships do not have to register under any specific legislation. Self-help groups are not compelled to register, but if they want to become a corporate entity, then they have to be registered under a specific law*.

\*in the UK, there are specific laws covering: Companies, Co-operatives and Community Benefit Societies and Charities.

**Corporatocracy** - a term used to depict an economic and political system controlled by corporations and/or corporate interests. This is different from 'corporatism', which is the organization of society into groups with common interests.

**Democratic control** - means a system of control based upon equivalence, whereby power is shared based on equal rights and each member has the power of only one vote.

**Demutualisation** - is the term used to describe the process of converting SHEs into investor-controlled companies. Many SHEs throughout the world have been demutualised, a form of corporate appropriation. Many building societies and agricultural co-ops in the UK and many consumer co-ops in European countries have been lost in this way—often as a direct result of the loss of member-control.

**Enterprise** - an organization, engaged in the trade of goods or services, normally running within the context of the market. (This definition includes both enterprises working with the object of generating profit and those run not-for-profit).

**Equivalence** - means equal in value—in votes, voice, responsibilities, opportunities, justice and individual human respect and dignity. In the context of SHEs, it means that in all dealings with members the criterion of equivalence shall apply, with all members treated on an equal basis. Note: This replaces the goal of profit maximization that motivates commercial businesses, which is often based upon individual transactions, where it's common to offer secret deals to some people while charging individual customers whatever price they think they can get away with.

**Equitable** - means dealing fairly and equally with all concerned.

**Federal - (A).** An enterprise where the members are other SHEs, (for example a wholesale supply enterprise supplying its members that operate retail shops).

**Form of enterprise** (A) - means one of a wide range of economic structures, the form is decided by the motivation driving its creation, for example - the generation of profit, the achievement of a specific charitable outcome, or, in the case of a self-help enterprise, to get a better deal for members. Each form of enterprise calls for a specific model that will supply the framework for its operation. There can be different types of each form of enterprise.

**Margin** - means the difference between all of the costs incurred the selling price of goods or services. The margin essential to trade and end up with a surplus to cover not only the direct cost of producing or supplying the goods or services but also any indirect costs involved. Indirect costs may include the depreciation of any assets used and provision for any risks involved with the transaction (e.g. the cost of goods unsold, a fall in the value of stocks held, shoplifting/theft, and bad debts). It is usual to talk about 'gross margin' (the margin added to the cost of goods bought) and 'net margin' (the margin that is left after all direct costs involved are taken into consideration).

**Market economy** - means an economy in which the allocation of resources is decided only by the supply and the demand for them. This is a theoretical concept; this because of every country, even those favouring corporatocracy places restrictions on the ownership and exchange of some specific services, commodities, and goods.

**Member** – in the context of SHEs, means a legal person duly registered under the rules of the enterprise.

**Member control** - in the context of SHEs, means that the people setting the overall direction and the most important policies of the enterprise are responsible to the membership. Also, that all major decisions about the purpose and constitution/rules of the enterprise are made only by the members constituted in a general meeting. The bulk of persons directing the affairs of the enterprise are appointed, by and from, the membership. Member control also implies democratic control, based on one member/one vote.

**Mutant enterprises** - is one that uses a name that implies that it's a genuine self-help enterprise when in fact this is no longer the case. Instead, they have become enterprises that primarily serve the interests of those running them.

**Mutual** - is a term used to describe some types of SHEs, especially those working within the financial sector, such as building societies, credit unions, and mutual insurance societies. The main thing that often differentiates them from other types of self-help enterprise is that in many financial mutuals, members don't hold individual 'shares' (qualifying investments). Instead, their activities are financed by using members' savings held by their SHEs or raised from the contributions of members; for example, by regular insurance premiums in an insurance mutual. One of the simplest types of mutual is the savings and loan club, where all members save a regular amount, and each member in return becomes eligible to take a loan from the club. The fact is that all SHEs rely upon a mutual form of ownership and its members need to cooperate.

**Not-for-profit enterprises** - (often known as 'non-profit organizations') are enterprises that do not have as their goal the generation of profits for their owners but to achieve other specific aims. Nevertheless, not-for-profit enterprises cannot survive if they regularly make losses. Not-for-profit enterprises come in two main forms, those generating a surplus that is donated to a charity or other cause, and those conducting their enterprise in a manner that directly furthers its cause. SHEs may be regarded as 'not-for-profit enterprises' because their purpose is to achieve specific outcomes, as determined by their members. At the discretion of the members, any surplus arising from their operations may be distributed according to the members' direction, subject only to any limitations imposed by its rules and the relevant legislation.

**Objective** - means something that our efforts and actions are intended to achieve. In this book, a distinction is made between 'strategic aims' (forming part of a long-term/strategic purpose) and operational objectives (shorter-term objectives, achieving outcomes along the way towards the achievement of the strategic aims).

**Oversight** - means responsibility for supervision, via a system of structural checks, utilised whenever those running an enterprise are different from its owners. A vigorous system of oversight is essential because without it the owners are highly likely to discover that the main benefits arising from their enterprise are ending up in the hands of those running it. ('the owners' means 'the shareholders' in the case of a company, and it means 'the members' in the case of a self-help enterprise.)

**Par-value** - means that the value of an item stays unchanged, e.g. the price paid when buying an item is still the same when it's sold or cashed-in.

**Patronage** - means giving financial or other support to individuals or groups. Such dependency usually results in creating some form of reliance, often a feeling of indebtedness or obligation to the organization, and to the individuals dispensing it.

**Policy** - means a series of guidelines setting out how a specific goal is to be achieved, often defining the tactics that may or may not to be used. Policies can be separately named as 'foundation policies' and 'operational policies', the former being those that ensure the implementation of an organization's vital foundations and the latter being those that relate to the routine running of the enterprise.

**Primary-level self-help enterprise** - means an enterprise that works at the first level (for example running a single village shop) and where members are typically individuals.

**Process** - means a series of actions or steps taken to achieve a specified outcome.

**Profit** - means money gained in a business transaction. 'Profit' is not a moral issue, but a practical choice based on the function of an enterprise.

**Provident** - means having or showing wise foresight for future needs or events, and exercising care in planning, e.g. saving money for use in case of future emergencies or unforeseen circumstances (sometimes referred to as 'long-termism').

**Resource optimisation** - means making full productive use of all tangible assets. Examples include maximising the utilisation of space in all buildings, securing the best achievable levels of stock turnover, using finance productively, and achieving no less than a market level of return on all finance employed. Within a self-help enterprise, the management should focus on resource optimisation rather than the profit maximization that drives a commercial enterprise.

**Self-help enterprises** - (SHEs) encompass cooperatives of all types*, credit unions, building societies, savings & loan associations, friendly societies, community benefit societies, insurance mutuals, social clubs, and many other kinds of enterprises based upon the practice of mutual action. The differences between them lie in the specific practices that each type adopts to meet its specific purposes.

\* Including, but not limited to, cooperatives of consumers of all manner of goods and services, farmers, or growers (producers), members of communities, tenants, workers, students, artists, artisans, professionals, residents, and users and providers of all manner of health and social services.

**Social Economy** (The) - includes a wide range of enterprises that trade primarily for social and environmental purposes. Although many commercial businesses have some social aims, social enterprises are distinctive because their purpose is central, and any profits are reinvested to sustain and further their mission for positive change. Derived from the French économie sociale (first recorded in about 1900), it describes a sector of the economy that covers a wide range of community, voluntary and not-for-profit activities, as distinct from the commercial business sector. SHEs are markedly different from any of the other types of enterprise grouped within the social economy. The term may be helpful when seeking to support the joint interests of this broad sector of the economy but classifying SHEs as 'social enterprises may cause people to become confused about their true function.

**Social enterprise** - describes one of a broad range of enterprises that trade primarily for social and environmental aims. Although many commercial businesses have some social aims, social enterprises are distinctive because their purpose is central, usually reinvesting any profits to sustain and further their mission. Social enterprises can be structured as a 'for-profit' or 'non-profit' and may take various legal forms, depending on the country and the legal forms available.

**Social engineering** - refers to efforts to influence attitudes and social behaviours on a large scale, (whether by governments, media, or private groups) to produce desired characteristics in a target population. Attempts to undertake social engineering can cause organizations to conform with a predetermined perspective; for example, by changing the stakeholder groups represented on the main board of an enterprise.

**Sovereignty** - means the full right and power of an organization to govern itself without interference from outside sources or bodies.

**Stakeholders** - are the group of persons affected by the activities of an enterprise, generally said including its customers, suppliers, workforce, management, bankers, investors. An extended range of stakeholder groups also includes the community in which the enterprise operates, the government, and future generations. Not all stakeholders have a direct financial interest in the enterprise, but all stakeholders stand to gain from (or be adversely affected by) the activities of the enterprise.

**Stewardship** - embodies responsible planning and management of resources, which are part of the concept of sustainability.

**Strategy** - is a plan of action designed to achieve a long-term or overall aim.

**Surplus** - is the sum left-over after all costs, current and expected, are deducted from income received.

**Sustainable** - means a resource that can be used without being completely used up or destroyed, especially the property of maintaining diversity, for example, varied species, and being productive indefinitely.

**System** - A human system means a set of interacting and interdependent practices, procedures, and habits that work together with the aim of achieving specified outcomes. A Complete system is one that includes all the practices necessary to achieve the overall objective of the system.

# INDEX

## A

## B

## Q

## R

www.ingramcontent.com/pod-product-compliance
Lightning Source LLC
Chambersburg PA
CBHW071248220526
45468CB00001B/35